Twice-Told Proverbs

Twice-Told Proverbs
and the
Composition of the Book of Proverbs

Daniel C. Snell

Eisenbrauns
Winona Lake, Indiana
1993

Library of Congress Cataloging-in-Publication Data

Snell, Daniel C.
    Twice-told Proverbs and the composition of the book of Proverbs /
Daniel C. Snell.
        p.   cm.
    Includes bibliographical references and index.
    ISBN 0-931464-66-8
    1. Bible. O.T. Proverbs—Criticism, interpretation, etc.
I. Title.
BS1465.2.S644 1993   92-46623
223′.7066—dc20   CIP

For Katie Barwick,

who eludes clichés

Contents

Preface

Indolence, interruption, business, and pleasure, all take their turns of retardation; and every long work is lengthened by a thousand causes that can, and ten thousand that cannot, be recounted. Perhaps no extensive and multifarious performance was ever effected within the term originally fixed in the undertaker's mind. He that runs against Time has an antagonist not subject to casualties.

Johnson, on the time it took Pope to translate the Iliad

This study began in a graduate seminar that I taught at the University of Michigan in the spring of 1977. I became intrigued with the problem of repetition in the Book of Proverbs and presented the students in the seminar with my tentative results as they presented me with their term papers.

In March 1980 I gave a short paper on the topic at the American Oriental Society meeting in San Francisco. In 1980 I was granted a National Endowment for the Humanities Fellowship to look further into the Book of Proverbs, and my first effort was devoted to revising my short paper on the problem of repetition. In preparation for the fellowship year I prepared a Hebrew word index to the Book of Proverbs with the help of a research grant from Barnard College. This index is the basis for the study. In 1985 a University of Oklahoma Research Council grant allowed me to have my graduate student Garold Mills check the entire index against the text of Proverbs for accuracy.

Professors James Crenshaw of Duke University, Edwin M. Good of Stanford University, and Edward Greenstein of the Jewish Theological Seminary read earlier versions of this study and offered useful suggestions. Greenstein especially gave an earlier draft a very detailed reading and suggested recasting the study into one not just of repetition but of the composition of the Book of Proverbs. These scholars are not responsible for my errors, nor do they necessarily agree with my views.

In January 1989 I gave a short paper based on this study to the Oklahoma–Kansas Hebrew Bible Colloquium in Stillwater, Oklahoma, and I received many stimulating suggestions from the scholars present. The late Professor John Gammie of the University of Tulsa and Professor Leo Perdue, then of Phillips University, were especially helpful. James Eisenbraun and his readers, Theodore Hildebrandt, Michael O'Connor, and David Aiken, offered many suggestions, which I have tried to incorporate.

The final revision was done in the spring of 1990 at the National Humanities Center in North Carolina, to the staff and librarians of which I am most grateful. Dr. Kent Mulliken, the center's associate director, kindly gave me bibliographic help in connection with Samuel Johnson. Professor David Levy of the University of Oklahoma promptly sent me materials that I had compiled in Oklahoma, and Professor Gary Cohen of the same institution was tireless in

his encouragement. Professor Philip Stadter of the University of North Carolina was kind enough to review my translations from the Greek and saved me from several errors.

To all of the persons and institutions mentioned here I extend my thanks. Indolence, interruption, business, and pleasure have retarded this particular race with Time, and without help from all these quarters the race could not have been attempted. Responsibility for errors remains my own.

The dedication is an imperfect reflection of my feelings.

List of Tables and Charts

Sources of Epigraphs

Preface   Samuel Johnson, *Lives of the English Poets* (introduction by Warren L. Fleischauer; Chicago: Regnery, 1955), p. 262

1   Samuel Johnson, *Lives of the English Poets* (introduction by Warren L. Fleischauer; Chicago: Regnery, 1955), p. 3

2   Samuel Johnson, *Lives of the English Poets* (introduction by Warren L. Fleischauer; Chicago: Regnery, 1955), p. 4

3   James Boswell, *The Life of Samuel Johnson* (introduction by Herbert Askwith; New York: Modern Library, 1945), p. 705

4   James Boswell, *The Life of Samuel Johnson* (introduction by Herbert Askwith; New York: Modern Library, 1945), p. 351

Excursus   Samuel Johnson, *Lives of the English Poets* (introduction by Warren L. Fleischauer; Chicago: Regnery, 1955), p. 96

5   James Boswell, *The Journal of a Tour to the Hebrides with Samuel Johnson* (edited by Allan Wendt; Boston: Houghton Mifflin, 1965), p. 136

6   James Boswell, *The Life of Samuel Johnson* (introduction by Herbert Askwith; New York: Modern Library, 1945), p. 1042

7   Samuel Johnson, *Poems* (edited by Edward L. McAdam Jr. and George Milne; Yale Edition of the Works of Samuel Johnson 6; New Haven: Yale University Press, 1964), pp. 263–64

8   James Boswell, *The Journal of a Tour to the Hebrides with Samuel Johnson* (edited by Allan Wendt; Boston: Houghton Mifflin, 1965), p. 142

1

Introduction

Those writers who lay on the watch for novelty could have little hope of greatness; for great things cannot have escaped former observation. [The Metaphysical poets'] attempts were always analytic; they broke every image into fragments; and could no more represent, by their slender conceits and labored particularities, and prospects of nature, or the scenes of life, than he who dissects a sunbeam with a prism can exhibit the wide effulgence of a summer room.

—Johnson, on Abraham Cowley

The Book of Proverbs is a tantalizing legacy. It tantalizes us with hints at its origins and original uses. It makes reference to familiar historical personages as well as to unfamiliar. One would think that these references would allow us to date the book or at least to say something about its composition, but this has not in fact been the case.

Perhaps we should take to heart Samuel Johnson's warning that "great things cannot have escaped former observation." Certainly in the present instance there is the possibility that some scholar of an earlier age has already compiled the information that this volume conveys. But it is now clear to me that if someone did it earlier, everyone since has forgotten it, and so it must now be done again. And yet Johnson is quite right that, whatever one thinks of the Metaphysical poets, fragmenting analysis does sometimes deprive one of the larger picture. I am hopeful that this study will aid in visualizing the entire Book of Proverbs.

The teachings of the Book of Proverbs are mostly not at issue in this study. This is not because I am not interested in the teachings and what they tell about Israelite society, but because I believe that understanding the way the book came together is preliminary to understanding its teachings.

Here and in what follows I shall frequently allude to statements by the incomparable Dr. Samuel Johnson because his own more modern wise sayings so frequently strike me as being, in the words of Sir Walter Raleigh (1861–1922), "an embodiment of corporate tradition and the settled wisdom of the ages."[1] Part of Johnson's skill with words derived from his interest in creating the broadest generalization possible on any subject; Johnson shared this interest

---

1. Quotation in S. Johnson, *Lives of the English Poets, Selections* (ed. W. Fleischauer; Chicago: Regnery, 1955) vi.

1

with many of the people who assembled the Book of Proverbs. There is no doubt that Dr. Johnson would approve of anything that led people to pay more attention to Scripture. And if by citing his words I can add levity and entertainment to dour instruction, Dr. Johnson's memory will be well served.[2]

The Book of Proverbs has at least two different kinds of material in it. There are instructions that represent themselves as commonsense teachings from parents to sons, and there are one-line aphorisms that seem to have no particular social context. The initial form-critical task has proved relatively easy; almost all of the material can be classed as one or the other of these types. And yet this classification does not actually bring scholars any nearer to understanding the *Sitz im Leben* of each kind of saying.[3]

The book has thirteen identifiable sections, which do not always correspond to the present-day chapter divisions, but which may once have been independent collections. Some of these have headlines associating them with famous women and men of the past, some of whom are no longer well known. Relatively little has been done in recent years to explain the existence of individual collections, and in fact R. B. Y. Scott has argued that the collection divisions are meaningless.[4] His point is that the individual collections have no unifying ideological context or other characteristics, aside from the form-critical similarity of using the instruction or the aphoristic form. His findings are certainly correct insofar as they are descriptive, and yet one has the feeling that the collections do have some historical significance, even if additions have been made since they were compiled.

Biblical scholarship has failed to arrive at a consensus on what indications about composition mean. There is limited agreement about the composition of the book, but that agreement appears to be based not upon a systematic study of the book but upon more general feelings developed through study over the last century.

The Book of Proverbs is worth more concentrated effort. This is especially true because it clearly presents a set of assumptions about the way the world works and the way individuals should behave. It is rare in the Hebrew Bible that one finds such a concentrated set of norms. It is also rare to find those norms applying to everyday life rather than to unusual or criminal situations, as in the Law. This aspect of the book has perhaps not received quite the emphasis it ought to have, though it has been analyzed as a class ethic for upper-class young men.[5]

---

2. F. W. Bate underlines the tendency of Johnson (which increased in his later work) to use aphorism or maxim (*The Achievement of Samuel Johnson* [New York: Oxford University Press, 1955] 29); Bate sees this as a result of Johnson's compulsion "to distil experience into the most condensed generalization possible" (p. 22). This apparently made him a memorable conversationalist. His passion for scientific inquiry as well as for proverbial thought made Johnson a pivotal figure and an appropriate writer to quote in a study such as this, which attempts to apply scientific-analytical methods to the remains of proverbial thought.

3. On this problem see R. Murphy, "Assumptions and Problems in Old Testament Wisdom Research," *Catholic Biblical Quarterly* 29 (1967) 407–18; and idem, *Wisdom Literature* (The Forms of the Old Testament Literature 13; Grand Rapids: Eerdmans, 1981), of which pp. 47–82 are a form-critical listing of the material in Proverbs.

4. R. B. Y. Scott, "Wise and Foolish, Righteous and Wicked," in *Studies in the Religion of Ancient Israel* (Vetus Testamentum Supplement 23; Leiden: Brill, 1972) 146–65.

5. B. W. Kovacs, "Is There a Class-Ethic in Proverbs?" in *Essays in Old Testament Ethics: J. Philip Hyatt, In Memoriam* (ed. J. L. Crenshaw and J. T. Willis; New York: Ktav, 1974) 171–89.

The importance of the book for its view of Hebrew society has not been sufficiently explored, to some extent because of the uncertain nature of its origins. If the book arose as an imitation of Egyptian wisdom literature, some of its concerns might not even reflect an Israelite milieu, and it ought not then to be used to sketch a view of everyday life in Israel. An Egyptian connection can most clearly be seen in Proverbs 22:17–24:22, a selection of sayings loosely translated from the Egyptian *Instruction of Amenemope*.[6] The existence of this work, more closely connected to the Bible than any other ancient Near Eastern composition, causes scholars to wonder what other aspects of the book might derive from the Nile rather than from the Jordan. If it proves possible to clarify the relationships among the various collections and to provide a plausible explanation of the way the book came together, we might diminish the uncertainties that derive from the book's international contacts.

The book is also of considerable interest because of the current study of the books of Ecclesiastes and Job. Both of these books appear to react against some of the ideas of the Book of Proverbs, though one cannot be sure whether their authors were directly aware of the Book of Proverbs as it now stands. R. N. Whybray's study of the vocabulary of the wisdom tradition, which he calls the intellectual tradition, emphasizes the close relationship between Proverbs and the books that appear to criticize Proverbs' basic assumptions.[7]

In the present study I wish to turn to the text of the book for the purpose of reconstructing the history of its composition. I started by compiling a word index of the book, in which the complete verse containing each word was affixed in photocopy to an index card. I then examined previous analyses of the composition of the book, searching for explanations of the dominant and significant phenomenon of repetition (chapters 2–3). The ways in which the Septuagint, the Greek translations of the Hebrew Bible, deals with repetition have also been taken into consideration (excursus). I classified the kinds of repetition observed (chapter 4) and cataloged the repeated verses (chapter 5).

The catalog allowed me to create several charts (pp. 64–69) clarifying the affinities among the collections in the book and also to draw conclusions about the relative chronology of the compilation of the book (chapter 6). I then proceeded to reexamine the question of composition and to propose a new theory (chapter 7). I believe that repeated verses do in fact hold the only key we are ever likely to have for understanding the history of composition. I hope, therefore, that my investigations will serve as a basis for future work in understanding the history of the wisdom tradition in its other biblical manifestations and also in analyzing the social and economic history of Israel exemplified in Proverbs.

The words that occur in repeated verses or parts of verses have been collected in the first index, as well as a wide selection of clichés that appear more than once in the book. Though I have

---

6. On Egyptian wisdom collections in general, see I. Grumach, *Untersuchungen zur Lebenslehre des Amenope* (Munich/Berlin: Deutscher Kunstverlag, 1972); and W. McKane, *Proverbs* (Old Testament Library; Philadelphia: Westminster, 1970) 51–150. D. C. Simpson, "The Hebrew Book of Proverbs and the Teachings of Amenophis," *Journal of Egyptian Archaeology* 12 (1926) 232–39, is still fundamental in listing the parallels between Proverbs and the *Instruction of Amenemope*. See R. Williams, "The Sages of Egypt in Recent Study," *Journal of the American Oriental Society* 101 (1981) 1–19, a critical survey of the literature.

7. R. N. Whybray, *The Intellectual Tradition in the Old Testament* (Beihefte zur Zeitschrift für die Alttestamentliche Wissenschaft 135; Berlin/New York: de Gruyter, 1974).

not found it useful to trace the affinities of clichés in the various collections, it seems helpful to display in an easily accessible way this byproduct of my investigations. A second index lists the repeated verses and clichés in order of occurrence in the book.[8]

---

8. My title itself contains a cliché. It occurs in a positive sense in a proverb known as early as 1577, "A good tale may be twice told" (quoted in W. G. Smith and F. P. Wilson, eds., *The Oxford Dictionary of English Proverbs* [Oxford: Clarendon, 1970] 802b). But it may be best remembered from Shakespeare's negative usage in *King John* 3:4:108: "Life is as tedious as a twice-told tale." Nathaniel Hawthorne in his first collection of short stories, *Twice Told Tales* (1837), was doubtless thinking of the proverb rather than of Shakespeare's line.

2

Theories of Composition

Yet great labor, directed by great abilities, is never wholly lost.
—Johnson

Israeli scholar Jehoshua Grintz, in his stimulating 1968 article "The Proverbs of Solomon," contributed the first serious analysis of the method used in putting together the Book of Proverbs.[1] Although the study cannot be said to have been neglected, it has not received the attention it deserves, probably because of its publication in Modern Hebrew, which is still a neglected language among biblicists. From his study of shared features in chapters 1–9, 10:1–22:16, and chapters 25–29, he develops theories about the affinities among the collections and about a two-stage history of the composition of the book.

Among the features Grintz observes are repeated verses of various sorts, but he refuses to speculate on the reason the repetitions occur (p. 91 below). He listed what he calls "expressions" in the collections. His term *expression* (Hebrew, הבעה) includes some of what I would call proverbial clichés (for a fuller treatment of the word *cliché* see pp. 16–18 below), but it also seems to include unusual words. He catalogs expressions occurring in only one collection, and then he lists those which appear in more than one collection.

Grintz concludes that many features of language are shared between the sections represented by chapters 1–9 and 10:1–22:16, but the latter section is similar in both content and language to chapters 25–29 (p. 111 below). His findings regarding similarities may be depicted graphically as follows (the alphabetic letters used to symbolize the collections were assigned by Grintz):

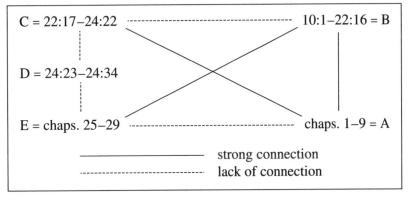

---

1. "משלי שלנה', "*Lešonenu* 33:4 (1968) ברורים בשאלת היחס שבין שלושת הקבצים בס' משלי המיוחסים לשלמה 243–69. The article is translated in full in an appendix to the present work. Further references to Grintz's article are cited by page number from the appendix below. In contrast J.-P. Mathieu, "Les deux collections salomoniennes," *Laval Théologie et Philosophie* 19 (1963) 171–78, is a brief and partial sketch.

TABLE 1. *Collections in the Book of Proverbs*

According to Grintz		*According to Snell*	
A	1:1–9:18	A	1:1–5:23, 6:20–9:18
B	10:1–22:16	A_6	6:1–19
C	22:17–24:22	B_1	10:1–14:25
D	24:23–34	B_2	14:26–16:15
E	25:1–29:27	B_3	16:16–22:16
F	30:1–14	C_E	22:17–23:11
G	30:15–33	C_H	23:12–24:22
H	31:1–9	D	24:23–34
I	31:10–31	E	25:1–29:27
		F_1	30:1–14
		F_2	30:15–33
		F_3	31:1–9
		F_4	31:10–31

Grintz summarizes his findings by saying, "The canonical order of the book is, as it appears, also the historical order" (p. 114 below). According to him a first edition of Proverbs included chapters 1–9 and 10:1–22:16 as well as 22:17–24:23; a second edition included 24:23–34, chapters 25–29, and possibly the other small collections as well. Grintz is inclined to date the second and final edition of the whole book in Hezekiah's time (p. 114 below). Table 1 summarizes Grintz's ordering of the collections (left side), and my own conclusions on the makeup of the collections (right side) provide the sigla used in the following chapters.

The major problem with Grintz's efforts is that he is not as precise as one could wish about distinctions between the kinds of expressions he is comparing, and so I find myself disagreeing with his theories about the affinities among the collections. For example, Grintz categorizes as an expression the parallel words *father* and *mother*, a parallelism which occurs often in the Book of Proverbs. Even though this category of expression may well be an example of a cliché, it does not really demonstrate the same level of affinity between collections as completely repeated verses do, such as Prov 20:16 and 27:13, which Grintz also includes in his category "expressions".[2] My own approach has been to define rigorously what it is I am comparing and to exclude proverbial clichés when the question of the affinity of the collections arises. (See chapter 4 for a more thorough examination of the distinction between cliché and repeated verses.)

Some of Grintz's findings also seem to be open to question. I do not wish at this time to tackle the problem of the section affinities which he poses, since I will return to them at the end of this study. But I do want to point out here some logical difficulties with his explanations.

The first thing to be said is that affinities between collections do not necessarily indicate the contemporaneity of collections, as Grintz claims (p. 111 below). Chapters 1–9 could have been familiar with 10:1–22:16 through the literary record and could have been influenced by them without their being composed by the same persons or in the same period.

---

2. See the entries for *father/mother* (p. 121, below) and the repeated verse (p. 35).

Second, Grintz's assertion (p. 106 below) that the school is the *Sitz im Leben* for Proverbs is perhaps more problematic today than it was when Grintz wrote. But what he says is still true, that chapters 1–9 and 22:17–24:23 are written in the instruction form.[3]

Grintz's conclusion (p. 111 below) that there is almost no relation between 10:1–22:16 and 22:17–24:23 or 24:24–34 is an important point of which more will be made later. Grintz is saying that the collection translated loosely from Egyptian is not related to 10:1–22:16 or 24:24–34, the collections that immediately surround it.

Another conjecture of his, on the other hand, the idea that chapters 25–29 must have been temporarily lost (p. 111 below), seems absurd. It emphasizes the connections among the "Solomonic" collections but does not explain anything. Josiah's finding of the scroll in the temple in 2 Kings 22 and the discovery of the Dead Sea Scrolls show that texts could be hidden and found again, but literary affinities do not make it necessary to posit such hiding.[4]

Again, Grintz's assertion that one person arranged the first two collections (p. 112 below) remains to be demonstrated, but I do not know how one would begin to do so. Evidence of language similarities could derive from other circumstances than the texts' having a single compositor.

Grintz's supposition that Solomon's time was a time of wisdom (p. 113–14 below) has in the interim been undermined by R. B. Y. Scott's demonstration that the stories of Solomon's wisdom are of a "marvellous" cast and probably are not as old as other elements in 1 Kings.[5] The argument conjecturing Canaanite influence on Proverbs 1–9, which arose out of W. F. Albright's 1955 article, also seems thinner today. Based on that argument, some might argue for an early date for Proverbs, but, as Albright himself saw, "Canaanite" culture continued into the Christian era and covered too many years to be helpful in dating collections.[6]

---

3. On schools see A. Lemaire, *Les Écoles et la Formation de la Bible dans l'ancien Israël* (Göttingen: Vandenhoeck & Ruprecht, 1981); and especially J. L. Crenshaw, "Education in Ancient Israel," *Journal of Biblical Literature* 104 (1985) 601–15. N. Shupak ("The *Sitz im Leben* of the Book of Proverbs in the Light of a Comparison of Biblical and Egyptian Wisdom Literature," *Revue biblique* 94 [1987] 98–119) argues that a similar vocabulary shows that the Israelites borrowed the idea and form of schools from Egypt. I am doubtful that this is necessarily the case.

4. Note that this terminology is not original with Grintz. A. Baumgartner (*Étude critique sur l'État du Texte du Livre des Proverbes* [Leipzig: Drugulin, 1890] 261) recalled that midrashic sources, commenting on Proverbs 25:1, asserted that the Book of Proverbs had been "hidden" (Hebrew גנוז), that is, regarded as noncanonical, for some time before it was accepted.

5. See R. B. Y. Scott, "Solomon and the Beginnings of Wisdom in Israel," in *Wisdom in Israel and in the Ancient Near East Presented to Professor Harold Henry Rowley* (ed. M. Noth and D. W. Thomas; Vetus Testamentum Supplements 3; Leiden: Brill, 1955) 262–79; and R. N. Whybray, "Wisdom Literature in the Reigns of David and Solomon," in *Studies in the Period of David and Solomon* (ed. T. Ishida; Winona Lake, Indiana: Eisenbrauns, 1982) 13–26.

6. W. F. Albright, "Some Canaanite-Phoenician Sources of Hebrew Wisdom," in *Wisdom in Israel and in the Ancient Near East Presented to Professor Harold Henry Rowley* (ed. M. Noth and D. W. Thomas; Vetus Testamentum Supplements 3; Leiden: Brill, 1955) 1–15. Albright's summary does not accord with Grintz's conclusion. Albright wrote, "In a nutshell my opinion with regard to the provenience and date of Proverbs is that its entire content is probably pre-exilic, but that much of the Book was handed down orally until the fifth century B.C., when we know from Elephantine that Jews were interested in literature of this kind" (p. 13). On possible Phoenician influence see, further, M. Dahood, "The Phoenician Contribution to Biblical Wisdom Literature," in *The Role of the Phoenicians in the Interaction of Mediterranean Civilization* (ed. W. Ward; Beirut: American University, 1968) 123–52.

Grintz's contention that the present order of the sections within Proverbs is the historical order is possible but still far from proven (p. 114 below). Certainly, biblical books can "grow" at the end, as he is suggesting; the accretion of Isaiah seems fairly clear. But biblical books can also grow at the beginning, if, for example, the priestly creation story in Genesis 1–2 is to be understood in that way.

Most other researchers have a different view, but none has developed it as systematically as Grintz did, and he is to be credited for directly attacking the problem. The current view seems to be that 10:1–22:16 is probably the oldest part of the book. This view is based partly on its attribution to Solomon and partly on the fact that these chapters are made up of one-line sayings and are therefore simpler in structure than the instructions, which are composed of larger units of thought.[7]

The other aspect of the composition of the book that seems generally agreed upon is that chapters 1–9 were composed after most of the book had been assembled and were intended as a prologue to it. There is some question about whether this happened before or after the exile in 587 B.C.E.[8] It should be noted, too, that Egyptian material shows no development from sentence literature to instruction form, and so there is no form-critical reason to assert that this first collection really must be latest just because it is in the instruction form.[9]

Further, it seems to be agreed that the other collections are mainly later than 10:1–22:16 but earlier than chapters 1–9. Patrick Skehan, however, maintained that the compositor of chapters 1–9, who was also the final editor, added the very end of chapter 31, the acrostic poem about the woman of valor.[10]

The view that the collections (aside from 10:1–22:16) are late seems to be supported by the organization of the book in the Septuagint, possibly from the third century B.C.E. The different order there indicates that the order of the collections in 24:23–34, chapters 25–29, and chapters 30:1–31:9 was not firmly set when the translation was completed. At the very least, the Septuagint order argues that these collections circulated as individual collections.[11]

The MT and Septuagint arrangements of the book are shown on p. 9. The Septuagint's order causes one to speculate that, at some period after 1:1–24:22 had attained its present arrangement, the positions of 24:23–34 and chapters 25–29 were not yet set. Later tradition, as represented by the MT, placed 24:23–34 and chapters 25–29 differently in relation to the indi-

---

7. See, for example, U. Skladny, *Die ältesten Spruchsammlungen in Israel* (Göttingen: Vandenhoeck & Ruprecht, 1962) 5–7; and Mathieu, "Les deux collections salomoniennes," 177–78, who sees Proverbs 25–29 as preserving some older forms of sayings in Prov 10:1–22:16 but assembled at a later date.

8. See C. Kayatz, *Studien zu Proverbian 1–9* (Neukirchen-Vluyn: Neukirchener Verlag, 1966), arguing for an earlier date.

9. See the study of ᶜ*Onchsheshonqy's Instruction* in W. McKane, *Proverbs* (Old Testament Library; Philadelphia: Westminster, 1970) 117–50.

10. P. Skehan, "A Single Editor for the Whole Book of Proverbs," in *Studies in Israelite Poetry and Wisdom* (Catholic Biblical Quarterly Monograph Series 1; Washington, D.C.: Catholic Biblical Association, 1971) 15–26; repr. in J. L. Crenshaw (ed.), *Studies in Ancient Israelite Wisdom* (New York: Ktav, 1976) 329–40. For possible late dates of the small collections, see L. Alonso Schökel and J. Vilchez Lindez, *Proverbios* (Madrid: Cristiandad, 1984) 104–5.

11. Against R. B. Y. Scott, "Wise and Foolish, Righteous and Wicked," in *Studies in the Religion of Ancient Israel* (Vetus Testamentum Supplement 23; Leiden: Brill, 1972) 150–51.

```
MT                          Septuagint
1–9                         same
10:1–22:16                  same
22:17–24:22                 same
                            30:1–14
24:23–34                    same
25–29
30:1–14
30:15–33                    same
31:1–9                      same
                            25–29
31:10–31                    same
```

vidual sections of chapters 30–31. The result of this is to cause modern students to surmise that both 24:23–34 and chapters 25–29 were composed later than 1:1–22:16, and that the relative lateness of chapters 25–29 may also be deduced from the headline mentioning Hezekiah, King of Judah, who reigned from 715 to 687/686 B.C.E., more than two centuries after Solomon.[12]

The consensus view can be summarized briefly as follows. The parts of the book were composed and joined in the following order: 10:1–22:16, 22:17–24:22, chapters 1–9, (24:23–34, chapters 25–29, chapters 30–31), the actual order of composition of the collections in parentheses being unknown. This order would not be accepted by all, as we will see below. But earlier students did not have available to them data about the propensity of the collections toward using repeated elements and about the affinities among the collections in using these elements. These data will allow a fresh approach to the question of the composition of the book.

Before using these data, one must consider what they might mean and why the repetitions might have arisen. What I propose to do is to take one characteristic of the Book of Proverbs—its propensity toward repetition—and study it in detail to see what it might tell about the composition of the book. But to do that one must have a clear view of what repetition is and how exactly it occurs. Actually, I will fail at explaining repetition, but because repetition shows that sections of the book had in one way or another an affinity for each other, I will still be able to speculate in a more informed way than before about the way the book came together. In spite of my problems with Grintz's work, I happily admit that he was the first to see that such an approach was possible and was likely to bear fruit.[13]

---

12. See R. N. Whybray, *The Intellectual Tradition in the Old Testament* (Beiheft zur Zeitschrift für die Alttestamentliche Wissenschaft 135; Berlin/New York: de Gruyter, 1974) 57. For the few other deviations in the Greek from the MT's ordering, see H. B. Swete, *An Introduction to the Old Testament in Greek* (1914; repr. New York: Ktav, 1968) 233. The significance of the omission of Prov 20:14–22 from the Greek will be considered below in the excursus.

13. In fact, I came across Grintz's work only after mine was more or less complete, so it comes as a confirmation of my approach rather than serving as its inspiration.

3

Theories about Repetition

Sir, it will be much exaggerated in public talk: for, in the first place, the common people do not accurately adapt their thoughts to the objects; nor, secondly, do they accurately adapt their words to their thoughts; they do not mean to lie; but, taking no pains to be exact, they give you very false accounts. A great part of their language is proverbial. If anything rocks at all, they say it *rocks like a cradle*; and in this way they go on.

—Johnson, after Boswell's remarks about an earthquake

Everyone who has read through the Book of Proverbs realizes that verses in the book sometimes occur more than once. But not everyone is agreed on what this phenomenon means or even on whether it has any significance. Dr. Johnson's observation that, in everyday speech, clichés, and especially proverbial clichés, proliferate even when they are inappropriate is still true today, and it contributes to a view that such proliferation is a kind of error. As we will see below, modern students have sometimes reacted similarly to repetition in the Book of Proverbs.

At this point I want to ask the following questions: (1) Is this repetition significant? (2) What are the reasons posited by other scholars for repetition and how could one test these reasons, and do some of them seem more probable than others?

First, is the repetition within Proverbs significant? Some suppose that it is meaningless, a scribal oversight, especially if no pattern can be seen in the repetitions. Or some might speculate that there were many small causes for repetition from which significant generalizations cannot be made. By way of analogy, repetitions in Psalms may be due to various poetic needs in the course of writing the various poems. But in Psalms, repetition actually shows an awareness of poetic clichés and may show affinity between collections insofar as whole passages are repeated. And the repetition of units of several lines is a major factor in arguments about the compilation of the Book of Psalms.[1]

---

1. Psalm 14, for example, is the same as Psalm 53, though they are only seven verses long; the former uses Yahweh and the latter uses אלהים for God. Also, Psalm 40:13–17 is the same as Psalm 70, and Psalm 108's thirteen verses are found in Ps 57:7–11 and 60:5–12. On the final assemblage of that book see G. H. Wilson, *The Editing of the Hebrew Psalter* (Chico, California: Scholars Press, 1985).

Comparative evidence also argues that repetition has significance. No other collections of aphorisms from the Near East have the extensive internal repetition that is in evidence in the Book of Proverbs; that is, they tend not to repeat sentences within what seems to be the same collection. For example, between 15% and 19% of the sentences in Edmund Gordon's Sumerian proverb collections appear in other collections, but none is actually repeated within the same collection.[2] Representing a different time, Dimitri Gutas's study of the Arabic gnomologia translated from Greek shows a very high percentage of sayings that are found in other collections and even in the Hebrew Bible itself, but apparently only one is actually repeated within the collection which Gutas studied.[3]

In contrast, in the Hebrew Book of Proverbs there seems to be a substantial number of sayings repeated among the various collections, and, more importantly, a striking volume of internal, or apparently internal, repetitions within the individual collections. It seems highly unlikely that this is merely an oversight on the part of editors or scribes; it must have some significance.

The second question, concerning the reasons for repetition, has received four answers. The traditional answer is that repetition is the result of literary cleavage similar to the doublettes in the Pentateuch: that is, various collections that circulated independently were joined to form the book, and the editors who did the joining respected the integrity of the contents of the collections even though some of the sayings consequently were used more than once. This is the view taken by Eissfeldt and has been followed widely elsewhere.[4]

The hypothesis of literary cleavage can be criticized on the grounds that even within the major collections, which are set off by their headlines, there is repetition. Proponents of the literary-cleavage theory speculate that editors created these marked collections from smaller unmarked collections. But inevitably such reasoning is circular: if repetition stems from literary cleavage, then repetition remains the major indication that there is literary cleavage. Such criticism may be labeled arbitrary due to the unavailability of collections earlier than those found in the Masoretic Bible.[5] One way to check this hypothesis is to observe whether repeated sayings occur in close

---

2. The data, from E. I. Gordon, *Sumerian Proverbs* (Philadelphia: University Museum, 1959) 25 and 153–54, are as follows: collection 1 has 202 sentences, of which 39 (or 19%) are found elsewhere; collection 2 has 164 (or 166) sentences of which 25 (or 15%) are found elsewhere. Other collections have fewer sharings. For a sampling, see also E. I. Gordon, "Sumerian Proverbs: 'Collection Four,'" *Journal of the American Oriental Society* 77 (1957) 67–79, esp. 67 and 69; and idem, "Sumerian Animal Proverbs and Fables: 'Collection Five,'" *Journal of Cuneiform Studies* 12 (1958) 1–21, 43–75, esp. 2–3.

3. See D. Gutas, *Greek Wisdom Literature in Arabic Translation: A Study of the Graeco-Arabic Gnomologia* (American Oriental Series 60; New Haven: American Oriental Society, 1975), especially the tables of concordance, pp. 483–90 for Arabic collections, and 490–92 for Greek. For the repeated saying, see p. 431 and note Gutas's comment, "The compiler promptly noted this following S 56 [Gutas's sigla for a saying by Socrates; this particular saying is also attributed to Plato]: 'Some people, though, say that this is one of Plato's sayings.'" One may argue that the Arabic compiler was simply more careful and self-conscious than the compiler(s) of Proverbs, but it appears that some repetition in Proverbs goes beyond sloppiness to some sort of significance. F. Delitzsch notes that his colleague H. L. Fleischer in 1836 had suggested an analogy between the repetitions in the Book of Proverbs and those among the Arabic proverb collections (*Biblical Commentary on the Proverbs of Solomon* [Edinburgh: T. & T. Clark, 1894] 1:26 n. 1; see also p. ix).

4. O. Eissfeldt, *The Old Testament: An Introduction* (trans. P. R. Ackroyd; New York: Harper & Row, 1965) 472.

5. I do not wish to accuse G. E. Bryce of arbitrariness; his proposal deserves consideration, but he does use what I regard as a cliché—and in its later occurrence a clearly mangled one (in 25:2b and 25:27b)—as part of his argument for setting off this "book" ("Another Wisdom-'Book' in Proverbs," *Journal of Biblical Literature* 91 [1972] 145–57).

proximity to each other on a regular basis. If they do, or if they do in some parts of the book, it would seem that the hypothesis of literary cleavage could be ruled out at least for those parts of the book, though it might hold for other parts.

Patrick Skehan put forward a second and quite ingenious explanation of repetition.[6] He argues that verses were repeated by a final editor of the book who did not see fit to respect the integrity of the individual collections but who wanted to achieve a correspondence between the number of verses and the numerical value of the names that stand at the beginning of the book, Solomon, son of David, king of Israel. The numerical values are as follows:

שלמה	=	300 + 30 + 40 + 5	=	375
דוד	=	4 + 6 + 4	=	14
ישראל	=	10 + 300 + 200 + 1 + 30	=	541
			Total	930

Skehan notes that 375, the value of Solomon's name, is the same as the number of verses in the major collection in the book, 10:1–22:16. In Skehan's own count there are now 932 separate sayings in the book, although the Masoretic verse divisions net only 915. Skehan believes that the loci for the final editor's additions were at the beginning of collection 10:1–22:16 and in the middle of that collection, around chapter 15, where he observes a number of verses also found elsewhere.[7]

This suggestion is attractive because it does not have recourse to hypothetical earlier collections. But Skehan's counting of the sayings may be disputed and does not correspond to the verse divisions, which are very late and which also show some variation regarding what is considered a verse. The collections at the end of the book do not number each independent clause separately, while those toward the beginning of the book tend to number each clause. The late medieval enumerator must have gotten bored!

The major impediment to the acceptance of Skehan's hypothesis is that, as he himself points out, the use of the Hebrew alphabet with numerical values is not attested until a late date.[8] Skehan notes that the attention to the alphabet afforded in the acrostic poem in 31:10–31 may be in-

---

6. P. Skehan, "A Single Editor for the Whole Book of Proverbs," in *Studies in Israelite Poetry and Wisdom* (Catholic Biblical Quarterly Monograph Series 1; Washington, D.C.: Catholic Biblical Association, 1971) 15–26; repr. in *Studies in Ancient Israelite Wisdom* (ed. J. L. Crenshaw; New York: Ktav, 1976) 329–40. The fact that Prov 10:1–22:16 has 375 verses (the same as the numerical value of the name *Solomon*) and that Proverbs 25–29 has 136 (like the name of *Hezekiah*) was first observed in a short note by P. Behnke ("Spr 10,1. 25,1," *Zeitschrift für die Alttestamentliche Wissenschaft* 16 [1896] 122), as pointed out by S. Perry (*Structural Patterns in Proverbs 10:1–22:16: A Study in Biblical Hebrew Stylistics* [Ph.D. diss., University of Texas, 1987] 57). Perry notes that Skehan did not acknowledge Behnke's priority, if he was aware of it. Behnke was unwilling to guess at the meaning of his discoveries.

7. Note also that Skehan wishes to read into the headline of 25:1 an indication of the size of the section comprising chapters 25–29. He reads יחזקיה instead of the MT's חזקיה to get the number 140, which approximates the 138 verses into which the MT divides the section; see Skehan, *Studies in Israelite Poetry and Wisdom*, 17 n. 7, and in more detail his essay "Wisdom's House," pp. 27–45 in the same volume, esp. pp. 43–45. These theories are explored further by Stephen Brown, "The Structure of Proverbs 10:1–22:16" (Paper delivered at the annual meeting of the Society of Biblical Literature, 1988), which I have through the courtesy of Ted Hildebrandt. Brown argues that Skehan's division into "columns" of 25 verses each is supported by chiasms within each "column."

8. According to *Gesenius' Hebrew Grammar* (ed. E. Kautzsch; trans. A. E. Cowley; Oxford: Clarendon, 1910), §5k, the first use of Hebrew letters for numbers is on some Maccabean coins dated to 140/139 B.C.E.

dicative of the concerns of the final editor. The correspondence between the numerical value of Solomon's name and the number of verses in 10:1–22:16 is interesting, however, and clearly in the Egyptian collection there is an awareness of the number of sayings being transmitted.[9]

Skehan's hypothesis remains attractive, but, even if an earlier date for the numerical use of the alphabet were to be attested, its use in Proverbs would remain essentially a matter of conjecture, since there does not seem to be any way to substantiate it. The scholar would have to question whether the final editor was interested in the objectively seen bulk of the book and whether the editor might have freely inserted sayings to meet the proposed goal.

A third possible explanation, suggested by James L. Crenshaw, is that repetition is present simply for emphasis. R. Carlson argues that repetitions in the prose story of Elijah owe their existence not to literary cleavage but to the desire of the narrator to emphasize what is repeated.[10]

Robert Alter's study of poetry examines the uses of repetition in some detail, though not with regard to the Book of Proverbs in particular. Alter argues that repetition is used to achieve "a focusing, a heightening, a concretization, a development of meaning."[11] I would include all of these functions under the general rubric of emphasis, though obviously in particular cases the term *emphasis* may turn out to be too broad a description of what is intended.

In the chapter on Proverbs, Alter has many useful things to say about the compactness of one-line verses. Though he mentions the possibility that some repetition derives from the practice of proverb-capping, where a teacher presents a half-verse which students are then expected to cap with an appropriate ending, he does not commit himself to that as an explanation for repetition. He does draw attention to "a certain quality of predictability, of mechanical variation on a fixed set of themes" that may make repetition common.[12]

The idea that verses are repeated for emphasis is hard to test. One would have to understand the content of the saying and determine whether that saying was likely to be one that the ancients would have wished to emphasize. But in trying to weigh this likelihood, one would be influenced by the content of the rest of the book. It might be possible to disprove the emphasis hypothesis if a repeated saying were found that seemed to contradict what we understand to be the basic premises of the book or of Hebrew ethics. But such a case of repetition would obviously show only that a specific case was not intended for emphasis. It would not show that other sayings were not repeated for emphasis. And when one considers the possibility that repetition derives from poetic or rhetorical motives, then it is necessary to study the context of each repetition in a commentarylike exposition. This is clearly of great value, and Raymond Van Leeuwen's study of chapters 25–27 is in many ways a model of what can be accomplished.[13]

A fourth possible explanation, suggested by Bendt Alster for the Sumerian *Instructions of Shuruppak*, is that repetition is the result of some sort of oral formulaic composition, analogous

---

9. Prov 22:20: "Have I not written for you thirty [sayings] about admonition and knowledge?" Note also R. N. Whybray's division of Proverbs 1–9 into ten discourses on the basis of introductory formulas; see *Wisdom in Proverbs* (Studies in Biblical Theology 45; London: SCM, 1965) 33–52.

10. Crenshaw, personal correspondence regarding an earlier draft of this study. R. A. Carlson's study is "Élie à L'Horeb," *Vetus Testamentum* 19 (1969) 416–39, esp. 432.

11. R. Alter, *The Art of Biblical Poetry* (New York: Basic Books, 1985) 29.

12. Ibid., 163–84; the quotation is from p. 163.

13. R. C. Van Leeuwen, *Context and Meaning in Proverbs 25–27* (Atlanta: Scholars Press, 1988).

to what is found in the Homeric poems.[14] The slipperiness of oral transmission has been underlined recently in New Testament studies by Werner Kelber, who argues that verbatim repetition is not an essential part of oral transmission. He writes, "The formulaic quality of oral speech must not suggest mechanized learning processes, and oral clichés are not to be confused with literal consistency."[15] It is difficult to determine whether a piece of written literature was transmitted orally. But repetition of clichés is a common device used by modern composers of oral material.

The idea that verses are repeated as part of a method of oral formulaic composition must be tested by looking at contexts, to see whether, for example, the same pattern of repetitions occurs together more than once. But the lack of such a pattern would not necessarily prove that oral composition techniques were not being used. The Book of Proverbs lacks the relative coherence of the *Instructions of Shuruppak*, and it may be that the other Sumerian proverb collections are not as unified either. Inevitably, this hypothesis will also remain to some extent unprovable since no two scholars would agree on what is oral and what is not oral in biblical poetry, especially in biblical gnomic sayings. This problem is complicated, as it is in Sumerian, by the fact that, though oral techniques may have given rise to the "original" composition, it is writing techniques that have transmitted and preserved the compositions.[16]

There may be other useful hypotheses that might reasonably be proposed, but to test them and to devise new theories it is necessary first to describe clearly the repetitions in the Book of Proverbs and the locations of the repeated verses.

---

14. That is, Alster thinks that, like *Dumuzi's Dream*, the *Instructions of Shuruppak* were fixed when they were written down for the first time, at least as early as Abu Salabikh (about 2600 B.C.E.), but that the oral technique went on unchanged even though the composition had been written. Hence Alster writes, "Insofar as we may be able to interpret them as meaningful poems, not merely schematic compilations, we must conclude that they were created by literate people who utilized an oral technique of composition" (*Studies in Sumerian Proverbs* [Copenhagen: Akademisk, 1975] 81). He sees even the less clearly coherent Sumerian collections as "proverb poems" using oral material: "It must be remembered that, if by proverb collection we understand a more or less systematically organized documentary collection of sayings, either collected from literary sources, or among the folk, then such collections seem in general to be absent from the ancient world. However, if we extend the designation proverb collection to include also such literary poems which mainly are composed by means of freely used proverbial material, then we will find ample documentation in the ancient literatures" (p. 14).

15. W. Kelber, *The Oral and Written Gospel: The Hermeneutics of Speaking and Writing in the Synoptic Tradition, Mark, Paul, and Q* (Philadelphia: Fortress, 1983) 27. Kelber goes on, "Oral formulas, clichés, and commonplaces assure remembering and transmission. At the same time, oral formulas, clichés, and commonplaces are changeable, adaptable, and interchangeable." Compare, for the study of aphorisms and proverbs in the same material, J. D. Crossan, *In Fragments: The Aphorisms of Jesus* (San Francisco: Harper & Row, 1983). Both references in this note are through the courtesy of Leo Perdue.

16. Traditional explanations for repetition are summarized by W. O. E. Oesterley, *The Book of Proverbs* (Westminster Commentaries; London: Methuen, 1929) xvii–xviii: (1) small collections containing the same or similar proverbs may have been joined together; (2) the "sage may have purposely used the same saying more than once in order to adapt it to a different context"; (3) "a well-known saying might have been used twice over by the same collector, but altered slightly in order to suit a different context"; (4) "a saying may have been an oral one originally, and have been inaccurately quoted"; and (5) the text may have been corrupted. Oesterly concludes that nearly identical sayings "must either be due to carelessness, or they may be the work of a later scribe who overlooked the fact that they had already been utilized." These explanations are essentially the same as the ones analyzed above, except for Skehan's numerological hypothesis. For Oesterly, repetition seems to be a mistake that has to be explained away. But I contend that the practice of repeated verses is so widespread in the book that such a view cannot be correct.

4

How Are Verses Repeated?

> We may know historical facts to be true, as we may know facts in common life to be true. Motives are generally unknown. We cannot trust to the characters we find in history, unless when they are drawn by those who knew the persons; as those, for instance, by Sallust and by Lord Clarendon.
>
> —Johnson

We are less sure today than Johnson was about the accessibility of historical facts, but it is still true that motives elude even historians' acquaintances. And yet a clear description of the "historical facts"—in the case of Proverbs, a statistical analysis of the use of words—may allow us to reconstruct more clearly the way in which Proverbs was compiled. We will certainly never get close to understanding the motives of the editors without such a description. To that descriptive task we now turn.

There are two main ways in which sayings are repeated in the Book of Proverbs: sometimes a whole verse is reflected in a whole verse elsewhere in the book and sometimes only half the verse is reflected in another half-verse elsewhere. There are also cases which show a correspondence between half of one verse and the whole of another. A few sayings share similar syntax without sharing vocabulary; these sayings may be conscious or semiconscious recollection of an earlier proverb.[1]

My goal is to present these data in a way that will make it possible for people with other theories of the composition of the book and more comparative materials at hand to use the book's

---

1. The most recent attempt at a list of repeated verses is apparently C. Steuernagel's *Lehrbuch der Einleitung in das Altes Testament* (Tübingen: Mohr, 1912) 679–80, which list is clearly incomplete. He lists about 133 verses, and I have found 200 involved in various kinds of repetition. Compare also C. H. Toy, *Proverbs* (International Critical Commentary; Edinburgh: T. & T. Clark, 1899) vii–viii. R. B. Y. Scott in his brilliant article, "Wise and Foolish, Righteous and Wicked" in *Studies in the Religion of Ancient Israel* (Vetus Testamentum Supplement 23; Leiden: Brill, 1971) 146–65, recognizes a distinction between wholly repeated and half-repeated verses, but he also includes as a separate category verses in which very similar thoughts are differently expressed (p. 151). I do not consider these verses real cases of repetition, and it seems to me that choosing them is being more subjective than I am willing to be in this study. Also, Scott ignores repetitions between the collections in which one-line sayings predominate and other collections, though he recognizes that there are some (p. 152). Furthermore, he does not consider the clichés systematically, though he does discuss a few of them (e.g., pp. 156, 161).

distinctive qualities rather than to be baffled by them. It is not clear whether these different sorts of repetition are the products of the different social milieux of the writers or the products of different goals and different situations in life; to answer such questions would be the task of traditional form criticism. My purpose here, however, is first to present the data as I perceive them and then to see whether they are significant in reconstructing the book's composition.

Related to the typology of repetition is the phenomenon I call the proverbial cliché. The usual way of identifying possible repetitions has been the lexical operation of surveying pairs of words that occur together. From this survey, however, it can be seen that although some word pairs occur in sayings that also share other words, some do not. It is impossible to be sure that such pairs really are clichés, habitually used and folksy sounding, relevant expressions. But it is obvious that the only way to identify such potential clichés in a dead language is to catalog instances in which two or more words appear in the same sentence and seem related to each other. That is what I have tried to do in the index of repeated verses and clichés (pp. 119–38 below).

In English a cliché is "a trite phrase or expression," where "trite" means "hackneyed or boring from much use."[2] But of word pairs that occur more than once in Proverbs, one can only say that they are much used, not necessarily that they are hackneyed. It is also quite likely that there are other phrases that occur only once in Proverbs that may have sounded hackneyed to contemporary listeners; it may be possible to identify some of these through the study of other biblical books, especially those that on other grounds are thought to be part of the wisdom tradition. But here I want to use, insofar as possible, purely objective criteria to define a core vocabulary within the Book of Proverbs. It is inevitable that I have missed some word pairs and longer phrases because they occur only in repeated verses. I tried to index all words in repeated verses, but I have not done so for proverbial clichés. I did make an effort to catalog these, but there are a great many of them, and their significance for showing possible affinities among parts of the book seems to be much less than that of the repeated verses.

I believe, nonetheless, that the repeated verses and the clichés are both parts of the same phenomenon, which is the method of expression of the wisdom thinkers. That way of expression may also have been common among other parts of Israelite society, and it clearly included many of the clichés used by other writers of Biblical Hebrew.

Students of the book will have two opposite objections to my selection of clichés, both of which are quite legitimate: either that too many word pairs have been called clichés here, or that not enough have. I will briefly defend what I have done against each objection.

Some will say that I have considered too many word pairs to be clichés because I have usually made separate entries for words that appear to us to be virtually synonymous, for example ערום 'clever' and חכם 'wise' (see pp. 133 and 125 below). The question to be asked is whether there is a difference between linking 'clever' with 'fool' and linking 'wise' with 'fool', both of which occur as separate entries in my index. Probably not. I admit that occasionally I have combined synonyms that seem completely similar when they occur in the same contexts: an example of this is my classification of שמר נפשו 'guard oneself' and נצר נפשו 'keep oneself' as the same cliché (p. 137).

---

2. *Webster's Ninth New Collegiate Dictionary* (Springfield, Massachusetts: Merriam, 1985).

Also, I have created separate entries for verses that share a cliché with some verses and also share the cliché and some more words with other verses. An example would be the many verses that share the cliché תועבת יהוה 'an abomination to Yahweh' (p. 138). Four of them contrast that phrase with רצונו 'his desire' or, more loosely, 'what he wants'. Undoubtedly I have not recognized all of these more closely related verses, and that may lead others to count more clichés than I have.

Those who would find more clichés might be using synonyms as equivalents. For example, since מטר 'downpour' and גשם 'rain' are synonyms, some scholars would classify both אין גשם (25:14) and מטר . . . אין (28:3) as the same cliché. But I find the syntax and sense of these two verses dissimilar and have not included them together as a cliché. There are other cases where two words are used in two different verses but have not been included here because I felt that the words really were unrelated.[3] My criterion for deciding relatedness was whether the words occurred in grammatical relation to each other, in proximity to one another, or seemed related in sense.

After compiling the initial index of clichés, I began to resurvey the book to see if I could not find more that were less closely related to each other. Surveying only the letters of the alphabet ב through ח, I found an additional 122 pairs of words that occur together in two or more verses but which were not so closely related to each other as those in the index. Clearly this process could have been carried through to the end of the alphabet, but the result of it would not have been to isolate many real clichés. It seems to me mere happenstance that, for example, בעל 'lord' and נפש 'soul' occur together twice, in 1:19 and 23:2. But others might have included the occurrences of לב 'heart' and גבה 'high' in 16:5 and 18:12.

Probably in all this I have ended up relying on my feeling for the Biblical Hebrew language, which is fairly unreliable since I am not a native speaker. But I believe that my decisions are not arbitrary ones, and I have attempted to explain them in the notes to the index of clichés.

The problem arises of how to distinguish a cliché of several words from a repeated saying or a half-repeated saying (with perhaps one or two dissimilar words). What I have tried to do is to classify verses or half-verses as repeated if the sense of the whole clause is essentially the same in both instances; if it is not, I have classed the saying contained in it as a cliché.

The problems caused by this approach may be illustrated by an example that uses what is probably a cliché, בנה בית 'build a house'. The phrase occurs as follows in the book:

חכמות בנתה ביתה חצבה עמרדיה שבעה	9:1	Wisdom built her house, set up her seven pillars.
חכמות נשים בנתה ביתה ואולת בידיה תהרסנו	14:1	The wisdom of women built her house, but foolishness in her hand will destroy it.
בחכמה יבנה בית ובתבונה יתכונן	24:3	With wisdom a house is built, and with understanding it is established.
הכן בחוץ מלאכתך ועתדה בשדה לך אחר ובנית ביתך	24:27	Establish your work outside and prepare it in a field of yours; afterwards you build your house.

---

3. Other verses that might contain clichés, but which I have rejected, include 11:14 (רב־עם) and 14:28 (רב־עם); 10:15 (עז, מחתה) and 10:29 (מחתה, מעז); 13:11 and 28:8 (הון, קבץ); 15:31 and 19:23 (לין, חיים); 17:2 and 19:14 (משכיל, נחלה); 6:4, 10:10, 22:9, 23:26, and 23:31 (נתן, עין); 17:4 and 29:12 (מקשיב, שקר).

These include, incidentally, all the occurrences of the verb בנה in the book. I have classified the relation between 9:1 and 14:1 as that of a half-repeated verse with one dissimilar word since 14:1 specifies 'the wisdom of *women*' instead of the personified 'Wisdom' as subject. I have classified the relation between these two and 24:3 as that of a half-repeated verse with two dissimilar words since 'wisdom' is preceded by a preposition, is spelled differently, is not the subject of the sentence, and בנה is in the passive in 24:3. But because all three key words do occur in 24:3, I feel that it is essentially the same saying in spite of the differences. Prov 24:27 does not mention wisdom and the verb is in the second person; it and the others share only the cliché.

I initially attempted to classify clichés by their number of words and kinds of affinities, but I concluded that these distinctions were probably meaningless because synonyms for either term in a two-word cliché are frequently used; it does not seem reasonable to say that additional synonyms really change the classification, though they may edge the verse toward being a wholly repeated verse.

It seems likely that my distinctions in kinds of repetition are for the most part purely descriptive and not reflective of the concerns of the compositors, except perhaps where certain types of repetition cluster in the book. I have concentrated on the repeated verses and half-verses only because their affinities to each other are clearer, not because I see them as a separate phenomenon from clichés. They are simply easier to study.

This study was prepared without the use of a computer for indexing and, therefore, it may be possible quite easily to devise an exhaustive index of clichés with that aid.[4] Still, I think that such a listing would be less important for understanding the affinities of parts of the book than using repeated verses, and I believe I have an exhaustive list of such verses.

TYPES OF REPETITION

The various categories of repetition are discussed below. The verses cited here are merely representative of each category; see chapter 5 for a complete listing.

1.0 Whole verses repeated with spelling variations (6 sets).

Here I have also included the instances in which verses differ only in having spelling variations or the insertion of the prefix -וְ 'and'. For example:

מִי־פֶּתִי יָסֻר הֵנָּה חֲסַר־לֵב אָמְרָה לּוֹ   9:4   Who is simple, let him turn aside to here; one lacking sense, she speaks to him.

---

4. Computer study will serve as a check on my method, but it will not be a substitute for the creative search for similarities. See the preliminary computer-aided work of Steven Perry: *Structural Patterns in Proverbs 10:1–22:16: A Study in Biblical Hebrew Stylistics* (Ph.D. diss., University of Texas, 1987); reference courtesy of Ted Hildebrandt. But notice that when Perry deals with catchwords (p. 193), he discovers only one instance (the play on איש and אשה in 11:16–17) not noted by Boström in 1928 (see G. Boström, *Paronomasi i den äldre hebreiska Maschallitteraturen* [Lund: Gleerup/Leipzig: Harrassowitz, 1928]).

מי־פתי יסר הנה וחסר־לב ואמרה לו   9:16   Who is simple, let him turn aside to here, and one lacking sense, and she speaks to him.

1.1 Whole verses repeated with one dissimilar word (6 sets).

The dissimilar words are usually synonyms or additional words that seem to add little new to the sense. For example:

עד שקרים לא ינקה ויפיח כזבים לא ימלט   19:5   A witness of lies will not be declared innocent, and a testifyer of falsehoods will not escape.

עד שקרים לא ינקה ויפיח כזבים יאבד   19:9   A witness of lies will not be declared innocent, and a testifyer of falsehoods will perish.

1.2 Whole verses repeated with two dissimilar words (11 sets).

Many of the dissimilar words are synonymous, but others are not. For example:

טוב־רש הולך בתמו מעקש שפתיו והוא כסיל   19:1   Better is a poor one who walks in his simplicity than a crooked one of lips, and he a fool.

טוב־רש הולך בתמו מעקש דרכים והוא עשיר   28:6   Better is a poor one who walks in his simplicity than a crooked one of ways, and he a rich one.

1.3 Whole verses repeated with three dissimilar words (9 sets).

Some of the dissimilar words are closely related to each other; for example, 16:2 and 21:2 express the same idea but use the plural versus the singular of דרך 'way' and use synonyms in the other dissimilar words:

כל־דרכי־איש זך בעיניו ותכן רוחות יהוה   16:2   All the ways of a man are pure in his eyes, but Yahweh is an estimator of spirits.

כל־דרך־איש ישר בעיניו ותכן לבות יהוה   21:2   Each way of a man is upright in his eyes, but Yahweh is an estimator of hearts.

1.4 Whole verses repeated with four or more dissimilar words (10 sets).

Here the sayings deviate further from each other, and yet the similar meanings lead me to think that the sayings are more closely related than verses that share only a pair of words. The extreme case is 19:25 and 21:11, which actually have only three words in common and differ in syntax, but the other words are synonymous and the sense is precisely the same in each verse:

לץ תכה ופתי יערם והוכיח לנבון יבין דעת   19:25   A scoffer you hit, and a simple one gets smart; and correct an understanding one, he understands knowledge.

בענש־לץ יחכם־פתי ובהשכיל לחכם יקח־דעת   21:11   In the punishment of a scoffer a simple one gets wise, and in the enlightenment of a wise one he gets knowledge.

2.0 Half-verses repeated with spelling variations (16 sets).

Here and in the other instances of half-repeated verses I have also included cases in which verses may share words in the nonidentical half-verse, if such words appear to be synonyms of words in the identical half-verse. A problematic example that I have classified under category 1.2 above (but which some may have wanted to place here) is 1:8 and 6:20, where the dissimilar half-verses both refer to 'your father':

שמע בני מוסר אביך ואל־תטש תורת אמך	1:8	Hear, my son, the discipline of your father, and do not neglect the teaching of your mother.
נצר בני מצות אביך ואל־תטש תורת אמך	6:20	Guard, my son, the command of your father, and do not neglect the teaching of your mother.

A clearer example is the following:

חכם־לב יקח מצות ואויל שפתים ילבט	10:8	One wise of heart gets commands, but a fool of lips will be thrust down.
קרץ עין יתן עצבת ואויל שפתים ילבט	10:10	One who winks an eye gives trouble, but a fool of lips will be thrust down.

Such cases sometimes approach those of completely repeated sayings with two or three words dissimilar, but the distinction is usually clear.

2.1 Half-verses repeated with one dissimilar word (20 sets).

Here the problem I mentioned above comes into play, of whether to classify such sayings as half-verses or merely as clichés. I have tried to keep in this category sayings that seem to be synonymous in meaning, and I have relegated to the status of clichés those that do not seem to be synonymous. An extreme case is 13:1b and 13:8b where 'scoffer' and 'poor man' do not seem synonymous, at least not to the modern reader:

בן חכם מוסר אב ולץ לא־שמע גערה	13:1	A wise son is a discipline of a father, but a scoffer does not hear scolding.
כפר נפש־איש עשרו ורש לא־שמע גערה	13:8	The ransom of the soul of a man is his wealth, but a poor one does not hear scolding.

Because the rest of the half-verse is the same, I prefer to allow the possibility that in a compositor's mind these categories of people were not dissimilar.

2.2 Half-verses repeated with two dissimilar words (22 sets).

An example of sayings related in this way may be found in the discussion above of 9:1, 14:1, and 24:3, using 'build a house'. Obviously, as fewer and fewer words are shared, the meanings of sayings may be rather different. Prov 22:29 as a whole argues that quickness in work is a good quality; 29:20 as a whole says that quickness in speech is hopelessly bad—but their lexical and syntactic similarities situate them together:

חזית איש מהיר במלאכתו לפני־מלכים יתיצב | 22:29 You have observed a man hasty in his work—
בל־יתיצב לפני חשכים | before kings he will stand; he will not stand before low ones.

חזית איש אץ בדבריו תקוה לכסיל ממנו | 29:20 You have observed a man quick in his words—there is more hope for a fool than him.

3.0 Half-verses repeated in whole verse with each word in the half-verse appearing in the whole (4 sets).

Again, the general sense of all or many of these sayings is similar, but the distinctions I propose do seem to exist. A complex example, which I take to be one case of whole repetition and one of half-whole repetition, follows:

מאזני מרמה תועבת יהוה ואבן שלמה רצונו | 11:1 | Scales of deception are an abomination to Yahweh, and a complete stone is his desire

תועבת יהוה אבן ואבן ומאזני מרמה לא־טוב | 20:23 } 1.2 | An abomination to Yahweh is a stone and a stone, and scales of deception are not good.

אבן ואבן איפה ואיפה תועבת יהוה גם־שניהם | 20:10 } 3.0 | A stone and a stone, a grain measure and a grain measure are an abomination to Yahweh—also both of them.

Prov 11:1a seems to have both its elements used in the separate clauses of 20:23, and 20:23a has both its elements in the two halves of 20:10. The question which arises in this category especially is whether it is possible to say anything about which saying was likely to have been formulated earlier. I do not see that we can answer that question merely by looking at the verses as they now stand, though it is conceivable that the contexts of the sayings in the book may make some speculations possible in this regard.

3.1 and **3.2** Half-verses repeated in whole verses with one (3.1–6 sets) and with two dissimilar words (3.2–1 set).

As with the half-verses themselves, these categories are sometimes unclear. The extreme case is 20:8 and 20:26a, which share only two words, though the general sense seems to be the same:

מלך יושב על־כסא־דין מזרה בעיניו כל־רע | 20:8 | A king sitting on a throne of judgment scatters with his eyes all evil.

מזרה רשעים מלך חכם וישב עליהם אופן | 20:26 | A wise king scatters bad ones, and returns upon them a wheel.

4.0 Syntactically related verses.[5]

Two verses from the category which I define as *A is B and C is D* (4.3) may serve as an example of the entire category:

---

5. By *syntax* I mean "the way in which words are put together to form phrases, clauses, or sentences" (*Webster's Ninth Collegiate Dictionary*). Some might prefer the use of the term *rhetoric*, but it is in my opinion vaguer, "a type or mode of language or speech," (ibid). Also, M. O'Connor criticizes a broad use of "rhetoric" (*Hebrew Verse Structure* [Winona Lake, Indiana: Eisenbrauns, 1980] 10).

כי נר מצוה ותורה אור ודרך חיים תוכחות מוסר   6:23 For commandment is a lamp and instruction is
                                                     light, and the way of life is the corrections of
                                                     discipline.

שקר החן והבל היפי אשה יראת־יהוה היא תתהלל   31:30 Grace is a lie, and beauty a puff of breath;
                                                     a woman fearing Yahweh will be praised.

I have not included here the many instances of antonymous parallelism that characterizes many
verses, especially in chapters 10–15. I have only included other typical constructions that occur
more than once. Some of the verses cited are also repeated in one way or another, but they are included here because they share a syntactical pattern with other verses but do not share vocabulary with them. It is certain that I have not caught all possible instances of each syntactical form
since there is no systematic lexical way to find them. I have discussed elsewhere some of the
problems with the most numerous type of syntactical form noted here, which I call the double-
verb form (4.2), and others have studied the various "Better . . . than . . ." forms (4.5, 4.8).[6] It
seems possible that such peculiarities may also be a way to trace influences of the wisdom tradition beyond Proverbs.[7]

We do not know if perhaps some of the sayings in the book were at some stage real folk
proverbs as part of an oral tradition, but it is intriguing to note that A. Dundes has found that in
such proverbs there appear "to be a finite number of proverb compositional or architectural formulas," and he mentions formulas with "Better . . . than. . . ."[8] Dundes sees oral proverbs as
consisting of a topic and then a comment, with some proverbs being primarily identificational
("Money talks") while others are oppositional ("Hindsight is better than foresight"). He sees a
continuum running from proverbs that do not stress opposites to those that do.[9] It is possible
that further study of the syntax of the Book of Proverbs with Dundes' views in mind would be
quite fruitful.

---

6. D. C. Snell, "Notes on Love and Death in Proverbs," in *Love and Death in the Ancient Near East: Essays in
Honor of Marvin H. Pope* (ed. J. H. Marks and R. M. Good; Guilford, Connecticut: Four Quarters, 1987) 165–68;
and G. S. Ogden, "The 'Better'-Proverb (*Tōb-Spruch*), Rhetorical Criticism, and Qoheleth," *Journal of Biblical Literature* 96 (1977) 489–505.

7. Clearly more can be done in this regard within the Book of Proverbs itself, using perhaps transformational
grammar or constituent and unit analysis (as in O'Connor, *Hebrew Verse Structure*), as Ted Hildebrandt suggests in
a personal communication.

8. A. Dundes, "On the Structure of the Proverb," in *Analytic Essays in Folklore* (The Hague: Mouton, 1975)
105.

9. Ibid., 108, 114–15; the examples are from pp. 109 and 111.

Excursus: Repeated Verses in the Septuagint

I will not engage myself in an invidious comparison by opposing one passage to another—a work of which there would be no end, and which might be offensive without use.

—Johnson, on English versions of the *Aeneid*

The earliest translation of the Book of Proverbs is the Septuagint, and it is of interest to compare how the repeated verses identified below are translated into Greek. Since none of the translators is still alive, we may safely oppose passages one to another without giving offense. In 1979 Jack Berezov examined many of the instances of repetition and suggested that the translators were actually avoiding translating repeated sayings in the same way because of their esthetic judgment that repetition was inelegant.[1]

A survey of the Greek translation indicates that there is a range of ways of handling repeated verses in the book. Some of them are either omitted or simply translated with different words. But in most instances the translators made some effort to reflect the Hebrew repetition.

Table 2 shows the numbers of words that are similar or the same in repetitions classified according to the kinds of repetition that are seen in Hebrew. I compiled the table by comparing each instance of repetition in chapter 5 with the Septuagint and noting the use of the same words or similar words in the repeated instances. I call a word "similar" if it is from the same Greek root but in a different form or a different case. Table 2 shows that there is in fact a variety of ways of dealing with repeated verses in the Septuagint. No verse is actually completely repeated, though several come very close, including the following:

10:1~15:20 (category 1.2):

10:1	Υἱὸς σοφὸς εὐφραίνει πατέρα,
	υἱὸς δὲ ἄφρων λύπη τῇ μητρί.
	A wise son gladdens a father,
	but a stupid son is a sorrow to the mother.
15:20	υἱὸς σοφὸς εὐφραίνει πατέρα,
	υἱὸς δὲ ἄφρων μυκτηρίζει μητέρα αὐτοῦ.
	A wise son gladdens a father,
	but a stupid son mocks his mother.

---

1. Jack L. Berezov, "Remarks on the LXX Translation of Duplicate Proverbs," in *Society of Biblical Literature Abstracts 1979* (ed. P. Achtemeier; Missoula: Scholars Press, 1979) 65. Dr. Berezov kindly sent me a full copy of his paper, which he has not yet published. Note also that G. Gerleman says that the Septuagint of Proverbs avoids even synonymous parallelism, a key feature of the Masoretic Text of Proverbs ("The Septuagint Proverbs as a Hellenistic Document," *Oudtestamentische Studiën* 8 [1950] 17). I am not concerned here with double translations within the Septuagint such as were treated by C. T. Fritsch, "The Treatment of the Hexaplaric Signs in the Syro-Hexaplar of Proverbs," *Journal of Biblical Literature* 72 (1953) 169–81, where individual verses, half-verses, phrases, and words appear to have been translated twice within the same Septuagint verse.

TABLE 2. *Hebrew Repeated Verses with*

Number of Greek Words That Are the Same or Similar

	0	1	2	3	4
Category (see chap. 5)					
1.0	18:8~26:22 20:16~27:13				22:3~27:12
1.1			2:16~7:5	23:18~24:14b	
1.2	19:1~28:6		2:2~5:1		1:25~1:30 3:2~9:11 13:14~14:27 19:24~26:15
1.3	10:2~11:4	8:35~18:22	16:2~21:2	6:24~7:5 15:13~17:22	
1.4		11:14~15:22 12:13~29:6 12:23~13:16~15:2	2:3~8:1 13:16~15:2 15:16~16:8 19:25~21:11	21:9~21:19~25:24 26:1~26:8	2:16~6:24 22:2~29:13
2.0		6:15b~29:1b 10:29b~21:15b 15:33b~18:12b 17:15b~20:10b 26:7b~26:9b	10:8b~10:10b 11:14b~24:6b	4:4b–5~7:2a 10:15a~18:11a 13:9b~24:20b 17:3a~27:21a 22:28a~23:10a 23:3a~23:6b	6:19a~14:5b 10:6b~10:11b
2.1	3:21a~4:21a 11:13a~20:19a 13:1b~13:8b 20:18b~24:6a	8:35b~12:2a~18:22b 16:12b~25:5b~29:14b 19:29b~26:3b 20:11b~21:8b	1:9a~4:9a 11:2b~13:10b 15:14a~18:15a 15:18a~29:22a 15:22b~24:6b	9:1a~14:1a 12:14a~13:2a 19:12a~20:2a 28:12b~28:28a	3:31a~24:1a 15:8a~21:27a
2.2	3:7b~16:6b 6:15a~24:22a 12:15a~16:2a~21:2a 22:14a~23:27a 24:12b~24:29b	10:13b~26:3b 11:14a~29:18a 16:12b~20:28b~25:5b~29:14b 17:15a~24:24a 18:9b~28:24b 22:29a~29:20a 24:23b~28:21a	11:6a~12:6b 12:14a~13:2a~18:20a 16:18a~18:12a	1:7a~9:10a 1:8a~4:1a 9:1a~14:1a~24:3a	6:8a~30:25b
3.0	19:13b~27:15			4:10b~9:11 19:9~21:28a	20:10~20:23a
3.1	16:31a~20:29 20:20a~30:11	6:14~16:28a	3:3b~7:3 14:17a~14:29		
3.2		20:8~20:26a			
Total No. of Sets = 112	16	22	19	20	13
% of Total Sets	14	20	17	18	12

Same or Similar Greek Words

	Number of Greek Words That Are the Same or Similar				
	5	6	7	8	9
Category (see chap. 5)					
1.0		9:4~9:16	14:12~16:25	21:9~25:24	
1.1	19:5~19:9	2:1~7:1	5:7~7:24 6:11~24.34		6:10~24:33–34
1.2		11:1~20:23		10:1~15:20	1:8~6:20 4:20~5:1 12:11~28:19
1.3	10:28~11:7	22:13~26:13	26:12~29:20		3:15~8:11
1.4					
2.0	5:7a~7:24a~8:32a				
2.1	11:21a~16:5b				
2.2	18:4a~20:5a 26:4a~26:5a	16:17b~19:16a			
3.0					
3.1			13:3a~21:23		
3.2					
Total No. of Sets = 112	6	5	5	2	5
% of Total Sets	5	4	4	2	4

5:7a~7:24a~8:32a (category 2.0):

5:7   νῦν οὖν, υἱέ, ἄκουέ μου
        καὶ μὴ ἀκύρους ποιήσῃς ἐμοὺς λόγους·
        So now, son, listen to me,
        and do not make my words invalid.

7:24   νῦν οὖν, υἱέ, ἄκουέ μου
        καὶ πρόσεχε ῥήμασιν στόματος μου·
        So now, son, listen to me,
        and attend to the sayings of my mouth.

8:32   νῦν οὖν, υἱέ, ἄκουέ μου.
        So now, son, listen to me.[2]

6:19a~14:5b (category 2.0):

6:19   ἐκκαίει ψεύδη μάρτυς ἄδικος
        καὶ ἐπιπέμπει κρίσεις ἀνὰ μέσον ἀδελφῶν.
        An unjust witness kindles lies,
        and he sends disputes into the midst of brothers.

14:5   μάρτυς πιστὸς οὐ ψεύδεται
        ἐκκαίει δὲ ψεύδη μάρτυς ἄδικος.
        A trustworthy witness does not lie,
        but an unjust witness kindles lies.

15:8a~21:27a (category 2.1):

15:8   θυσίαι ἀσεβῶν βδέλυγμα κυρίῳ,
        εὐχαὶ δὲ κατευθυνόντων δεκταὶ παρ᾽ αὐτῷ
        The sacrifices of impious ones are an abomination to the Lord,
        but the vows of those who keep straight are acceptable to Him.

21:27 θυσίαι ἀσεβῶν βδέλυγμα κυρίῳ·
        καὶ γὰρ παρανόμως προσφέρουσιν αὐτάς.
        The sacrifices of impious ones are an abomination to the Lord,
        for they lawlessly present them.

Though no other repeated verses are as close as the above, in the great majority of cases in which the Hebrew has some sort of repetition, the Septuagint also indicates by its wording that it is repeating an earlier verse at least to some extent. An example of one such case may serve to represent many. In Hebrew, 14:12 is precisely repeated in 16:25 (category 1.0), and, though less tidy in Greek, it is obviously still a repetition:

14:12 ἔστιν ὁδὸς ἣ δοκεῖ ὀρθὴ εἶναι παρὰ ἀνθρώποις,
        τὰ δὲ τελευταῖα αὐτῆς ἔρχεται εἰς πυθμένα ᾅδου
        There is a way which seems to be straight for men,
        but its ends go into the depths of Hades.

---

2. 8:32b is missing in most Septuagint manuscripts. See the notes in A. Rahlfs, *Septuaginta* (Stuttgart: Württembergische Bibelanstalt, 1935) 2:197.

16:25   εἰσὶν ὁδοὶ δοκοῦσαι εἶναι ὀρθαὶ ἀνδρί,
        τὰ μέντοι τελευταῖα αὐτῶν βλέπει εἰς πυθμένα ᾅδου.
        There are ways seeming to be straight to a male,
        but their ends look into the depths of Hades.

In this case much of the same vocabulary is used, and the point is clearly the same, but only four words are precisely repeated in both verses.[3]

The apparent randomness of repetition in the Septuagint Proverbs may appear less problematic if we look at the relatively few instances of Hebrew repeated pairs that in the Septuagint have no identical or similar Greek words (column "0" in table 2). This may help to establish whether we are likely to prefer the Greek text and its underlying version or the Masoretic Text. The basic question is whether the Greek text might be better than the Masoretic. To answer that question each of the verses ought to be examined in its context. But when at least one word is repeated in Greek, I am inclined to see an effort on the part of the translators to reflect the MT at least in some small way. On the other hand, if there were no repeated words in Greek, the possibility of a different underlying text would seem stronger. The following sixteen instances (column "0" in table 2) lack a single shared word in Greek:

1.0	18:8~26:22	See below for the text and translation.
	20:16~27:13	The Septuagint omits 20:16; in fact, all of 20:14–22 is omitted in the Greek.
1.2	19:1~28:6	The Septuagint omits 19:1.
1.3	10:2~11:4	The Septuagint omits 11:4. These verses are rather near each other in the text, and the translators probably would have been aware that the Hebrew text was repetitious. If they were trying to avoid repetition, they probably would have omitted the second of these.
2.1	3:21a~4:21a	These verses are only a chapter apart, and translators might have consciously tried to vary the language.

3:21   Υἱέ, μὴ παραρρυῇς,
       τήρησον δὲ ἐμὴν βουλὴν καὶ ἔννοιαν,
       Son, do not be careless,
       but heed my counsel and good sense.

4:21   ὅπως μὴ ἐκλίπωσίν σε αἱ πηγαί σου,
       φύλασσε αὐτὰς ἐν σῇ καρδίᾳ·
       So that your sources not fail you,
       keep them in your heart.

| | 11:13a~20:19a | The Septuagint omits 20:19a. |
| | 13:1~13:8 | These verses are near each other in the text. |

---

3. Gillis Gerleman suggests that the MT's "roads of death" was changed to "depths of Hades" for Greek metrical reasons (*Studies in the Septuagint, 3: Proverbs* [Lund: Gleerup, 1956] 16).

13:1 υἱὸς πανοῦργος ὑπήκοος πατρί,
    υἱὸς δὲ ἀνήκοος ἐν ἀπωλείᾳ.
    A cunning son is obedient to a father,
    but a disobedient son is in destruction.

13:8 λύτρον ἀνδρὸς ψυχῆς ὁ ἴδιος πλοῦτος,
    πτωχὸς δὲ οὐχ ὑφίσταται ἀπειλήν.
    The ransom of a man's soul is his own wealth,
    but a beggar does not support a threat.

20:18b~24:6a   The Septuagint omits 20:18b.

2.2   3:7b~16:6b   The Septuagint omits 16:6.

6:15a~24:22a   See below for text and translation.

12:15a~16:2a~21:2a   See below for text and translation.

22:14a~23:27a   The verses are near each other in the text.

22:14 βόθρος βαθὺς στόμα παρανόμου,
    ὁ δὲ μισηθεὶς ὑπὸ κυρίου ἐμπεσεῖται εἰς αὐτόν.
    A deep trench is the mouth of a lawless one,
    but one hated by the Lord will fall into it.

23:27 πίθος γὰρ τετρημένος ἐστὶν ἀλλότριος οἶκος,
    καὶ φρέαρ στενὸν αλλότριον·
    For a pierced jar is the house of someone else,
    and a cistern of someone else is narrow.[4]

24:12b~24:29b   The verses are near each other, though not so near in the Septuagint as their present number would indicate since a translation of the MT's 30:1–14 intervenes (see the chart of the Septuagint's order on p. 9).

24:12 ἐὰν δὲ εἴπῃς Οὐκ οἶδα τοῦτον,
    γίνωσκε ὅτι κύριος καρδίας πάντων γινώσκει,
    καὶ ὁ πλάσας πνοὴν πᾶσιν αὐτὸς οἶδεν πάντα,
    ὃς ἀποδίδωσιν ἑκάστῳ κατὰ τὰ ἔργα αὐτοῦ.
    If you say, I do not know that,
    Know that the Lord knows the hearts of everyone,

---

4. On the meaning of this verse see Gerleman, *Studies in the Septuagint, 3: Proverbs*, 33, who suggests that the Greek term implies a house with bad housekeeping on the basis of possible influence of Xenophon, *Oeconomicus* 7:40 (Loeb Classical Library):

οὐχ ὁρᾷς, . . . οἱ εἰς τὸν τετρημένον πίθον ἀντλεῖν λεγόμενοι
ὡς οἰκτείρονται, ὅτι μάτην πονεῖν δοκοῦσι;

Don't you see how they who "draw water in a leaky jar," as the saying goes,
are pitied, because they seem to labor in vain?

Xenophon is a more likely source than Plato, *Gorgias* 493b (Loeb Classical Library):

φοροῖεν εἰς τὸν τετρημένον πίθον ὕδωρ

(these . . . wretched. . .) will carry water into their leaky jar.

and the one who formed the breath for everyone knows all
   things,
one who returns to each one according to his work.

24:29 μη εἴπης ὑΟν τρόπον ἐχρήσατό μοι χρήσομαι αὐτῶ,
     τείσομαι δὲ αὐτὸν Ἁ με ἰδίκησεν.
Do not say, In the manner in which he dealt with me
     I shall deal with him,
but I shall repay him the things that he has
     unjustly done to me.

3.0   19:13b~27:15   For text and translation see below.

3.1   16:31a~20:29   For text and translation see below.

      20:20a~30:11   The Septuagint omits 20:20.

Thus seven of the sixteen verses are simply omitted from the Greek translation, including four from section 20:14–22, which seems to cluster with repetitions in Hebrew. The five pairs that are near to each other in the present shape of the book may have kept translators from using similar words if their goal was to avoid repetition.

There are five other cases from the above list where both verses have been preserved in the Septuagint. These verses are not near each other, and they use no similar words in translating. The translations of the Septuagint are as follows):

1.0   18:8~26:22   The Hebrew has a difficult word, מתלהמים, which may have been
                          מהלומות 'blows', and both verses in Greek have something about
                          hitting. Another difficult word, נרגן 'grumbler', does not actually seem
                          to show up in either Greek verse. Because of the odd meaning of 18:8b,
                          it is hard to see it as reflecting a better Hebrew text.[5]

      18:8   Ὀκνηροὺς καταβάλλει φόβος,
             ψυχαὶ δὲ ἀνδρογύνων πεινάσουσιν.
             Fear strikes down timid ones,
                  but souls of effeminate ones will hunger.

      26:22 λόγοι κερκώπων μαλακοί,
             οὗτοι δὲ τύπτουσιν εἰς ταμίεια σπλάγχνων.
             Words of tricky ones are soft,
                  but these beat into storehouses of the inmost parts.

2.2   6:15a~24:22a   Though different words are used to express suddenness, it appears that
                          the same Hebrew version may underlie both verses even though the
                          Greek verses diverge in meaning.

      6:15a διὰ τοῦτο ἐξαπίνης ἔρχεται ἡ ἀπώλεια αὐτοῦ,
             διακοπὴ καὶ συντριβὴ ἀνίατος.

---

5. Procopius of Gaza (d. 538) saw the effeminate ones in Prov 18:8 as people who unhealthily mix the audacity of men with the timidity of women; J.-P. Migne, *Patrologia Graeca* 87 (Paris, 1865), cols. 1405–6. His is a fair, though sexist, explanation of a difficult Greek text, but it does not ring true as an adequate expression of the Hebrew.

Because of that suddenly comes his destruction,
a breach and an incurable ruin.

24:22a ἐξαίφνης γὰρ τείσονται τοὺς ἀσεβεῖς,
τὰς δὲ τιμωρίας ἀμφοτέρων τίς γνώσεται;
For on a sudden they take vengeance on the impious,
but the retribution of both who will know?

12:15a~16:2a~21:2a The general sense of the first halves of these verses is the same, even though none of the same words is used in all three verses. There is no reason to prefer their version to the Hebrew. 16:2b seems to deviate widely from the Hebrew, which is the same as in 21:2b—perhaps to avoid a repetition.

12:15a ὁδοὶ ἀφρόνων ὀρθαὶ ἐνώπιον αὐτῶν,
εἰσακούει δὲ συμβουλίας σοφός.
The roads of fools are upright before them,
but a wise one hearkens to consultation.

16:2a πάντα τὰ ἔργα τοῦ ταπεινοῦ φανερὰ παρὰ τῷ θεῷ,
οἱ δὲ ἀσεβεῖς ἐν ἡμέρᾳ κακῇ ὀλοῦνται.
All the works of the lowly are manifest before god,
but the impious ones perish in the evil day.

21:2a πᾶς ἀνὴρ φαίνεται ἑαυτῷ δίκαιος,
κατευθύνει δὲ καρδίας κύριος.
Each man appears just to himself,
but the Lord makes hearts straight.

3.0   19:13~27:15 Although no similar words are used, each element in the Greek can be seen to reflect something in the Hebrew, except for 19:13b, which seems to be only vaguely related to the strifes of women of the Hebrew.

19:13b αἰσχύνη πατρὶ υἱὸς ἄφρων,
καὶ οὐχ ἁγναὶ εὐχαὶ ἀπὸ μισθώματος ἑταίρας.
A shame to a father is a foolish son,
and vows from the hire of a courtesan are not upright.

27:15 σταγόνες ἐκβάλλουσιν ἄνθρωπον ἐν ἡμέρᾳ χειμερινῇ ἐκ τοῦ
οἴκου αὐτοῦ,
ὡσαύτως καὶ γυνὴ λοίδορος ἐκ τοῦ ἰδίου οἴκου.
Drops cast out a man in a winter day from his house;
in like manner also an abusive woman (casts out) from her
own house.

3.1   16:31a~20:29 Each element in the Greek corresponds, if only loosely, with an element in the Hebrew. One could wonder if σοφία 'wisdom' in 20:29a replaces כח 'strength' in the underlying text. But it does not seem to me that the Greek has a better reading.[6]

16:31a στέφανος καυχήσεως γῆρας,
ἐν δὲ ὁδοῖς δικαιοσύνης εὑρίσκεται

---

6. There is another case with two words the same, but the words are merely the definite article and the disjunctive particle δε:

> A crown of boasting is old age—
> in ways of justice it is found.

20:29 κόσμος νεανίαις σοφία,
      δόξα δὲ πρεσβυτέρων πολιαί.

> An honor for young men is wisdom,
> but glory of old men is gray hairs.

More work on the individual repeated pairs will enlarge upon these preliminary findings considerably. But in general Berezov is right that there was a tendency to avoid repeating words in Greek that are repeated in Hebrew. This avoidance was not rigid, however, and there are instances in verses that are close to each other where a considerable amount of repetition is tolerated in the Greek, even if the repetition is not as consistent as in the MT. For example 9:4~9:16 (1.0) have six shared words in Greek, and 19:5~19:9 (1.1) have five shared words in Greek.[7] But, although

---

2.0 10:8b~10:10b

10:8b σοφὸς καρδίᾳ δὲξεται ἐντολάς,
      ὁ δὲ ἄστεγος χείλεσιν σκολιάζων ὑποσκελισθήσεται.

> A wise one in [his] heart will accept commands,
> but the crooked one unable to control [his] lips will be tripped up.

10:10 ὁ ἐννεύων ὀφθαλμοῖς μετὰ δόλου συνάγει ἀνδράσι λύπας
      ὁ δὲ ἐλέγχων μετὰ παρρησίας εἰρηνοποιεῖ.

> The one who gives approving signs with [his] eyes with treachery
>   brings together pain for men.
> but one who corrects with frankness makes peace.

The translation of 10:8b approaches the Hebrew more closely than does that of 10:10b. BH³ and BHS suggest the latter is the original form of the Hebrew, but aside from the esthetic argument and the fact that the Syriac, as it frequently does, follows the Greek, there does not really seem to be any reason to prefer the Greek. The Targum, the Vulgate, and Saadia Gaon all follow the MT in v. 10b. Compare the translation of 10:10 by Gerleman, "Septuagint Proverbs as a Hellenistic Document," 16: "He that winks with his eyes deceitfully, procures grief for men, / but he that reproves boldly is a peacemaker."

---

7. 1.0 9:4~9:16

9:4 Ὅς ἐστιν ἄφρων, ἐκκλινάτω πρός με·
      καὶ τοῖς ἐνδεέσι φρενῶν εἶπεν

> Who is foolish, let him turn aside to me,
> and she speaks to those lacking minds.

9:16 Ὅς ἐστιν ὑμῶν ἀφρονέστατος, ἐκκλινάτω πρός με·
      ἐνδεέσι δὲ φρονήσεως παρακελεύομαι λέγουσα

> Who of you is most foolish, let him turn aside to me;
> I exhort those lacking sense.

1.1 19:5~19:9

These verses are rather close to each other in the text, even though such proximity may sometimes have been a motivation for the translators to avoid close repetition.

19:5 μάρτυς ψευδὴς οὐκ ἀτιμώρητος ἔσται,
      ὁ δὲ ἐγκαλῶν ἀδίκως οὐ διαφεύξεται.

> A false witness will not be unpunished,
> and one who brings a charge unjustly will not escape.

19:9 μάρτυς ψευδὴς οὐκ ἀτιμώρητος ἔσται·
      ὃς δ' ἂν ἐκκαύσῃ κακίαν, ἀπολεῖται ὑπ' αὐτῆς.

there is some toleration for repeating individual words, there is essentially none for repeating entire verses. It is hard not to see in this penchant a conscious, esthetic decision by the translators to avoid the repetition that dominates the Hebrew.

Berezov himself is adamant that his study has uncovered a characteristic of the Greek translators, not of a Hebrew text differing from the MT. "The absence of these duplications

---

> A false witness will not be unpunished,
>   and one who, if he kindles evil, perishes because of it.

Proximity is also true of the following six pairs, all of which share several words. This instance has three identical words and one similar:

2.0   10:6b~10:11b

10:6b   εὐλογία κυρίου ἐπὶ κεφαλὴν δικαίου,
          στόμα δὲ ἀσεβῶν καλύψει πένθος ἄωρον.
          The blessing of the Lord is on the head of the just one,
              but the mouth of the impious ones will cover untimely grief.

10:11b   πηγὴ Ζωῆς ἐν χειρὶ δικαίου,
          στόμα δὲ ἀσεβοῦς καλύψει ἀπώλεια.
          A spring of life is in the hand of a just one,
              but disaster will cover the mouth of the impious one.

2.0   23:3a~23:6b

This pair has four identical words:

23:3a   εἰ δὲ ἀπληστότερος εἶ, μὴ ἐπιθύμει τῶν ἐδεσμάτων αὐτοῦ,
          ταῦτα γὰρ ἔχεται Ζωῆς ψευδοῦς.
          Even if you are rather greedy, do not desire his foods,
              for these are attached to false life.

23:6b   μὴ συνδείπνει ἀνδρὶ βασκάνῳ
          μηδὲ ἐπιθύμει τῶν βρωμάτων αὐτοῦ·
          Do not dine with a malicious man,
              nor desire his meats.

2.1   28:12b~28:28a

This pair has three identical words:

28:12b   διὰ βοήθειαν δικαίων πολλὴ γίνεται δόξα,
          ἐν δὲ τόποις ἀσεβῶν ἁλίσκονται ἄνθρωποι.
          With help of just ones glory becomes much,
              but in the places of impious ones men are ruined.

28:28a   ἐν τόποις ἀσεβῶν στένουσι δίκαιοι,
          ἐν δὲ τῇ ἐκείνων ἀπωλείᾳ πληθυνθήσονται δίκαιοι.
          In the places of impious ones just ones are in difficulty,
              but in the destruction of them just ones will be increased.

2.2   26:4a~26:5a

This pair has five identical words—three important words and two particles:

26:4a   μὴ ἀποκρίνου ἄφρονι πρὸς τὴν ἐκείνου ἀφροσύνην,
          ἵνα μὴ ὅμοιος γένῃ αὐτῷ·
          Do not answer a fool in response to that one's folly,
              lest you become similar to him.

26:5a   ἀλλὰ ἀποκρίνου ἄφρονι κατὰ τὴν ἀφροσύνην αὐτοῦ,
          ἵνα μὴ φαίνηται σοφὸς παρ' ἑαυτῷ.
          But answer a fool according to his folly,
              lest he seem wise to himself.

from the Greek," he writes, " . . . does not indicate that they were likewise missing from the He-brew *Vorlage*. On the contrary, because we can attribute these modifications to the particular characteristics of the LXX translation, our investigation gives evidence that these duplications lay before the Greek translator."[8] I share Berezov's views and regard repetition as a basic and original feature of the book.

| 3.0 20:10~20:23a | This pair has two identical words and two similar. Note that, since the Septuagint omits 20:14–22, these verses are only four verses apart in the text. |

20:10 στάθμιον μέγα καὶ μικρὸν καὶ μέτρα δισσά,
 ἀκάθαρτα ἐνώπιον κυρίου καὶ ἀμφότερα.
 A big and little weight and twofold measures
 are both impure before the Lord.

20:23a βδέλυγμα κυρίῳ δισσὸν στάθμιον,
 καὶ Ζυγὸς δόλιος οὐ καλὸν ἐνώπιον αὐτοῦ.
 An abomination to the Lord is a twofold weight,
 and a deceitful balance-beam is not good before Him.

| 3.1 14:17a~14:29 | This pair has one identical word and two similar. See Gerleman, *Studies in the Septuagint, 3: Proverbs*, 20, for a translation of 14:17. |

14:17a ὀξύθυμος πράσσει μετὰ ἀβουλίας,
 ἀνὴρ δὲ φρόνιμος πολλὰ ὑποφέρει.
 One quick to anger acts with thoughtlessness,
 but a sensible male bears many things.

14:29 μακρόθυμος ἀνὴρ πολὺς ἐν φρονήσει,
 ὁ δὲ ὀλιγόψυχος ἰσχυρῶς ἄφρων.
 A patient male is great in intention,
 but the faint-hearted/feeble-minded is exceedingly foolish.

8. Berezov, "LXX Translation of Duplicate Proverbs," 8. This is certainly the thrust of Gerleman's findings in "Septuagint Proverbs as a Hellenistic Document" and *Studies in the Septuagint, 3: Proverbs*; see also A. Kaminka, "Septuaginta und Targum zu Proverbia," *Hebrew Union College Annual* 8–9 (1931–32) 169–91, esp. 169–70; and A. Baumgartner, *Étude critique sur l'État du Texte du Livre des Proverbs* (Leipzig: Drugulin, 1890) 250: "We do not believe ourselves obligated to suppose a text very essentially different from ours [the MT]" ("Nous ne nous croyons pas obligé de supposer un texte bien essentiellement différent du nôtre"). Note also the observation of T. Boman (*Das hebräische Denken im Vergleich mit dem griechischen* [7th ed.; Göttingen: Vandenhoeck & Ruprecht, 1983] 178) that in argument Biblical Hebrew prefers the method "of repetition, through which one continually hammers away at one appropriate point" ("die der Wiederholung, durch die man auf einen geeigneten Punkt immer wieder loshämmert").

5

Catalog of Repeated Verses

It is being concentrated which produces high convenience.
—Johnson, on the advantages of having dense population and discouraging emigration

Johnson was contending that cities and countries that are densely populated seem to enjoy the most amenities. In this study, I hope that the concentration of repetition will produce convenience as we discuss this phenomenon in the Book of Proverbs.

The verses in the book that appear to be repeated in various ways are collected in this chapter. Dissimilar elements are marked with ████, similar elements with ████ (in the Hebrew only, not in the translation). Notes explain my classification of the verses and show where else the verse seems to be repeated. The fact that one verse may be repeated in more than one way does not necessarily prove that the typology of verse repetition, as assigned below, was in the minds of the people who decided verses would appear more than once in the book. Many verses cited here also have groups of two or more words together that occur elsewhere and that might have been clichés. This phenomenon has not been consistently noted in the catalog, but it argues that there is a great deal of continuity in the language of the book. Unfortunately it has usually been impossible to deal with philological problems in the repeated verses, except insofar as they are elucidated by the existence of a parallel verse.

Verses are presented according to the typology suggested in chapter 4. Related verses are given in the order in which the earliest of them occurs in the book (e.g., 3:2 and 9:11 appear together before 4:20 and 5:1).

My own wooden translations are included for the benefit of the non-Hebraicist. The Revised Standard Version and other responsible translations do not always take care to assure that exactly the same words are used in translating the repeated verses, and so the close relationships between verses are obscured. Since repetition is a dominant feature of the book, a translation that does mirror such similarities is a desideratum.

1.0   WHOLE VERSES REPEATED WITH SPELLING VARIATIONS (6 SETS)

מִי־פֶתִי יָסֻר הֵנָּה חֲסַר־לֵב אָמְרָה לּוֹ	9:4	Who is simple, let him turn aside to here, one lacking sense; she speaks to him.
מִי־פֶתִי יָסֻר הֵנָּה וַחֲסַר־לֵב וְאָמְרָה לּוֹ	9:16	Who is simple, let him turn aside to here, and one lacking sense, and she speaks to him.
יֵשׁ דֶּרֶךְ יָשָׁר לִפְנֵי־אִישׁ וְאַחֲרִיתָהּ דַּרְכֵי־מָוֶת	14:12	There is a road upright before a man, but its end is the roads of death.
יֵשׁ דֶּרֶךְ יָשָׁר לִפְנֵי־אִישׁ וְאַחֲרִיתָהּ דַּרְכֵי־מָוֶת	16:25	(Translation exactly the same.)
דִּבְרֵי נִרְגָּן כְּמִתְלַהֲמִים וְהֵם יָרְדוּ חַדְרֵי־בָטֶן	18:8	Words of a grumbler are like dainty morsels, but they descend into the innermost parts of the belly.
דִּבְרֵי נִרְגָּן כְּמִתְלַהֲמִים וְהֵם יָרְדוּ חַדְרֵי־בָטֶן	26:22	(Translation exactly the same.)
לְקַח־בִּגְדוֹ כִּי־עָרַב זָר וּבְעַד נָכְרִים חַבְלֵהוּ	20:16	Take his cloak since he went surety for a stranger, and for a foreigner extract a pledge from him.
קַח־בִּגְדוֹ כִּי־עָרַב זָר וּבְעַד נָכְרִיָּה חַבְלֵהוּ	27:13	(Translation exactly the same.)
טוֹב לְשֶׁבֶת עַל־פִּנַּת־גָּג מֵאֵשֶׁת מִדְיָנִים וּבֵית חָבֶר	21:9	It is better to sit on the corner of a roof than a woman of strifes and a noisy house.
טוֹב שֶׁבֶת עַל־פִּנַּת־גָּג מֵאֵשֶׁת מִדְיָנִים וּבֵית חָבֶר	25:24	(Translation exactly the same.)
עָרוּם רָאָה רָעָה וְיִסְתָּר וּפְתָיִים עָבְרוּ וְנֶעֱנָשׁוּ	22:3	A smart one saw an evil and hid, but simple ones went over and were punished.
עָרוּם רָאָה רָעָה נִסְתָּר פְּתָאִים עָבְרוּ נֶעֱנָשׁוּ	27:12	A smart one saw an evil, hid; simple ones went over, were punished.

20:16 / 27:13   Both verses have odd forms for what should be נכרי. Probably the feminine should be emended in 27:13, as suggested in BH[3] and BHS. The form in 20:16 is not likely to be a masculine plural; perhaps it is one of those mysterious *m* forms like those found in Ugaritic; see C. H. Gordon, *Ugaritic Textbook* (Rome: Pontifical Biblical Institute, 1965) §11:4–5, 8; and (for Hebrew) H. D. Hummel, "Enclitic *Mem* in Early Northwest Semitic, Especially Hebrew," *Journal of Biblical Literature* 76 (1957) 85–107, who does not catalog 20:16 as a possible instance of *m*-form usage (reference courtesy of Edward L. Greenstein).

21:9 / 25:24   These verses relate also to 21:19 (see category 1.4) and share syntax with 19:1 and 28:6 (see 4.8). The translation "noisy house" relies on the etymology suggested by J. J. Finkelstein, "Hebrew HBR and Semitic *HBR," *Journal of Biblical Literature* 75 (1956) 328–31.

1.1 WHOLE VERSES REPEATED WITH ONE DISSIMILAR WORD (6 SETS)

בְּנִי אִם־תִּקַּח אֲמָרָי וּמִצְוֹתַי תִּצְפֹּן אִתָּךְ	2:1	My son, if you take my words, and my commands you treasure with you.
בְּנִי שְׁמֹר אֲמָרָי וּמִצְוֹתַי תִּצְפֹּן אִתָּךְ	7:1	My son, guard my words, and my commands you treasure with you.
לְהַצִּילְךָ מֵאִשָּׁה זָרָה מִנָּכְרִיָּה אֲמָרֶיהָ הֶחֱלִיקָה	2:16	To save you from a strange woman, from a foreign one who makes smooth her words.
לְשָׁמְרְךָ מֵאִשָּׁה זָרָה מִנָּכְרִיָּה אֲמָרֶיהָ הֶחֱלִיקָה	7:5	To guard you from a strange woman, from a foreign one who makes smooth her words.
וְעַתָּה בָנִים שִׁמְעוּ־לִי וְאַל־תָּסוּרוּ מֵאִמְרֵי־פִי	5:7	And now, sons, listen to me, and do not deviate from the words of my mouth.
וְעַתָּה בָנִים שִׁמְעוּ־לִי וְהַקְשִׁיבוּ לְאִמְרֵי־פִי	7:24	And now, sons, listen to me, and attend to the words of my mouth.
מְעַט שֵׁנוֹת מְעַט תְּנוּמוֹת מְעַט חִבֻּק יָדַיִם לִשְׁכָּב וּבָא־כִמְהַלֵּךְ רֵאשֶׁךָ וּמַחְסֹרְךָ כְּאִישׁ מָגֵן	6:10–11	A little sleeping, a little snoozing, a little folding of hands to lie down, and your poverty will come like a highwayman, and your want like an insolent man.
מְעַט שֵׁנוֹת מְעַט תְּנוּמוֹת מְעַט חִבֻּק יָדָיִם לִשְׁכָּב וּבָא־מִתְהַלֵּךְ רֵישֶׁךָ וּמַחְסֹרֶיךָ כְּאִישׁ מָגֵן	24:33–34	(Translation the same except that *like* is omitted from the second verse.)
עֵד שְׁקָרִים לֹא יִנָּקֶה וְיָפִיחַ כְּזָבִים לֹא יִמָּלֵט	19:5	A witness of lies will not be declared innocent, and a testifier of falsehoods will not escape.
עֵד שְׁקָרִים לֹא יִנָּקֶה וְיָפִיחַ כְּזָבִים יֹאבֵד	19:9	A witness of lies will not be declared innocent, and a testifier of falsehoods will perish.
כִּי אִם־יֵשׁ אַחֲרִית וְתִקְוָתְךָ לֹא תִכָּרֵת	23:18	But indeed there is an end, and your hope will not be cut off.

2:1 / 7:1 This case illustrates the problems of categorizing repetitions. The one different word in 7:1 corresponds to two in 2:1; but they both seem to fill the same syntactic slot in the statement.

2:16 / 7:5 Both verses are also related to 6:24, but less closely (see 1.4).

5:7 / 7:24 Both verses are related to 8:32a (see 2.0).

19:5 / 19:9 These verses are related to 21:28a (see 3.0). They are also related to 6:19a ~ 14:5b (see 2.0), but, since their vowel pointing is different, I have classified the words they share as synonymous clichés. For the translation of יפיח as a noun ('perjurer'), see William McKane, *Proverbs: A New Approach* (Old Testament Library; Philadelphia: Westminster/London: SCM, 1970) 240, 529; and W. Bühlmann, *Vom rechten Reden und Schweigen* (Freiburg: Universitätsverlag/Göttingen: Vandenhoeck & Ruprecht, 1976) 95–96.

אִם־מָצָאתָ וְיֵשׁ אַחֲרִית וְתִקְוָתְךָ לֹא תִכָּרֵת 24:14b If you have found [it], and there is an end,
and your hope will not be cut off.

1.2 WHOLE VERSES REPEATED WITH TWO DISSIMILAR WORDS (11 SETS)

שְׁמַע בְּנִי מוּסַר אָבִיךָ וְאַל־תִּטֹּשׁ תּוֹרַת אִמֶּךָ 1:8 Hear, my son, the discipline of your father,
and do not neglect the teaching of your mother.

נְצֹר בְּנִי מִצְוַת אָבִיךָ וְאַל־תִּטֹּשׁ תּוֹרַת אִמֶּךָ 6:20 Guard, my son, the command of your father,
and do not neglect the teaching of your mother.

וַתִּפְרְעוּ כָל־עֲצָתִי וְתוֹכַחְתִּי לֹא אֲבִיתֶם 1:25 And you have let loose all my advice,
and my correction you have not wanted.

לֹא־אָבוּ לַעֲצָתִי נָאֲצוּ כָּל־תּוֹכַחְתִּי 1:30 They did not want my advice;
they despised all my correction.

לְהַקְשִׁיב לַחָכְמָה אָזְנֶךָ תַּטֶּה לִבְּךָ לַתְּבוּנָה 2:2 To listen with your ears to wisdom,
incline your heart to understanding.

בְּנִי לְחָכְמָתִי הַקְשִׁיבָה לִתְבוּנָתִי הַט־אָזְנֶךָ 5:1 My son, to my wisdom listen;
to my understanding incline your ear.

כִּי אֹרֶךְ יָמִים וּשְׁנוֹת חַיִּים וְשָׁלוֹם יוֹסִיפוּ לָךְ 3:2 For length of days and years of life
and peace they will add to you.

כִּי־בִי יִרְבּוּ יָמֶיךָ וְיוֹסִיפוּ לְּךָ שְׁנוֹת חַיִּים 9:11 For with me your days will increase,
and years of life will be added for you.

בְּנִי לִדְבָרַי הַקְשִׁיבָה לַאֲמָרַי הַט־אָזְנֶךָ 4:20 My son, to my words listen;
to my sayings incline your ear.

בְּנִי לְחָכְמָתִי הַקְשִׁיבָה לִתְבוּנָתִי הַט־אָזְנֶךָ 5:1 My son, to my wisdom listen;
to my understanding incline your ear.

בֵּן חָכָם יְשַׂמַּח־אָב וּבֵן כְּסִיל תּוּגַת אִמּוֹ 10:1 A wise son makes a father happy,
and a foolish son is a sorrow of his mother.

1:8 / 6:20 1:8a is related to 4:1a (see 2.2). Up to this point in the catalog the RSV has reflected similar elements with similar translations, but in 1:8 it reads "reject" and in 6:20 "forsake" for the verb I translate "neglect."

1:25 / 1:30 Perhaps these should be categorized differently since the positions and, of course, the persons of the verbs have been switched in the two verses. These verses appear close to each other, however, and it seems likely that the repetition is an intentional variation on the same theme, probably for emphasis.

2:2 / 5:1 5:1 relates also to 4:20 (in this section). The different forms and the use of *my son* in 5:1 might lead others to classify 2:2 and 5:1 as less closely related than I do.

3:2 / 9:11 9:11 is also related to 4:10b (see 3.0).

4:20 / 5:1 5:1 is also related to 2:2 (see 1.2).

בֵּן חָכָם יְשַׂמַּח־אָב וּכְסִיל אָדָם בּוֹזֶה אִמּוֹ	15:20	A wise son makes a father happy, and a fool of a man despises his mother.
מֹאזְנֵי מִרְמָה תּוֹעֲבַת יְהוָה וְאֶבֶן שְׁלֵמָה רְצוֹנוֹ	11:1	Scales of deceit are an abomination of Yahweh, and a complete stone is his desire.
תּוֹעֲבַת יְהוָה אֶבֶן וָאָבֶן וּמֹאזְנֵי מִרְמָה לֹא־טוֹב	20:23	An abomination of Yahweh is a stone and a stone, and scales of deceit are not good.
עֹבֵד אַדְמָתוֹ יִשְׂבַּע־לָחֶם וּמְרַדֵּף רֵיקִים חֲסַר־לֵב	12:11	One who works his land will have enough bread, but one who runs after empty things lacks sense.
עֹבֵד אַדְמָתוֹ יִשְׂבַּע־לָחֶם וּמְרַדֵּף רֵקִים יִשְׂבַּע־רִישׁ	28:19	One who works his land will have enough bread, but one who runs after empty things will have enough poverty.
תּוֹרַת חָכָם מְקוֹר חַיִּים לָסוּר מִמֹּקְשֵׁי מָוֶת	13:14	The teaching of a wise one is a source of life for turning aside from traps of death.
יִרְאַת יְהוָה מְקוֹר חַיִּים לָסוּר מִמֹּקְשֵׁי מָוֶת	14:27	The fear of Yahweh is a source of life for turning aside from traps of death.
טוֹב־רָשׁ הוֹלֵךְ בְּתֻמּוֹ מֵעִקֵּשׁ שְׂפָתָיו וְהוּא כְסִיל	19:1	Better is a poor one who walks in his simplicity than a crooked one of his lips, and he a fool.
טוֹב־רָשׁ הוֹלֵךְ בְּתֻמּוֹ מֵעִקֵּשׁ דְּרָכַיִם וְהוּא עָשִׁיר	28:6	Better is a poor one who walks in his simplicity than a crooked one of ways, and he a rich one.
טָמַן עָצֵל יָדוֹ בַּצַּלָּחַת גַּם־אֶל־פִּיהוּ לֹא יְשִׁיבֶנָּה	19:24	A lazy one hides his hand in the plate; also to his mouth he does not return it.
טָמַן עָצֵל יָדוֹ בַּצַּלָּחַת נִלְאָה לַהֲשִׁיבָה אֶל־פִּיו	26:15	A lazy one hides his hand in the plate; he is unable to return it to his mouth.

1.3 WHOLE VERSES REPEATED WITH THREE DISSIMILAR WORDS (9 SETS)

יְקָרָה הִיא מִפְּנִיִּים וְכָל־חֲפָצֶיךָ לֹא יִשְׁווּ־בָהּ	3:15	It is more valuable than corals, and all your desires will not equal it.
כִּי־טוֹבָה חָכְמָה מִפְּנִינִים וְכָל־חֲפָצִים לֹא יִשְׁווּ־בָהּ	8:11	For better is wisdom than corals, and all desires will not equal it.

12:11 / 28:19   28:19 seems to be a cleverer and more elegant verse since it repeats the verb in the first clause. I doubt, however, that we can say that it was therefore original or would have seemed a better saying to the ancients.

13:14 / 14:27   This pair is a prime example for those who wish to see a development in proverbial thought away from human knowledge toward reliance on God; see McKane, *Proverbs*, 474. But here we are interested in formal similarities, and these verses are obviously related.

19:1 / 28:6   Both verses seem syntactically related to 21:9, 21:19, and 25:24 (see 4.8).

3:15 / 8:11   The subject of 3:15 is חכמה 'wisdom' (from 3:13).

לִשְׁמָרְךָ מֵאֵשֶׁת רָע מֵחֶלְקַת לָשׁוֹן נָכְרִיָּה	6:24	To guard you from a woman of evil, from the smoothness of tongue of a foreign one.
לִשְׁמָרְךָ מֵאִשָּׁה זָרָה מִנָּכְרִיָּה אֲמָרֶיהָ הֶחֱלִיקָה	7:5	To guard you from a strange woman, from a foreign one who makes smooth her words.
כִּי מֹצְאִי מָצָאִי חַיִּים וַיָּפֶק רָצוֹן מֵיהוָה	8:35	For one who finds me has found life, and he gets desire from Yahweh.
מָצָא אִשָּׁה מָצָא טוֹב וַיָּפֶק רָצוֹן מֵיהוָה	18:22	He has found a woman; he has found good, and he gets desire from Yahweh.
לֹא־יוֹעִילוּ אוֹצְרוֹת רֶשַׁע וּצְדָקָה תַּצִּיל מִמָּוֶת	10:2	The treasures of wickedness will not be of use, but righteousness saves from death.
לֹא־יוֹעִיל הוֹן בְּיוֹם עֶבְרָה וּצְדָקָה תַּצִּיל מִמָּוֶת	11:4	Wealth will not be of use in a day of wrath, but righteousness saves from death.
תּוֹחֶלֶת צַדִּיקִים שִׂמְחָה וְתִקְוַת רְשָׁעִים תֹּאבֵד	10:28	The expectation of righteous ones is joy, but the hope of bad ones will perish.
בְּמוֹת אָדָם רָשָׁע תֹּאבַד תִּקְוָה וְתוֹחֶלֶת אוֹנִים אָבָדָה	11:7	In the death of an evil man hope perishes, but the expectation of ——— has perished.
לֵב שָׂמֵחַ יֵיטִב פָּנִים וּבְעַצְּבַת־לֵב רוּחַ נְכֵאָה	15:13	A happy heart makes good a face, but in sadness of heart is a smitten spirit.
לֵב שָׂמֵחַ יֵיטִב גֵּהָה וְרוּחַ נְכֵאָה תְּיַבֶּשׁ־גָּרֶם	17:22	A happy heart makes good a healing, but a smitten spirit makes dry the bone.
כָּל־דַּרְכֵי־אִישׁ זַךְ בְּעֵינָיו וְתֹכֵן רוּחוֹת יְהוָה	16:2	All the ways of a man are pure in his eyes, but Yahweh is an estimator of spirits.
כָּל־דֶּרֶךְ־אִישׁ יָשָׁר בְּעֵינָיו וְתֹכֵן לִבּוֹת יְהוָה	21:2	Each way of a man is upright in his eyes, but Yahweh is an estimator of hearts.
אָמַר עָצֵל אֲרִי בַחוּץ בְּתוֹךְ רְחֹבוֹת אֵרָצֵחַ	22:13	A lazy one said, There is a lion outside; in the midst of open places I will be killed!
אָמַר עָצֵל שַׁחַל בַּדָּרֶךְ אֲרִי בֵּין הָרְחֹבוֹת	26:13	A lazy one said, There is a young lion on the road, a lion between open places.

6:24 / 7:5   6:24 is related to 2:16 (see 1.4); 7:5 is related to 2:16 (see 1.1).

8:35 / 18:22   The second halves of both verses are related to 12:2a (see 2.1), and the first halves are related to the many verses sharing the double-verb syntactical form (see 4.2).

10:28 / 11:7   What Crawford H. Toy wrote of 11:7 in 1899 is still true: "The true text of the second cl[ause] must be left undetermined" (*A Critical and Exegetical Commentary on the Book of Proverbs* [International Critical Commentary; Edinburgh: T. & T. Clark, 1899] 223). The versions all understand אונים, which usually means 'generative power', as 'evil persons': 'impious ones' (LXX), 'those who do turpitude' (Targum), 'bad people' (Peshitta), 'harassers' (Vulgate), and 'excessive ones' (Saadia Gaon).

16:2 / 21:2   The first halves of both verses are related to 12:15a (see 2.2).

רָאִיתָ אִישׁ חָכָם בְּעֵינָיו תִּקְוָה לִכְסִיל מִמֶּנּוּ   26:12
     You saw a man wise in his eyes—
       there is more hope for a fool than for him.

חָזִיתָ אִישׁ אָץ בִּדְבָרָיו תִּקְוָה לִכְסִיל מִמֶּנּוּ   29:20
     You observed a man quick in his words—
       there is more hope for a fool than for him.

1.4 WHOLE VERSES REPEATED WITH FOUR OR MORE DISSIMILAR WORDS (10 SETS)

כִּי אִם לַבִּינָה תִקְרָא לַתְּבוּנָה תִּתֵּן קוֹלֶךָ   2:3
     Surely, if you call to comprehension;
       to understanding you give your voice.

הֲלֹא חָכְמָה תִקְרָא וּתְבוּנָה תִּתֵּן קוֹלָהּ   8:1
     Does not wisdom call,
       and understanding give her voice?

לְהַצִּילְךָ מֵאִשָּׁה זָרָה מִנָּכְרִיָּה אֲמָרֶיהָ הֶחֱלִיקָה   2:16
     To save you from a strange woman,
       from a foreign one who makes smooth her words.

לִשְׁמָרְךָ מֵאֵשֶׁת רָע מֵחֶלְקַת לָשׁוֹן נָכְרִיָּה   6:24
     To guard you from a woman of evil,
       from the smoothness of tongue of a foreign one.

בְּאֵין תַּחְבֻּלוֹת יִפָּל עָם וּתְשׁוּעָה בְּרֹב יוֹעֵץ   11:14
     With no steersmanship a people falls,
       but salvation is in many counselors.

הָפֵר מַחֲשָׁבוֹת בְּאֵין סוֹד וּבְרֹב יוֹעֲצִים תָּקוּם   15:22
     Frustrate thoughts without confidential conversation,
       but with many counselors you will stand.

בְּפֶשַׁע שְׂפָתַיִם מוֹקֵשׁ רָע וַיֵּצֵא מִצָּרָה צַדִּיק   12:13
     In the sin of lips is a trap of a bad one,
       but a righteous one gets out from trouble.

בְּפֶשַׁע אִישׁ רָע מוֹקֵשׁ וְצַדִּיק יָרוּן וְשָׂמֵחַ   29:6
     In the sin of a bad man is a trap,
       but a righteous one gives a joyful cry and is happy.

אָדָם עָרוּם כֹּסֶה דָּעַת וְלֵב כְּסִילִים יִקְרָא אִוֶּלֶת   12:23
     A smart man covers knowledge,
       but the heart of fools calls out foolishness.

כָּל־עָרוּם יַעֲשֶׂה בְדָעַת וּכְסִיל יִפְרֹשׂ אִוֶּלֶת   13:16
     Each smart one acts in knowledge,
       but a fool spreads out foolishness.

26:12 / 29:20 29:20a is related to 22:29a (see 2.2).

2:3 / 8:1 Though the verb forms are the same in the two verses, 2:3 is in the 2d person, and 8:1 is in the 3d person.

2:16 / 6:24 Both verses are related to 7:5 (see 1.1 and 1.3).

11:14 / 15:22 11:14a is related to 29:18a (see 2.2) and 11:14b is related to 24:6b (see 2.0); 15:22b is also related to 24:6b (see 2.1).

12:13 / 29:6 There are really only three different words in this pair, but I have placed them here because of the slightly different use of רע 'bad one'.

לְשׁוֹן חֲכָמִים תֵּיטִיב דָּעַת וּפִי כְסִילִים יַבִּיעַ אִוֶּלֶת	15:2	The tongue of wise ones improves knowledge, but the mouth of fools pours forth foolishness.
טוֹב־מְעַט בְּיִרְאַת יְהוָה מֵאוֹצָר רָב וּמְהוּמָה בוֹ	15:16	Better is a little in the fear of Yahweh than a big treasure and confusion in it.
טוֹב־מְעַט בִּצְדָקָה מֵרֹב תְּבוּאוֹת בְּלֹא מִשְׁפָּט	16:8	Better is a little in righteousness than much produce without justice.
לֵץ תַּכֶּה וּפֶתִי יַעְרִם וְהוֹכִיחַ לְנָבוֹן יָבִין דָּעַת	19:25	A scoffer you hit, and a simple one gets smart, and correct an understanding one, he understands knowledge.
בַּעְנָשׁ־לֵץ יֶחְכַּם־פֶּתִי וּבְהַשְׂכִּיל לְחָכָם יִקַּח־דָּעַת	21:11	In the punishment of a scoffer a simple one gets wise, and in the enlightenment of a wise one he gets knowledge.
טוֹב לָשֶׁבֶת עַל־פִּנַּת־גָּג מֵאֵשֶׁת מִדְיָנִים וּבֵית חָבֶר	21:9	It is better to sit on the corner of a roof than a woman of strifes and a noisy house.
טוֹב שֶׁבֶת בְּאֶרֶץ־מִדְבָּר מֵאֵשֶׁת מִדְיָנִים וָכָעַס	21:19	It is better to sit in a land of wilderness than a woman of strifes and anger.
טוֹב שֶׁבֶת עַל־פִּנַּת־גָּג מֵאֵשֶׁת מִדְיָנִים וּבֵית חָבֶר	25:24	It is better to sit on the corner of a roof than a woman of strifes and a noisy house.
עָשִׁיר וָרָשׁ נִפְגָּשׁוּ עֹשֵׂה כֻלָּם יְהוָה	22:2	A rich one and a poor one met— Yahweh is the maker of all of them.
רָשׁ וְאִישׁ תְּכָכִים נִפְגָּשׁוּ מֵאִיר־עֵינֵי שְׁנֵיהֶם יְהוָה	29:13	A poor one and a man of oppressions met— Yahweh puts light in the eyes of both of them.
כַּשֶּׁלֶג בַּקַּיִץ וְכַמָּטָר בַּקָּצִיר כֵּן לֹא־נָאוֶה לִכְסִיל כָּבוֹד	26:1	Like snow in the summer and like rain in the harvesttime, thus is honor not becoming for a fool.
כִּצְרוֹר אֶבֶן בְּמַרְגֵּמָה כֵּן־נוֹתֵן לִכְסִיל כָּבוֹד	26:8	Like a bundle of stone in a heap [sling?], thus is one who gives honor to a fool.

15:16 / 16:8   Both verses syntactically resemble 12:9, 15:17, and 17:1 (see 4.5).

19:25 / 21:11   21:11 syntactically resembles 11:10, 28:28, and 29:2 (see 4.4).

21:9 / 21:19 / 25:24   21:9 is more closely related to 25:24 (see 1.0); all three verses syntactically resemble 19:1 and 28:6 (see 4.8).

22:2 / 29:13   Again one might argue that only three major elements differ between the two verses, but I have placed the pair here because 29:13 uses more words to say about the same thing as 22:2.

26:1 / 26:8   Both verses syntactically resemble others with ... כן ... כן (see 4.9). The hapax legomenon מרגמה in 26:8 has something to do with stones, but the image is uncertain; see McKane, *Proverbs*, 598, and J. de Fraine, "מרגמה (Prov. 26,8)," in *Fourth World Congress of Jewish Studies: Papers* (Jerusalem: World Union of Jewish Studies, 1967) 1:131–35, opting for "pile" of stones.

2.0 HALF-VERSES REPEATED WITH SPELLING VARIATIONS (16 SETS)

וַיֹּרֵנִי וַיֹּאמֶר לִי יִתְמָךְ־דְּבָרַי לִבֶּךָ שְׁמֹר מִצְוֹתַי וֶחְיֵה   4:4b   And he instructed me and said to me,
Let your heart take my words;
keep my commands, and live.

שְׁמֹר מִצְוֹתַי וֶחְיֵה וְתוֹרָתִי כְּאִישׁוֹן עֵינֶיךָ   7:2a   Keep my commands and live,
and my teaching like the pupil of your eye.

וְעַתָּה בָנִים שִׁמְעוּ־לִי וְאַל־תָּסוּרוּ מֵאִמְרֵי־פִי   5:7a   And now, sons, listen to me,
and do not deviate from the words of my mouth.

וְעַתָּה בָנִים שִׁמְעוּ־לִי וְהַקְשִׁיבוּ לְאִמְרֵי־פִי   7:24a   And now, sons, listen to me,
and attend to the words of my mouth.

וְעַתָּה בָנִים שִׁמְעוּ־לִי וְאַשְׁרֵי דְּרָכַי יִשְׁמֹרוּ   8:32a   And now, sons, listen to me,
and happy are they who keep my ways.

עַל־כֵּן פִּתְאֹם יָבוֹא אֵידוֹ פֶּתַע יִשָּׁבֵר וְאֵין מַרְפֵּא   6:15b   Because of that, suddenly will come his destruction;
instantly he will be broken, and there will be no healer.

אִישׁ תּוֹכָחוֹת מַקְשֶׁה־עֹרֶף פֶּתַע יִשָּׁבֵר וְאֵין מַרְפֵּא   29:1b   A man of corrections hardens the neck;
suddenly he will be broken, and there will be no healer.

יָפִיחַ כְּזָבִים עֵד שָׁקֶר וּמְשַׁלֵּחַ מְדָנִים בֵּין אַחִים   6:19a   A testifier of lies is a witness of falseness,
and one who sends strifes between brothers.

עֵד אֱמוּנִים לֹא יְכַזֵּב וְיָפִיחַ כְּזָבִים עֵד שָׁקֶר   14:5b   A witness of truthfulness does not lie,
and a testifier of lies is a witness of falseness.

בְּרָכוֹת לְרֹאשׁ צַדִּיק וּפִי רְשָׁעִים יְכַסֶּה חָמָס   10:6b   Blessings are for the head of a righteous one,
but the mouth of bad ones covers violence.

מְקוֹר חַיִּים פִּי צַדִּיק וּפִי רְשָׁעִים יְכַסֶּה חָמָס   10:11b   A source of life is the mouth of a righteous one,
but the mouth of bad ones covers violence.

חֲכַם־לֵב יִקַּח מִצְוֹת וֶאֱוִיל שְׂפָתַיִם יִלָּבֵט   10:8b   One wise of heart gets commands,
but a fool of lips will be thrust down.

קֹרֵץ עַיִן יִתֵּן עַצָּבֶת וֶאֱוִיל שְׂפָתַיִם יִלָּבֵט   10:10b   One who winks an eye gives trouble,
but a fool of lips will be thrust down.

4:4b / 7:2a The "he" of 4:4 is אבי 'my father' (from 4:3).

5:7a / 7:24a / 8:32a 5:7 and 7:24 are more closely related to each other (see 1.1).

6:15b / 29:1b 6:15a is related to 24:22a (see 2.2).

6:19a / 14:5b See note on 19:5/19:9 (p. 36 above) for the translation "testifier" for יפיח.

10:6b / 10:11b Since these verses are close to each other, perhaps this is a repetition for emphasis.

10:8b / 10:10b Again, this repetition may be for emphasis. It is an esthetic judgment that in 10:10b the RSV made here to follow the Greek translators (who apparently found repetition distasteful). See the excursus, pp. 23–33 above.

הוֹן עָשִׁיר קִרְיַת עֻזּוֹ מְחִתַּת דַּלִּים רֵישָׁם	10:15a	The wealth of a rich one is the village of his strength; the ruin of poor ones is their poverty.
הוֹן עָשִׁיר קִרְיַת עֻזּוֹ וּכְחוֹמָה נִשְׂגָּבָה בְּמַשְׂכִּיתוֹ	18:11a	The wealth of a rich one is the village of his strength; and like an inaccessible wall in his imagination.
מָעוֹז לַתֹּם דֶּרֶךְ יְהוָה וּמְחִתָּה לְפֹעֲלֵי אָוֶן	10:29b	A place of safety for simplicity is the way of Yahweh, but a ruin for those who do sin.
שִׂמְחָה לַצַּדִּיק עֲשׂוֹת מִשְׁפָּט וּמְחִתָּה לְפֹעֲלֵי אָוֶן	21:15b	It is joy for the righteous one to do justice, but a ruin for those who do sin.
בְּאֵין תַּחְבֻּלוֹת יִפָּל־עָם וּתְשׁוּעָה בְּרֹב יוֹעֵץ	11:14b	With no steersmanship a people falls, but salvation is in many counselors.
כִּי בְתַחְבֻּלוֹת תַּעֲשֶׂה־לְּךָ מִלְחָמָה וּתְשׁוּעָה בְּרֹב יוֹעֵץ	24:6b	For with steersmanship you make war for yourself, but salvation is in many counselors.
אוֹר־צַדִּיקִים יִשְׂמָח וְנֵר רְשָׁעִים יִדְעָךְ	13:9b	A light of righteous ones is joyful, but the lamp of bad ones will be extinguished.
כִּי לֹא־תִהְיֶה אַחֲרִית לָרָע נֵר רְשָׁעִים יִדְעָךְ	24:20b	For there will be no end for the evil one; the lamp of bad ones will be extinguished.
יִרְאַת יְהוָה מוּסַר חָכְמָה וְלִפְנֵי כָבוֹד עֲנָוָה	15:33b	The fear of Yahweh is the discipline of wisdom, and before honor humility.
לִפְנֵי־שֶׁבֶר יִגְבַּהּ לֵב־אִישׁ וְלִפְנֵי כָבוֹד עֲנָוָה	18:12b	Before a break the heart of a man is high, and before honor is lowliness.
מַצְרֵף לַכֶּסֶף וְכוּר לַזָּהָב וּבֹחֵן לִבּוֹת יְהוָה	17:3a	A crucible for silver and a furnace for gold, and a trier of hearts is Yahweh.
מַצְרֵף לַכֶּסֶף וְכוּר לַזָּהָב וְאִישׁ לְפִי מַהֲלָלוֹ	27:21a	A crucible for silver and a furnace for gold, and a man according to his praise.

11:14b / 24:6b   11:14 is related to 15:22 (see 1.4) and 11:14a is related to 29:18a (2.2); 24:6a is related to 20:18b (see 2.1). Both 11:14 and 24:6 could conceivably be classified as wholly repeated verses since they share the word תחבלות in their first clauses. But they seem to be saying slightly different things, and their second clauses are exactly the same, so I have placed them here.

15:33b / 18:12b   18:12a is related to 16:18a (see 2.2).

מַצְדִּיק רָשָׁע וּמַרְשִׁיעַ צַדִּיק תּוֹעֲבַת יְהוָה גַּם־שְׁנֵיהֶם

17:15b   One who declares righteous a bad one or one
who declares bad a righteous one—
both of them are an abomination of Yahweh.

אֶבֶן וָאֶבֶן אֵיפָה וְאֵיפָה תּוֹעֲבַת יְהוָה גַּם־שְׁנֵיהֶם

20:10b   A stone and a stone and a grain measure and a
grain measure—
both of them are an abomination of Yahweh.

אַל־תַּסֵּג גְּבוּל עוֹלָם אֲשֶׁר עָשׂוּ אֲבוֹתֶיךָ

22:28a   Do not move a border of a long time ago,
which your fathers made.

אַל־תַּסֵּג גְּבוּל עוֹלָם וּבִשְׂדֵי יְתוֹמִים אַל־תָּבֹא

23:10a   Do not move a border of a long time ago,
and in the fields of fatherless ones do not enter.

אַל־תִּתְאָו לְמַטְעַמּוֹתָיו וְהוּא לֶחֶם כְּזָבִים

23:3a   Do not desire his dainties,
since it is the bread of lies.

אַל־תִּלְחַם אֶת־לֶחֶם רַע עָיִן וְאַל־תִּתְאָו לְמַטְעַמֹּתָיו

23:6b   Do not eat the bread of one bad of eye,
and do not desire his dainties.

דַּלְיוּ שֹׁקַיִם מִפִּסֵּחַ וּמָשָׁל בְּפִי כְסִילִים

26:7b   Draw out the thighs from a lame one,
and an apt saying in the mouth of fools.

חוֹחַ עָלָה בְיַד־שִׁכּוֹר וּמָשָׁל בְּפִי כְסִילִים

26:9b   A thorn went up in the hand of a drunkard,
and an apt saying in the mouth of fools.

2.1 HALF-VERSES REPEATED WITH ONE DISSIMILAR WORD (20 SETS)

כִּי לִוְיַת חֵן הֵם לְרֹאשֶׁךָ וַעֲנָקִים לְגַרְגְּרֹתֶיךָ

1:9a   For a garland of grace they are for your head,
and necklaces for your throat.

תִּתֵּן לְרֹאשְׁךָ לִוְיַת־חֵן עֲטֶרֶת תִּפְאֶרֶת תְּמַגְּנֶךָּ

4:9a   She will give to your head a garland of grace;
a crown of beauty she will present you.

בְּנִי אַל־יָלֻזוּ מֵעֵינֶיךָ נְצֹר תֻּשִׁיָּה וּמְזִמָּה

3:21a   My son, let them not depart from your eyes;
keep resourcefulness and foresight.

אַל־יַלִּיזוּ מֵעֵינֶיךָ שָׁמְרֵם בְּתוֹךְ לְבָבֶךָ

4:21a   Let them not depart from your eyes;
guard them within your heart.

17:15b / 20:10b   17:15a is related to 24:24a (see 2.2) and 20:10 is related to 20:23a (see 3.0).

23:3a / 23:6b   The reference in 23:3 is to the ruler in Prov 23:1. Note the proximity of 23:3 and 23:6 in the MT.

26:7b / 26:9b   These verses occur close to each other in the text and may again be examples of repetition for emphasis. I see 26:7b as less problematic than the commentators do (e.g., Toy, *Book of Proverbs*, 474; and McKane, *Proverbs*, 597–98). If taken as it stands, it means, "You might as well take for yourself the understandably weak and useless thighs of a lame person; you'll be getting goods of equal value if you seek an apt saying from a fool."

1:9a / 4:9a   The subject of 1:9 is מוסר אביך 'your father's instruction' and תורת אמך 'your mother's teaching' (from v. 8). The subject of 4:9 is חכמה 'wisdom' (from v. 5).

3:21a / 4:21a   The subjects of 3:21 are חכמה 'wisdom', תבונה 'understanding', and דעת 'knowledge' (from vv. 19–20), although the RSV reverses the two clauses, making the nouns in 3:21b the subjects. The parallel in 4:21

אַל־תְּקַנֵּא בְּאִישׁ חָמָס וְאַל־תִּבְחַר בְּכָל־דְּרָכָיו	3:31a	Do not envy a man of violence, and do not choose any of his ways.
אַל־תְּקַנֵּא בְּאַנְשֵׁי רָעָה וְאַל־תִּתְאָו לִהְיוֹת אִתָּם	24:1a	Do not envy men of evil, and do not desire to be with them.
כִּי מֹצְאִי מָצָא חַיִּים וַיָּפֶק רָצוֹן מֵיהֹוָה	8:35b	For one who finds me has found life, and he gets desire from Yahweh.
טוֹב יָפִיק רָצוֹן מֵיהֹוָה וְאִישׁ מְזִמּוֹת יַרְשִׁיעַ	12:2a	A good one gets desire from Yahweh, but a man of deceits he declares guilty.
מָצָא אִשָּׁה מָצָא טוֹב וַיָּפֶק רָצוֹן מֵיהֹוָה	18:22b	He has found a woman; he has found a good thing, and he gets desire from Yahweh.
חָכְמוֹת בָּנְתָה בֵיתָהּ חָצְבָה עַמּוּדֶיהָ שִׁבְעָה	9:1a	Wisdom built her house; she has hewn her seven pillars.
חַכְמוֹת נָשִׁים בָּנְתָה בֵיתָהּ וְאִוֶּלֶת בְּיָדֶיהָ תֶהֶרְסֶנּוּ	14:1a	The wisdom of women built her house, but foolishness in her hand destroys it.
בָּא־זָדוֹן וַיָּבֹא קָלוֹן וְאֶת־צְנוּעִים חָכְמָה	11:2b	Excess comes, and calumny comes, but wisdom is with modest ones.
רַק־בְּזָדוֹן יִתֵּן מַצָּה וְאֶת־נוֹעָצִים חָכְמָה	13:10b	Only in excess does one give strife, but wisdom is with advised people.
הוֹלֵךְ רָכִיל מְגַלֶּה־סּוֹד וְנֶאֱמַן־רוּחַ מְכַסֶּה דָבָר	11:13a	One who spreads rumors reveals secret talk, but one who is trustworthy in spirit covers a matter.
גּוֹלֶה־סּוֹד הוֹלֵךְ רָכִיל וּלְפֹתֶה שְׂפָתָיו לֹא תִתְעָרָב	20:19a	One who reveals secret talk spreads rumors, and with one who deceives with his lips do not get involved.

---

seems to indicate that such a change is not necessary. My translation of 3:21b follows NJPSV. The subject of 4:21 is אמרי 'my words' (from v. 20).

    8:35b / 12:2a / 18:22b   8:35 and 18:22 are more closely related to each other (see 1.3) and to other verses with double-verb syntax (see 4.2). The antecedent of 8:35 is wisdom.

    9:1a / 14:1a   Both verses are also related to 24:3a (see 2.2). See the discussion of the cliché in chapter 4, pp. 17–18.

    11:2b / 13:10b   This pair could be classified differently because they also share זדון 'insolence', and they could be seen as wholly repeated verses with four dissimilar words. I have placed the pair here because their first clauses are rather different and the dissimilar words in their second clauses seem to be acoustic reflections of each other.

יָד לְיָד לֹא־יִנָּקֶה רָּע וְזֶרַע צַדִּיקִים נִמְלָט	11:21a	Immediately [lit.: hand to hand] a bad one will not be found innocent, but the seed of righteous ones escapes.
תּוֹעֲבַת יְהוָה כָּל־גְּבַהּ־לֵב יָד לְיָד לֹא יִנָּקֶה	16:5b	Each highness of heart is an abomination to Yahweh; immediately [lit.: hand to hand] it will not be found innocent.
מִפְּרִי פִי־אִישׁ יִשְׂבַּע־טוֹב וּגְמוּל יְדֵי־אָדָם יָשׁוּב לוֹ	12:14a	From the fruit of the mouth of a man he will have enough good, and the deed of the hands of a person returns to him.
מִפְּרִי פִי־אִישׁ יֹאכַל טוֹב וְנֶפֶשׁ בֹּגְדִים חָמָס	13:2a	From the fruit of the mouth of a man he will eat good, but the desire of deceivers is violence.
בֵּן חָכָם מוּסַר אָב וְלֵץ לֹא־שָׁמַע גְּעָרָה	13:1b	A wise son is a discipline of a father, but a scoffer does not hear scolding.
כֹּפֶר נֶפֶשׁ־אִישׁ עָשְׁרוֹ וְרָשׁ לֹא־שָׁמַע גְּעָרָה	13:8b	The ransom of the soul of a man is his wealth, but a poor one does not hear scolding.
זֶבַח רְשָׁעִים תּוֹעֲבַת יְהוָה וּתְפִלַּת יְשָׁרִים רְצוֹנוֹ	15:8a	The offering of bad ones is an abomination of Yahweh, but the prayer of upright ones is his desire.
זֶבַח רְשָׁעִים תּוֹעֵבָה אַף כִּי־בְזִמָּה יְבִיאֶנּוּ	21:27a	The offering of bad ones is an abomination; how much more so he brings it in depravity.
לֵב נָבוֹן יְבַקֶּשׁ־דָּעַת וּפְנֵי כְסִילִים יִרְעֶה אִוֶּלֶת	15:14a	The heart of an understanding one seeks knowledge, but the face of fools keeps company with foolishness.
לֵב נָבוֹן יִקְנֶה־דָּעַת וְאֹזֶן חֲכָמִים תְּבַקֶּשׁ־דָּעַת	18:15a	The heart of an understanding one acquires knowledge, and the ear of wise ones seeks knowledge.

11:21a / 16:5b M. Anbar, "Proverbes 11,21; 16,5: יד ליד, 'sur le champ,'" *Biblica* 53 (1972) 537–38, shows the meaning of the expression יד ליד 'hand to hand' to be 'immediately', by analogy to a similar expression in Mari Akkadian. Compare the references in *Chicago Assyrian Dictionary I/J*, s.v. *idu* A, 7:14b 4′. The sense is thus roughly the same as the expression in 6:15b ~ 29:1b (see 2.0).

12:14a / 13:2a Both verses are also related to 18:20a (see 2.2).

13:1b / 13:8b The physical proximity of these verses suggests a conscious effort to emphasize and to extend the idea.

15:14a / 18:15a 15:14b seems closely related to 12:23b, 13:16b, and 15:2b (see 1.4), but I have classified what they share as a cliché (see the index under כסיל, אולת). The relation between 15:14a and 18:15 might be classed as a case of half-and-whole-verse repetition, since 18:15b shares the last two words with 15:14a and both parts of 18:15 have the same meaning as 15:14a. But I have chosen to see this pair as half-repeated with a parallel synonym.

אִישׁ חֵמָה יְגָרֶה מָדוֹן וְאֶרֶךְ אַפַּיִם יַשְׁקִיט רִיב	15:18a	A man of anger causes strife, but patience quiets a dispute.
אִישׁ־אַף יְגָרֶה מָדוֹן וּבַעַל חֵמָה רַב־פָּשַׁע	29:22a	A man of wrath causes strife, and a person given to anger is great of sin.
הָפֵר מַחֲשָׁבוֹת בְּאֵין סוֹד וּבְרֹב יוֹעֲצִים תָּקוּם	15:22b	Frustrate thoughts without confidential conversation, but with many counselors you will stand.
כִּי בְתַחְבֻּלוֹת תַּעֲשֶׂה־לְּךָ מִלְחָמָה וּתְשׁוּעָה בְּרֹב יוֹעֵץ	24:6b	For with steersmanship you make war for yourself, but salvation is in many counselors.
תּוֹעֲבַת מְלָכִים עֲשׂוֹת רֶשַׁע כִּי בִצְדָקָה יִכּוֹן כִּסֵּא	16:12b	It is an abomination to kings to do evil, for with justice a throne is established.
הָגוֹ רָשָׁע לִפְנֵי־מֶלֶךְ וְיִכּוֹן בַּצֶּדֶק כִּסְאוֹ	25:5b	Remove a bad one before a king, and his throne is established with rightness.
מֶלֶךְ שׁוֹפֵט בֶּאֱמֶת דַּלִּים כִּסְאוֹ לָעַד יִכּוֹן	29:14b	A king who judges poor ones with truth— his throne is established forever.
נַהַם כַּכְּפִיר זַעַף מֶלֶךְ וּכְטַל עַל־עֵשֶׂב רְצוֹנוֹ	19:12a	A growling like a young lion is the anger of a king, but like dew on grass is his desire.
נַהַם כַּכְּפִיר אֵימַת מֶלֶךְ מִתְעַבְּרוֹ חוֹטֵא נַפְשׁוֹ	20:2a	A growling like a young lion is the wrath of a king; one who crosses it loses his soul.
נָכוֹנוּ לַלֵּצִים שְׁפָטִים וּמַהֲלֻמוֹת לְגֵו כְּסִילִים	19:29b	Penalties are prepared for the scoffers, and blows for the back of fools.
שׁוֹט לַסּוּס מֶתֶג לַחֲמוֹר וְשֵׁבֶט לְגֵו כְּסִילִים	26:3b	A whip is for the horse, a bridle for the ass, and a staff is for the back of fools.
גַּם בְּמַעֲלָלָיו יִתְנַכֶּר־נָעַר אִם־זַךְ וְאִם־יָשָׁר פָּעֳלוֹ	20:11b	Also in his deeds a lad is recognized, whether his act is pure and upright.
הֲפַכְפַּךְ דֶּרֶךְ אִישׁ וָזָר וְזַךְ יָשָׁר פָּעֳלוֹ	21:8b	Twisted is the way of a man and a stranger, but a pure one—his act is upright.

15:22b / 24:6b 15:22 is related to 11:14 (see 1.4), 24:6a is related to 20:18b (see 2.1), and 24:6b is also related to 11:14b (see 2.0).

16:12b / 25:5b / 29:14b All these verses are also related to 20:28b (see 2.2), and they might be classified as wholly repeated since they share the word מלך 'king' in their first clauses. I have placed them here because the first clauses all seem rather different from each other.

19:29b / 26:3b 26:3b is related to 10:13b (see 2.2).

20:11b / 21:8b Though the underlined words are the same here, their grammatical functions differ. זך 'pure' in 21:8b is the subject of the clause, while the subject of 20:11b is פעל 'act' of נער 'a lad' from the first half of the verse. The NJPSV construes the half-verses as similar: "The way of a man may be tortuous and strange, / Though his actions are blameless and proper" (21:8), which involves inserting *and* before *proper*.

מַחֲשָׁבוֹת בְּעֵצָה תִכּוֹן וּבְתַחְבֻּלוֹת עֲשֵׂה מִלְחָמָה	20:18b	Thoughts with advice are established, and with steersmanship make war.
כִּי בְתַחְבֻּלוֹת תַּעֲשֶׂה־לְּךָ מִלְחָמָה וּתְשׁוּעָה בְּרֹב יוֹעֵץ	24:6a	For with steersmanship you make war for yourself, but salvation is in many counselors.
בַּעֲלֹץ צַדִּיקִים רַבָּה תִפְאָרֶת וּבְקוּם רְשָׁעִים יְחֻפַּשׂ אָדָם	28:12b	In the rejoicing of righteous ones beauty increases, but in the rise of bad ones a man is sought.
בְּקוּם רְשָׁעִים יִסָּתֵר אָדָם וּבְאָבְדָם יִרְבּוּ צַדִּיקִים	28:28a	In the rise of bad ones a man hides, but in their perishing righteous ones increase.

2.2 HALF-VERSES REPEATED WITH TWO DISSIMILAR WORDS[1] (22 SETS)

יִרְאַת יְהוָה רֵאשִׁית דָּעַת חָכְמָה וּמוּסָר אֱוִילִים בָּזוּ	1:7a	The fear of Yahweh is the first thing of knowledge; wisdom and discipline fools despise.
תְּחִלַּת חָכְמָה יִרְאַת יְהוָה וְדַעַת קְדֹשִׁים בִּינָה	9:10a	The beginning of wisdom is the fear of Yahweh, and knowledge of the holy one is understanding.
שְׁמַע בְּנִי מוּסַר אָבִיךָ וְאַל־תִּטֹּשׁ תּוֹרַת אִמֶּךָ	1:8a	Hear, my son, the discipline of your father, and do not neglect the teaching of your mother.
שִׁמְעוּ בָנִים מוּסַר אָב וְהַקְשִׁיבוּ לָדַעַת בִּינָה	4:1a	Hear, sons, the discipline of a father, and listen to know understanding.
אַל־תְּהִי חָכָם בְּעֵינֶיךָ יְרָא אֶת־יְהוָה וְסוּר מֵרָע	3:7b	Do not be wise in your eyes; fear Yahweh and turn aside from evil.
בְּחֶסֶד וֶאֱמֶת יְכֻפַּר עָוֹן וּבְיִרְאַת יְהוָה סוּר מֵרָע	16:6b	With loving-kindness and truth, sin is covered over, and in the fear of Yahweh is turning aside from evil.

20:18b / 24:6a   24:6b is related to 11:14b (see 2.0) and to 15:22b (in this section).

28:12b / 28:28a   Because of their proximity to each other, these may be another case of repetition for emphasis. Both verses are syntactically related to 11:10, 21:11, and 29:2 (see 4.4).

1:8a / 4:1a   1:8 is related to 6:20 (see 1.2).

3:7b / 16:6b   The grammatical function of סור differs in these verses: in 3:7b it is an imperative, in 16:6b an infinitive.

1. The distinction between a pair of half-repeated verses and two instances of a cliché is one that others might make differently. I have tried to classify instances as half-repeated verses when the sense of the half-verses is essentially the same. If the verses seem not to be saying the same thing, I have relegated them to the status of clichés.

תָּכִין בַּקַּיִץ לַחְמָהּ אָגְרָה בַקָּצִיר מַאֲכָלָהּ	6:8a	It prepares its food in the summer, gathers in the harvesttime what it eats.
הַנְּמָלִים עַם לֹא־עָז וַיָּכִינוּ בַקַּיִץ לַחְמָם	30:25b	The ants are a people not strong, but they prepare in the summer their food.
עַל־כֵּן פִּתְאֹם יָבוֹא אֵידוֹ פֶּתַע יִשָּׁבֵר וְאֵין מַרְפֵּא	6:15a	Because of that, suddenly will come his destruction; instantly he will be broken, and there will be no healer.
כִּי־פִתְאֹם יָקוּם אֵידָם וּפִיד שְׁנֵיהֶם מִי יוֹדֵעַ	24:22a	For suddenly will arise their destruction, and the ruin of both of them, who knows?
חָכְמוֹת בָּנְתָה בֵיתָהּ חָצְבָה עַמּוּדֶיהָ שִׁבְעָה	9:1a	Wisdom built her house; she has hewn her seven pillars.
חַכְמוֹת נָשִׁים בָּנְתָה בֵיתָהּ וְאִוֶּלֶת בְּיָדֶיהָ תֶהֶרְסֶנּוּ	14:1a	The wisdom of women built her house, but foolishness in her hand destroys it.
בְּחָכְמָה יִבָּנֶה בָּיִת וּבִתְבוּנָה יִתְכּוֹנָן	24:3a	With wisdom a house is built, and with understanding it is established.
בְּשִׂפְתֵי נָבוֹן תִּמָּצֵא חָכְמָה וְשֵׁבֶט לְגֵו חֲסַר־לֵב	10:13b	In the lips of an understanding one, wisdom is found, but a staff is for the back of one lacking sense.
שׁוֹט לַסּוּס מֶתֶג לַחֲמוֹר וְשֵׁבֶט לְגֵו כְּסִילִים	26:3b	A whip is for the horse, a bridle for the ass, and a staff is for the back of fools.
צִדְקַת יְשָׁרִים תַּצִּילֵם וּבְהַוַּת בֹּגְדִים יִלָּכֵדוּ	11:6a	The righteousness of upright ones saves them, but in the desire of deceitful ones, they are caught.
דִּבְרֵי רְשָׁעִים אֱרָב־דָּם וּפִי יְשָׁרִים יַצִּילֵם	12:6b	The words of bad ones are an ambush of blood, but the mouth of upright ones saves them.
בְּאֵין תַּחְבֻּלוֹת יִפָּל־עָם וּתְשׁוּעָה בְּרֹב יוֹעֵץ	11:14a	With no steersmanship a people falls, but salvation is in many counselors.
בְּאֵין חָזוֹן יִפָּרַע עָם וְשֹׁמֵר תּוֹרָה אַשְׁרֵהוּ	29:18a	With no prophecy a people is let run wild, but one who keeps instruction—happy is he.

6:8a / 30:25b The subject of 6:8 is נמלה 'ant' (from 6:6).

6:15a / 24:22a 6:15b is related to 29:1b (see 2.0). The subject of 6:15 is אדם בליעל 'a worthless person' (from 6:12). The 3d-person pronominal suffixes in 24:22 refer to Yahweh and the king.

9:1a / 14:1a / 24:3a 9:1a is more closely related to 14:1a (see 2.1) than to 24:3a. See the discussion of the cliché in chapter 4, pp. 17–18.

10:13b / 26:3b 26:3b is related to 19:29b (see 2.1).

11:14a / 29:18a 11:14 is related to 15:22 (see 1.4) and 11:14b is related to 24:6b (see 2.0).

מִפְּרִי פִי־אִישׁ יִשְׂבַּע־טוֹב וּגְמוּל יְדֵי־אָדָם יָשׁוּב לוֹ

12:14a   From the fruit of the mouth of a man he will have enough good,
and the deed of the hands of a person returns to him.

מִפְּרִי פִי־אִישׁ יֹאכַל טוֹב וְנֶפֶשׁ בֹּגְדִים חָמָס

13:2a   From the fruit of the mouth of a man he will eat good,
but the desire of deceivers is violence.

מִפְּרִי פִי־אִישׁ תִּשְׂבַּע בִּטְנוֹ תְּבוּאַת שְׂפָתָיו יִשְׂבָּע

18:20a   From the fruit of the mouth of a man his belly will have enough;
of the produce of his lips he will have enough.

דֶּרֶךְ אֱוִיל יָשָׁר בְּעֵינָיו וְשֹׁמֵעַ לְעֵצָה חָכָם

12:15a   The way of a fool is upright in his eyes,
but one who listens to advice is wise.

כָּל־דַּרְכֵי־אִישׁ זַךְ בְּעֵינָיו וְתֹכֵן רוּחוֹת יְהוָה

16:2a   All the ways of a man are pure in his eyes,
but Yahweh is an estimator of spirits.

כָּל־דֶּרֶךְ־אִישׁ יָשָׁר בְּעֵינָיו וְתֹכֵן לִבּוֹת יְהוָה

21:2a   Each way of a man is upright in his eyes,
but Yahweh is an estimator of hearts.

תּוֹעֲבַת מְלָכִים עֲשׂוֹת רֶשַׁע כִּי בִצְדָקָה יִכּוֹן כִּסֵּא

16:12b   It is an abomination to kings to do evil,
for with justice a throne is established.

חֶסֶד וֶאֱמֶת יִצְּרוּ־מֶלֶךְ וְסָעַד בַּחֶסֶד כִּסְאוֹ

20:28b   Loving-kindness and truth keep a king,
and he sustains with loving-kindness his throne.

הָגוֹ רָשָׁע לִפְנֵי־מֶלֶךְ וְיִכּוֹן בַּצֶּדֶק כִּסְאוֹ

25:5b   Remove a bad one before a king,
and his throne is established with rightness.

מֶלֶךְ שׁוֹפֵט בֶּאֱמֶת דַּלִּים כִּסְאוֹ לָעַד יִכּוֹן

29:14b   A king who judges poor ones with truth—
his throne is established forever.

מְסִלַּת יְשָׁרִים סוּר מֵרָע שֹׁמֵר נַפְשׁוֹ נֹצֵר דַּרְכּוֹ

16:17b   The causeway of upright ones is to turn away from evil;
one who guards his soul keeps his way.

שֹׁמֵר מִצְוָה שֹׁמֵר נַפְשׁוֹ בּוֹזֵה דְרָכָיו יָמֻת

19:16a   One who keeps commandment keeps his soul;
one who despises his ways will die.

12:14a / 13:2a / 18:20a   I see 12:14a as slightly more closely related to 13:2a (see 2.1) than both verses are to 18:20a.

12:15a / 16:2a / 21:2a   16:2 is more closely related to 21:2 (see 1.3).

16:12b / 20:28b / 25:5b / 29:14b   I have classified 16:12b, 25:5b, and 29:14b under 2.1. It could be that the relation of 20:28b to those verses is better regarded as a cliché, perhaps involving מלך 'king' and כסא 'throne'. But because of the similar sense of 20:28b, I have placed it here. It might also be that סעד 'upholds' is related to the similar sounding לעד 'forever' in 29:14b.

16:17b / 19:16a   19:16a is syntactically similar to the many double-verb clauses noted in 4.2 below. 16:17b, of course, is also loosely related to them, since it uses two common synonyms for 'to keep'.

לִפְנֵי־שֶׁבֶר גָּאוֹן וְלִפְנֵי כִשָּׁלוֹן גֹּבַהּ רוּחַ	16:18a	Before a break is haughtiness, and before failure highness of spirit.
לִפְנֵי־שֶׁבֶר יִגְבַּהּ לֶב־אִישׁ וְלִפְנֵי כָבוֹד עֲנָוָה	18:12a	Before a break the heart of a man is high, and before honor is lowliness.
מַצְדִּיק רָשָׁע וּמַרְשִׁיעַ צַדִּיק תּוֹעֲבַת יְהוָה גַּם־שְׁנֵיהֶם	17:15a	One who declares righteous a bad one or one who declares bad a righteous one— both of them are an abomination to Yahweh.
אֹמֵר לְרָשָׁע צַדִּיק אָתָּה יִקְּבֻהוּ עַמִּים יִזְעָמוּהוּ לְאֻמִּים	24:24a	One who says to a bad one, You are righteous— peoples curse him, nations execrate him.
מַיִם עֲמֻקִּים דִּבְרֵי פִי־אִישׁ נַחַל נֹבֵעַ מְקוֹר חָכְמָה	18:4a	Deep water is the words of the mouth of a man, a stream flowing is the source of wisdom.
מַיִם עֲמֻקִּים עֵצָה בְלֶב־אִישׁ וְאִישׁ תְּבוּנָה יִדְלֶנָּה	20:5a	Deep water is advice in the heart of a man, and a man of understanding draws it forth.
גַּם מִתְרַפֶּה בִמְלַאכְתּוֹ אָח הוּא לְבַעַל מַשְׁחִית	18:9b	Also one who is slack in his work is a brother to one given to destroying.
גּוֹזֵל אָבִיו וְאִמּוֹ וְאֹמֵר אֵין־פָּשַׁע חָבֵר הוּא לְאִישׁ מַשְׁחִית	28:24b	One who robs his father and his mother and says, There is no sin, is a fellow to a destroying man.
שׁוּחָה עֲמֻקָּה פִּי זָרוֹת זְעוּם יְהוָה יִפּוֹל־שָׁם	22:14a	A deep pit is the mouth of foreign women; one cursed by Yahweh falls there.
כִּי־שׁוּחָה עֲמֻקָּה זוֹנָה וּבְאֵר צָרָה נָכְרִיָּה	23:27a	For a deep pit is a whore, and a narrow well is an alien one.
חָזִיתָ אִישׁ מָהִיר בִּמְלַאכְתּוֹ לִפְנֵי־מְלָכִים יִתְיַצָּב בַּל־יִתְיַצֵּב לִפְנֵי חֲשֻׁכִּים	22:29a	You have observed a man hasty in his work— before kings he will stand; he will not stand before low ones.
חָזִיתָ אִישׁ אָץ בִּדְבָרָיו תִּקְוָה לִכְסִיל מִמֶּנּוּ	29:20a	You have observed a man quick in his words— there is more hope for a fool than him.

16:18a / 18:12a   18:12b is also related to 15:33b (see 2.0).

17:15a / 24:24a   17:15b is related to 20:10b (see 2.0).

22:14a / 23:27a   The use of זונה 'whore' in parallelism to נכריה 'strange woman' seems to offer some evidence that the much decried "strange woman" of the first collection in Proverbs may sometimes be understood as a real harlot and not, as some have argued, a devotee of a fertility cult. Leo G. Perdue, *Wisdom and Cult* (Missoula: Scholars Press, 1977) 151 and elsewhere, supports this latter view, as does B. Lang, *Wisdom and the Book of Proverbs: A Hebrew Goddess Redefined* (New York: Pilgrim, 1986).

22:29a / 29:20a   29:20 is related to 26:12 (see 1.3). It may be that what 22:29a and 29:20a share is better classed as a cliché, since they take opposite views of their subject. But because they use synonymous terms, I have placed them here.

כִּי־תֹאמַר הֵן לֹא־יָדַעְנוּ זֶה הֲלֹא־תֹכֵן לִבּוֹת הוּא־יָבִין וְנֹצֵר נַפְשְׁךָ הוּא יֵדָע וְהֵשִׁיב לְאָדָם כְּפָעֳלוֹ	24:12b	For you say, See, we did not know this. Does not the estimator of hearts understand, and the keeper of your soul know, and return to a person according to his deed?
אַל־תֹּאמַר כַּאֲשֶׁר עָשָׂה־לִי כֵּן אֶעֱשֶׂה־לּוֹ אָשִׁיב לָאִישׁ כְּפָעֳלוֹ	24:29b	Do not say, As he did to me, thus I will do to him; I return to the man according to his deed.
הַכֵּר־פָּנִים בְּמִשְׁפָּט בַּל־טוֹב	24:23b	Favoritism [lit.: recognizing a face] in judgment is not good.
הַכֵּר־פָּנִים לֹא־טוֹב וְעַל־פַּת־לֶחֶם יִפְשַׁע־גָּבֶר	28:21a	Favoritism is not good, and about a crust of bread a man sins.
אַל־תַּעַן כְּסִיל כְּאִוַּלְתּוֹ פֶּן־תִּשְׁוֶה־לּוֹ גַם־אָתָּה	26:4a	Do not answer a fool according to his foolishness lest you be equal to him also you.
עֲנֵה כְסִיל כְּאִוַּלְתּוֹ פֶּן־יִהְיֶה חָכָם בְּעֵינָיו	26:5a	Answer a fool according to his foolishness lest he be wise in his own eyes.

**3.0   HALF-VERSES REPEATED IN WHOLE VERSE WITH EACH WORD IN
THE HALF-VERSE APPEARING IN THE WHOLE**[2] (4 SETS)

שְׁמַע בְּנִי וְקַח אֲמָרָי וְיִרְבּוּ לְךָ שְׁנוֹת חַיִּים	4:10b	Listen, my son, and take my words, and the years of life will increase for you.
כִּי־בִי יִרְבּוּ יָמֶיךָ וְיוֹסִיפוּ לְךָ שְׁנוֹת חַיִּים	9:11	For with me your days will increase, and years of life will be added for you.
עֵד שְׁקָרִים לֹא יִנָּקֶה וְיָפִיחַ כְּזָבִים יֹאבֵד	19:9	A witness of lies will not be declared innocent, and a testifier of falsehoods will perish.
עֵד־כְּזָבִים יֹאבֵד וְאִישׁ שׁוֹמֵעַ לָנֶצַח יְדַבֵּר	21:28a	A witness of falsehoods will perish, but a man who listens forever will speak.
הַוֹּת לְאָבִיו בֵּן כְּסִיל וְדֶלֶף טֹרֵד מִדְיְנֵי אִשָּׁה	19:13b	A destruction for his father is a foolish son, and a drip that drives away is the strifes of a woman.
דֶּלֶף טוֹרֵד בְּיוֹם סַגְרִיר וְאֵשֶׁת מִדְוָנִים נִשְׁתָּוָה	27:15	A drip that drives away on a day of heavy rain, and a woman of strifes are similar.

24:23b / 28:21a   24:23a is the headline of the collection attributed to the "wise ones," 24:23–24:34, referred to in the discussions here as collection D.

26:4a / 26:5a   These successive verses give the opposite advice, but their similar structure argues that they are two forms of the same saying. And their contiguity shows that they are meant to emphasize their subject in order to inspire critical thinking in readers.

4:10b / 9:11   9:11 is related to 3:2 (see 1.2).

19:9 / 21:28a   19:9 is related to 19:5 (see 1.1).

2. See the note on 15:14a~18:15a (p. 46 above).

אֶבֶן וָאֶבֶן אֵיפָה וְאֵיפָה תּוֹעֲבַת יְהוָה גַּם־שְׁנֵיהֶם	20:10	A stone and a stone and a grain measure and a grain measure— both of them are an abomination of Yahweh.
תּוֹעֲבַת יְהוָה אֶבֶן וָאָבֶן וּמֹאזְנֵי מִרְמָה לֹא־טוֹב	20:23a	An abomination of Yahweh is a stone and a stone, and scales of deception are not good.

3.1   HALF-VERSES REPEATED IN WHOLE VERSES WITH ONE DISSIMILAR WORD (6 SETS)

חֶסֶד וֶאֱמֶת אַל־יַעַזְבֻךָ קָשְׁרֵם עַל־גַּרְגְּרוֹתֶיךָ כָּתְבֵם עַל־לוּחַ לִבֶּךָ	3:3b	Let not loving-kindness and truth leave you; bind them on your throat; write them on the tablet of your heart.
קָשְׁרֵם עַל־אֶצְבְּעֹתֶיךָ כָּתְבֵם עַל־לוּחַ לִבֶּךָ	7:3	Bind them on your fingers; write them on the tablet of your heart.
תַּהְפֻּכוֹת בְּלִבּוֹ חֹרֵשׁ רָע בְּכָל־עֵת מִדְיָנִים יְשַׁלֵּחַ	6:14	Rebellions in his heart a bad one devises; at each time he sends forth strifes.
אִישׁ תַּהְפֻּכוֹת יְשַׁלַּח מָדוֹן וְנִרְגָּן מַפְרִיד אַלּוּף	16:28a	A man of rebellions sends forth strife, and a grumbler alienates an intimate friend.
נֹצֵר פִּיו שֹׁמֵר נַפְשׁוֹ פֹּשֵׂק שְׂפָתָיו מְחִתָּה־לוֹ	13:3a	One who guards his mouth keeps his soul; one who opens wide his lips is a ruin for him.
שֹׁמֵר פִּיו וּלְשׁוֹנוֹ שֹׁמֵר מִצָּרוֹת נַפְשׁוֹ	21:23	One who keeps his mouth and his tongue keeps his soul from troubles.
קְצַר־אַפַּיִם יַעֲשֶׂה אִוֶּלֶת וְאִישׁ מְזִמּוֹת יִשָּׂנֵא	14:17a	One short of patience does foolishness, and a man of bad plans is hated.
אֶרֶךְ אַפַּיִם רַב־תְּבוּנָה וּקְצַר־רוּחַ מֵרִים אִוֶּלֶת	14:29	One long of patience is great of understanding, but the short of spirit raises up foolishness.
עֲטֶרֶת תִּפְאֶרֶת שֵׂיבָה בְּדֶרֶךְ צְדָקָה תִּמָּצֵא	16:31a	A crown of beauty is gray hairs; in the way of righteousness is it found.
תִּפְאֶרֶת בַּחוּרִים כֹּחָם וַהֲדַר זְקֵנִים שֵׂיבָה	20:29	The beauty of young men is their strength, and the glory of old men is gray hairs.

20:10 / 20:23a   20:10b is related to 17:15b (see 2.0) and 20:23 is related to 11:1 (see 1.2).

    3:3b / 7:3   The classification of these verses is, unfortunately, a result of the verse division; actually, 3:3b is the equivalent of 7:3, but 3:3 contains three clauses instead of the usual two. The direct objects in 7:3 are מצותי 'my commands' and תורתי 'my teaching'.

    13:3a / 21:23   21:23 syntactically resembles the many other double-verb clauses noted in 4.2; 13:3a is related to them, too, since it uses common synonyms for 'to keep'.

    14:17a / 14:29   These verses occur near each other and thus may be repeated for emphasis.

מְקַלֵּל אָבִיו וְאִמּוֹ יִדְעַךְ נֵרוֹ בֶּאֱשׁוּן חֹשֶׁךְ   20:20a   One who curses his father and his mother—
his lamp is extinguished in the time of darkness.

דּוֹר אָבִיו יְקַלֵּל וְאֶת־אִמּוֹ לֹא יְבָרֵךְ   30:11   A generation that curses its father,
and its mother does not bless.

3.2   HALF-VERSES REPEATED IN WHOLE VERSES WITH TWO DISSIMILAR WORDS (1 SET)

מֶלֶךְ יוֹשֵׁב עַל־כִּסֵּא־דִין מְזָרֶה בְעֵינָיו כָּל־רָע   20:8   A king sitting on a throne of judgment
scatters with his eyes all evil.

מְזָרֶה רְשָׁעִים מֶלֶךְ חָכָם וַיָּשֶׁב עֲלֵיהֶם אוֹפָן   20:26a   A wise king scatters bad ones,
and returns upon them a wheel.

4.0   SYNTACTICALLY RELATED VERSES[3]

4.1   X, Y, AND Z[4] (3 VERSES)

לָקַחַת מוּסַר הַשְׂכֵּל צֶדֶק וּמִשְׁפָּט וּמֵישָׁרִים   1:3   To get discipline, wise conduct,
rightness, justice, and fairness.

רֹדֵף צְדָקָה וָחָסֶד יִמְצָא חַיִּים צְדָקָה וְכָבוֹד   21:21   One who chases after righteousness and loving-kindness
will find life, righteousness, and honor.

עֵקֶב עֲנָוָה יִרְאַת יְהוָה עֹשֶׁר וְכָבוֹד וְחַיִּים   22:4   After lowliness is the fear of Yahweh,
riches, and honor, and life.

4.2   DOUBLE VERB[5] (15 VERSES)

אִם־לַלֵּצִים הוּא־יָלִיץ וְלַעֲנָיִים יִתֶּן־חֵן   3:34a   If with regard to the scoffers, he scoffs,
but to the lowly he gives grace.

אֲנִי אֹהֲבֶיהָ אֵהָב וּמְשַׁחֲרַי יִמְצָאֻנְנִי   8:17a   I, those who love me I love,
and those who seek me find me.

20:8 / 20:26a Perhaps מלך 'king' and מזרה 'winnows' should merely be regarded as forming a cliché, but the general sense of both verses is the same. On the strange wheel in 20:26 see my note "The Wheel in Proverbs xx 26," *Vetus Testamentum* 39 (1989) 503–7.

3. I have collected here only a small sampling of syntactically similar verses. There are doubtless others.

4. These verses share the feature of presenting lists of synonymous nouns and therefore I call it the "x, y, z" form.

5. I have studied the double-verb form represented by these verses in my article, "Notes on Love and Death in Proverbs," in *Love and Death in the Ancient Near East: Essays in Honor of Marvin H. Pope* (ed. J. H. Marks and R. M. Good; Guilford, Conn.: Four Quarters, 1987) 165–68. One point noted there deserves repetition, that the double-verb

כִּי מֹצְאִי מָצָא חַיִּים וַיָּפֶק רָצוֹן מֵיהֹוָה	8:35a	For one who finds me has found life, and he gets desire from Yahweh.
אִם־חָכַמְתָּ חָכַמְתָּ לָּךְ וְלַצְתָּ לְבַדְּךָ תִשָּׂא	9:12a	If you get wise, you get wise for yourself, but [if] you scoff, alone you bear [it].
הוֹלֵךְ בַּתֹּם יֵלֶךְ בֶּטַח וּמְעַקֵּשׁ דְּרָכָיו יִוָּדֵעַ	10:9a	One who goes in simplicity goes securely, but one who makes crooked his ways will be known.
בָּא־זָדוֹן וַיָּבֹא קָלוֹן וְאֶת־צְנוּעִים חָכְמָה	11:2a	Excess comes, and calumny comes, but wisdom is with modest ones.
אֹהֵב מוּסָר אֹהֵב דָּעַת וְשֹׂנֵא תוֹכַחַת בָּעַר	12:1a	One who loves discipline loves knowledge, but one who hates reproof is stupid.
אֹהֵב פֶּשַׁע אֹהֵב מַצָּה מַגְבִּיהַּ פִּתְחוֹ מְבַקֶּשׁ־שָׁבֶר	17:19a	One who loves sin loves dispute; one who exalts his threshold seeks a break.
בְּבוֹא־רָשָׁע בָּא גַם־בּוּז וְעִם־קָלוֹן חֶרְפָּה	18:3a	In the coming of a bad one, comes also despising, and with calumny, scorn.
מָצָא אִשָּׁה מָצָא טוֹב וַיָּפֶק רָצוֹן מֵיהֹוָה	18:22a	He has found a woman; he has found good, and he gets desire from Yahweh.
שֹׁמֵר מִצְוָה שֹׁמֵר נַפְשׁוֹ בּוֹזֵה דְרָכָיו יָמֻת	19:16a	One who keeps commandment keeps his soul; one who despises his ways will die.
שֹׁמֵר פִּיו וּלְשׁוֹנוֹ שֹׁמֵר מִצָּרוֹת נַפְשׁוֹ	21:23	One who keeps his mouth and his tongue keeps his soul from troubles.
כִּי־יְהֹוָה יָרִיב רִיבָם וְקָבַע אֶת־קֹבְעֵיהֶם נָפֶשׁ	22:23b	For Yahweh will dispute their dispute and will deprive those who deprive them of life.

8:35a   8:35 is related to 18:22 (see 1.3) and to 12:2a (see 2.1).
11:2b   Related to 13:10b (see 2.1).
18:22   Related to 8:35 (see 1.3).
19:16a   Related to 16:17b (see 2.2).
21:23   Related to 13:3a (see 3.1).

form is known in Egypt. C. Kayatz, *Studien zu Proverbian 1–9* (Neukirchen: Neukirchener Verlag, 1966) 101–2, calls it the *reziproke Formel* and notes that Egyptian gods are sometimes the subjects of sentences like 8:17a, though the Israelite God is not. The form is popular in Proverbs probably because it expresses so well the basic idea of the book, indeed of most of the Bible, that human actions have direct consequences in reward and punishment. Another possible candidate for this category is 11:25, in which the last verb is probably to be emended and understood as the same as the earlier verb:

נפש־ברכה תדשן ומרוה גם־הוא יורא
A soul of blessing will get fat,
and one who waters will also be watered.

Note also 13:20b, where the last verb puns on the earlier verb: " . . . one who keeps company with fools has bad happen to him"; and 22:7, where the verbs *to borrow* and *to loan* are different stems of the same root, but their similarity carries no moral weight.

צֹפְנֶיהָ צָפַן־רוּחַ וְשֶׁמֶן יְמִינוֹ יִקְרָא	27:16a	Those who treasure her, treasure wind, and he calls his right hand oil.
בִּרְבוֹת רְשָׁעִים יִרְבֶּה־פָּשַׁע וְצַדִּיקִים בְּמַפַּלְתָּם יִרְאוּ	29:16a	In the increase of bad ones, sin increases, but righteous ones will look upon their fall.

4.3   A IS B; C IS D[6] (4 VERSES)

כִּי נֵר מִצְוָה וְתוֹרָה אוֹר וְדֶרֶךְ חַיִּים תּוֹכְחוֹת מוּסָר	6:23a	For commandment is a lamp and instruction is light, and the way of life is the corrections of discipline.
לֵץ הַיַּיִן הֹמֶה שֵׁכָר וְכָל־שֹׁגֶה בּוֹ לֹא יֶחְכָּם	20:1a	Wine is a scoffer and strong drink a brawler, and everyone who strays with it is not wise.
אַכְזְרִיּוּת חֵמָה וְשֶׁטֶף אָף וּמִי יַעֲמֹד לִפְנֵי קִנְאָה	27:4	Anger is cruel, and wrath a flood, and who can stand before jealousy?
שֶׁקֶר הַחֵן וְהֶבֶל הַיֹּפִי אִשָּׁה יִרְאַת־יְהוָה הִיא תִתְהַלָּל	31:30a	Grace is a lie, and beauty a puff of breath; a woman fearing Yahweh will be praised.

4.4   IN . . . IN . . . [7] (5 VERSES)

בְּטוּב צַדִּיקִים תַּעֲלֹץ קִרְיָה וּבַאֲבֹד רְשָׁעִים רִנָּה	11:10	In the good of righteous ones a village rejoices, but in the perishing of bad ones is joy.
בַּעֲנָשׁ־לֵץ יֶחְכַּם־פֶּתִי וּבְהַשְׂכִּיל לְחָכָם יִקַּח־דָּעַת	21:11	In the punishment of a scoffer a simple one gets wise, and in the enlightenment of a wise one he gets knowledge.
בַּעֲלֹץ צַדִּיקִים רַבָּה תִפְאָרֶת וּבְקוּם רְשָׁעִים יְחֻפַּשׂ אָדָם	28:12	In the rejoicing of righteous ones beauty increases, but in the rise of bad ones a man is sought.

27:16a   "Her" refers to "a woman of strifes" in Prov 27:15.
21:11   Related to 19:25 (see 1.4).
28:12b   Related to 28:28a (see 2.1).

6. These verses have the form "a is b, and c is d," and I call it the "double-noun" form. One extrabiblical analog is to be found in the Akkadian prayer to Ishtar, no. 1 (E. Ebeling, *Die akkadische Gebetsserie "Handerhebung"* [Berlin: Akademie-Verlag, 1953] 60–63, line 22): *napluski tašmû qibītki nūra*, which C. Wright (*The Literary Structure of Assyro-Babylonian Prayers to Ishtar* [Ph.D. diss., University of Michigan, 1979] 78) translates, "Obedience is what you look at, light is what you command."

7. This group shares the use of verbal nouns preceded by ‑בְ 'in' in both clauses. It has been studied by J. Berezov, *Single-Line Proverbs: A Study of the Sayings Collected in Proverbs 10–22:16 and 25–29* (Ph.D. diss., Hebrew Union College/Jewish Institute of Religion, 1987) 44.

בְּקוּם רְשָׁעִים יִסָּתֵר אָדָם וּבְאָבְדָם יִרְבּוּ צַדִּיקִים

28:28   In the rise of bad ones a man hides,
      but in their perishing, righteous ones increase.

בִּרְבוֹת צַדִּיקִים יִשְׂמַח הָעָם וּבִמְשֹׁל רָשָׁע יֵאָנַח עָם

29:2   In the increasing of righteous ones the people
        is happy,
      but in the ruling of a bad one a people
        groans.

4.5   BETTER . . . AND/IN . . . THAN . . . AND/IN . . . [8] (5 VERSES)

טוֹב נִקְלֶה וְעֶבֶד לוֹ מִמִּתְכַּבֵּד וַחֲסַר־לָחֶם

12:9   Better is one thought light of and has a slave
      than one taking on airs and lacking bread.

טוֹב־מְעַט בְּיִרְאַת יְהוָה מֵאוֹצָר רָב וּמְהוּמָה בוֹ

15:16   Better is a little in the fear of Yahweh
      than a big treasure and confusion in it.

טוֹב אֲרֻחַת יָרָק וְאַהֲבָה־שָׁם מִשּׁוֹר אָבוּס וְשִׂנְאָה־בוֹ

15:17   Better is a meal of vegetables and love there
      than a fattened ox and hatred with it.

טוֹב־מְעַט בִּצְדָקָה מֵרֹב תְּבוּאוֹת בְּלֹא מִשְׁפָּט

16:8   Better is a little in righteousness
      than much produce without justice.

טוֹב פַּת חֲרֵבָה וְשַׁלְוָה־בָהּ מִבַּיִת מָלֵא זִבְחֵי־רִיב

17:1   Better is a dry crust and well-being with it
      than a house full of the sacrifices of dispute.

4.6   A OF B IS C IN . . . [9] (2 VERSES)

אֶבֶן־חֵן הַשֹּׁחַד בְּעֵינֵי בְעָלָיו אֶל־כָּל־אֲשֶׁר יִפְנֶה יַשְׂכִּיל

17:8   The bribe is a precious stone in the eyes of its
        owner;
      everywhere he turns, he figures things out.

פַּלְגֵי־מַיִם לֶב־מֶלֶךְ בְּיַד־יְהוָה עַל־כָּל אֲשֶׁר יַחְפֹּץ יַטֶּנּוּ

21:1   The heart of a king is streams of water in the
        hand of Yahweh;
      wherever he wishes, he diverts it.

28:28a Related to 28:12b (see 2.1).

15:16 Related to 16:8 (see 1.4). The fact that 15:17 has the same form may show a conscious effort to bring together or to devise sayings in this form.

16:8 Related to 15:16 (see 1.4).

8. This group of verses is characterized by the form טוֹב . . . ב/ו . . . מִן . . . ב/ו . . . , in which the next-to-last element is something desirable and the last element is not. This feature sets them apart from the other group of טוֹב verses below (4.8).

9. These two verses share the following structure: two-word predicate nominative, subject, two-word prepositional phrase, preposition-generalizer-relative pronoun, subordinate verb, main verb.

4.7   WHO . . . ?[10] (3 VERSES)

רוּחַ־אִישׁ יְכַלְכֵּל מַחֲלֵהוּ וְרוּחַ נְכֵאָה מִי יִשָּׂאֶנָּה	18:14b	The spirit of a man holds his sickness, but a broken spirit, who can lift it?
רָב־אָדָם יִקְרָא אִישׁ חַסְדּוֹ וְאִישׁ אֱמוּנִים מִי יִמְצָא	20:6b	Many are the men who call a man his loving-kindness, but a man of trustworthiness who can find?
אֵשֶׁת־חַיִל מִי יִמְצָא וְרָחֹק מִפְּנִינִים מִכְרָהּ	31:10a	A woman of valor, who finds? And more distant than corals is her price.

4.8   BETTER . . . THAN . . . AND . . .[11] (5 VERSES)

טוֹב־רָשׁ הוֹלֵךְ בְּתֻמּוֹ מֵעִקֵּשׁ שְׂפָתָיו וְהוּא כְסִיל	19:1	Better is a poor one who walks in his simplicity than a crooked one of lips, and he a fool.
טוֹב לָשֶׁבֶת עַל־פִּנַּת־גָּג מֵאֵשֶׁת מִדְיָנִים וּבֵית חָבֶר	21:9	It is better to sit on the corner of a roof than a woman of strifes and a noisy house.
טוֹב שֶׁבֶת בְּאֶרֶץ־מִדְבָּר מֵאֵשֶׁת מִדְוָנִים וָכָעַס	21:19	It is better to sit in a land of wilderness than a woman of strifes and anger.
טוֹב שֶׁבֶת עַל־פִּנַּת־גָּג מֵאֵשֶׁת מִדְוָנִים וּבֵית חָבֶר	25:24	It is better to sit on the corner of a roof than a woman of strifes and a noisy house.
טוֹב־רָשׁ הוֹלֵךְ בְּתֻמּוֹ מֵעִקֵּשׁ דְּרָכַיִם וְהוּא עָשִׁיר	28:6	Better is a poor one who walks in his simplicity than a crooked one of ways, and he a rich one.

19:1   Related to 28:6 (see 1.2).
21:9   Related to 21:19 (see 1.4) and to 25:24 (see 1.0 and 1.4).
21:19   Related to 21:9 (see 1.4).
25:24   Related to 21:9 (see 1.0 and 1.4).
28:6   Related to 19:1 (see 1.2).

10. These verses all contain a rhetorical question with מי 'who?'; the answer in each case is presumably, "few persons in any generation."

11. These verses have the form טוב . . . מן . . . ו . . . . Unlike the טוב verses discussed above (4.5), the last two elements are both undesirable. It is not clear that the term בית חבר in 21:9 and 25:24 is negative; McKane, *Proverbs*, 554–55, translates simply "to share a house with a nagging wife." I prefer J. J. Finkelstein's suggestion that the phrase means a "noisy household" ("Hebrew HBR," 328–31), which would be undesirable. עשיר 'rich' in 28:6 is not undesirable, but עקש דרכים 'crooked of [two?] roads' is. The verse may not really belong with this group, but it clearly does not share the desirable/undesirable ending of the other group of טוב verses.

4.9   LIKE . . . THUS . . .[12] (7 VERSES)

כַּחֹמֶץ לַשִּׁנַּיִם וְכֶעָשָׁן לָעֵינָיִם כֵּן הֶעָצֵל לְשֹׁלְחָיו	10:26	Like vinegar to the teeth and like smoke to the eyes, thus is the sluggard to ones who send him.
כִּי כְּמוֹ־שָׁעַר בְּנַפְשׁוֹ כֶּן־הוּא אֱכֹל וּשְׁתֵה יֹאמַר לָךְ וְלִבּוֹ בַּל־עִמָּךְ	23:7	For like a gate in his soul, thus he is; Eat and drink, he says to you, but his heart is not with you.
כַּשֶּׁלֶג בַּקַּיִץ וְכַמָּטָר בַּקָּצִיר כֵּן לֹא־נָאוֶה לִכְסִיל כָּבוֹד	26:1	Like snow in the summer and like rain in the harvesttime, thus is honor not becoming for a fool.
כַּצִּפּוֹר לָנוּד כַּדְּרוֹר לָעוּף כֵּן קִלְלַת חִנָּם לֹא תָבֹא	26:2	Like a bird for wandering and like a swallow for flying, thus a gratuitous curse will not come.
כִּצְרוֹר אֶבֶן בְּמַרְגֵּמָה כֵּן־נוֹתֵן לִכְסִיל כָּבוֹד	26:8	Like a bundle of stone in a heap [sling?], thus is one who gives honor to a fool.
כְּצִפּוֹר נוֹדֶדֶת מִן־קִנָּהּ כֵּן־אִישׁ נוֹדֵד מִמְּקוֹמוֹ	27:8	Like a bird wandering from its nest, thus is a man wandering from his place.
כַּמַּיִם הַפָּנִים לַפָּנִים כֵּן לֵב־הָאָדָם לָאָדָם	27:19	Like water is the face to a face, thus is the heart of a person to a person.

10:26   This verse may be another form of 25:13, which is on the same subject and also begins with כְּ: "Like the coldness of snow in a day of harvest is a trustworthy messenger to ones who send him, and the desire of his lords he returns."

23:7   The subject is the stingy man (lit., the man with the bad eye) in 23:6.

26:1   Related to 26:8 (see 1.4).

26:8   Related to 26:1 (see 1.4).

12. These verses share the form . . . כֵן . . . כְּ. Verses with this syntax were briefly studied by Berezov, *Single-Line Proverbs*, 41–42 (listed on pp. 151–52).

6

Significance of Repetitions

> BOSWELL: Sir Alexander Dick tells me, that he remembers having a thousand people
> in a year to dine at his house; that is, reckoning each person as one, each time he
> dined there.
> JOHNSON: That, Sir, is about three a day.
> BOSWELL: How your statement lessens the idea.
> JOHNSON: That, Sir, is the good of counting. It brings everything to a certainty,
> which before floated in the air indefinitely.

It is now time to ask this question about twice-told proverbs: What might these repetitions mean? In organizing the answer to this question, I have divided Proverbs into the various collections, as well as a few smaller divisions.

In view of R. B. Y. Scott's frontal attack on the assumption that the collection headlines (and indeed the collections themselves) have meaning, it is important to point out some reasons for continuing to use them.[1] Scott is reacting to his interesting discovery that there is no concentration of either "secular" or "religious" sayings in any of the collections of one-line sayings. That is why he argues that the collections cannot be dated individually and should not even be evaluated as units, as U. Skladny attempted to do.[2] I completely agree with Scott that "it is . . . clear that the book of Proverbs in its present form is the end result of a long process of compilation."[3] But it does not follow that the collections have no significance.

First, the mere fact that there are headlines over some of the collections does show that someone thought they were distinct. As Scott observes, the collections may have grown by accretion, so that they now contain material from rather different times and groups.[4] But that is no

---

1. R. B. Y. Scott, "Wise and Foolish, Righteous and Wicked," in *Studies in the Religion of Ancient Israel* (Vetus Testamentum Supplement 23; Leiden: Brill, 1972) 146–65.

2. U. Skladny, *Die ältesten Spruchsammlungen in Israel* (Göttingen: Vandenhoeck & Ruprecht, 1962), esp. 67–86.

3. Scott, "Wise and Foolish," 147.

4. Scott writes, "The present Book of Proverbs is better seen as the end result of a centuries-long process of composition, supplementing, editing, and scribal transmission, a process which has blurred some lines of demarcation between its parts" (ibid., 150).

reason not to see in them cores of material that really were separate at some stage. Modern scholars may never be able to identify these cores, but it does not seem logical to reject the headlines and divisions as purely editorial.[5]

Second, the Greek translation of the Bible does order some of the collections differently, including chapters 25–29 (see chart on p. 9 above). One might consider this to be merely late evidence of editorial activity, but it seems quite as likely to be evidence that even at a late date some of the individual collections may have circulated as independent units.

It is fruitless, as Scott has shown, to try to characterize the ideologies of the collections, but there may be other aspects of them that can be characterized, notably their use of repetition. This seems potentially productive for determining affinities among the collections.

There is evidence of editorial activity, probably at a literary stage of the assembly of the book. As Scott does not explicitly point out, relatively little of this editorial activity had anything to do with ideological issues, the subject in which he is interested.[6] It seems important, regardless of the stand we take on ideological development or the lack of it, that if we want to reconstruct the history of composition of the book, we must gain a clearer view of just where the repetitions occur. In order to visualize this, I have divided the book into six main collections, with a total of thirteen smaller sections.

The first collection, which I label collection A, begins at the beginning of the book and runs to the last verse of chapter 9. This collection is attributed to Solomon in its headline. Omitted from it is the group of sayings comprising 6:1–19, because this group has generally been recognized as secondary to the instruction form of most of collection A. This small subsection I label A_6. One could further argue that not all of collection A is of a piece, since the last two chapters might be isolated due to their form and subject matter. But it seems useful to keep together the entire introductory discourse, since it is all couched in the instruction form and addresses an audience of affluent young men.

Collection B begins at 10:1 and runs through 22:16; it also is attributed to Solomon. It is customary to divide it into two parts, starting the division at 15:1, because the use of verses with two antithetical phrases seems to break down at approximately that point. But I have followed Skehan's suggestion and separated the sayings from 14:26 through 16:15 into a subdivision in an attempt to verify his idea that this subsection is a locus for additions by a final editor. Thus, this collection encompasses three parts that I call B_1, B_2, and B_3.

Collection C begins where the loose translation from the Egyptian *Instruction of Amenemope* begins, at 22:17. It is not clear whether there is a separate headline for this collection, but the parallels to *Amenemope* continue through 23:11, with some gaps.[7] I label the section that does have Egyptian parallels C_E, underlining its Egyptian nature. The rest of collection C appears to continue to 24:22 and does not have Egyptian parallels, with the possible exception of Prov 24:11, which Simpson suggests is related to *Amenemope* 11:6–7, although the parallel

---

5. Scott does admit that the headlines at 30:1 and 31:1 are significant, indicating that the contents of those sections did circulate independently of the rest of the book (ibid., 150).

6. See Scott, "Wise and Foolish," 152, for some examples of repeated verses that may have been revised for ideological reasons.

7. On the possible headline to the *Amenemope* section, see R. B. Y. Scott, *Proverbs, Ecclesiastes* (Anchor Bible 18; Garden City, New York: Doubleday, 1965) 135.

does not seem very obvious to me.[8] I call this second section, from 23:12 to 24:22, C_H to emphasize its apparently Hebrew origin.

Collection D is a small collection, set off by a headline identifying its contents as being "also of the wise ones," and runs from 24:23 through 24:34.

Collection E begins with a headline describing its contents as being proverbs of Solomon "which Hezekiah's men copied out."[9] It runs from 25:1 through the end of chapter 29.

Last, collection F contains two different headlines, attributing chapter 30 to a certain Agur and chapter 31 to a certain Lemuel. I separate each chapter into two parts. Sections 30:1–14 and 30:15–33 are divided in the Greek translation of the Bible.[10] I also divide the acrostic poem to the woman of valor, beginning at 31:10, which is generally recognized as distinct. Thus there are four parts, which I call F_1, F_2, F_3, and F_4. For a summary of the notations for collections see p. 6 above.

In the following charts each collection begins near the middle of the page and continues outward. Numbers below or to the left of the bold lines are chapter numbers. Numbers above or to the right of the bold lines are the verse numbers; "a" or "b" after the verse numbers indicates the first or second half of a verse.

The wheellike construction of the charts allows some important features to be seen clearly, such as the isolation of a collection or the close relations between two collections. The arrangement works less well when two collections share sayings but are physically far apart on the charts.

Chart 1 shows the category I have classified as whole verses repeated (1.0–1.4). Collection A seems to use less precise sorts of repetition to bind its parts together. Predictably, section 6:1–19 has no repetitions within the instruction material in collection A, though it does relate to the very end of collection D. Collection A has just one connection to a saying outside of it, at 18:22. As many have concluded on form-critical grounds, collection A is shown to be a self-contained unit, not directly related to the rest of the book, at least as far as whole-verse repetition is concerned.

Duplication (category 1.0) occurs only between collections B_1 and B_3 (one instance) and between B_3 and E (four instances). This datum contrasts with the distribution of the less precisely repeated sayings, which are shared more widely. Collection B shows some repetition within itself, but one gets the impression that repetition was not so important in this collection

8. See D. C. Simpson, "The Hebrew Book of Proverbs and the Teaching of Amenophis," *Journal of Egyptian Archaeology* 12 (1926) 232–39. Prov 24:11 reads: הצל לקחים למות ומטים להרג אם־תחשׂוך 'Save those taken to death, / and those tottering to murder if you hold back'. *Amenope* 11:6–7 reads: "Call not 'Sin' against a man, if the conditions of flight are concealed" (after I. Grumach, *Untersuchungen zur Lebenslehre des Amenope* [Munich/Berlin: Deutscher Kunstverlag, 1972] 70). M. Lichtheim, *Ancient Egyptian Literature* ([Berkeley: University of California, 1976] 2:153) and W. Kelly Simpson, *The Literature of Ancient Egypt* ([New Haven: Yale University Press, 1972] 250) read similarly.

9. Some scholars (such as Skladny, *Die ältesten Spruchsammlungen in Israel*, 57–65), regard chapters 28–29 as a separate collection on the basis of its ideological content, but there seems no extrinsic evidence for such a division. With Scott, I am wary of distinctions based on content. Compare J. L. Berezov, who denies that there is a basis for dividing chapters 25–29 (*Single-Line Proverbs: A Study of the Sayings Collected in Proverbs 10–22:16 and 25–29* [Ph.D. diss., Hebrew Union College–Jewish Institute of Religion, 1987] 82–83).

10. See the synopsis of the Septuagint order in chapter 2 above, p. 9.

as it was in collection A. Skehan's locus for possible additions by a final editor, B_2, does show a fair amount of affinity with B_1 and B_3, but it shares no whole verse with any other collection.

Collection C has one internal repetition but not in the part translated from Egyptian. The whole collection shares no complete verse with any other collection.

Collection D shares only two verses with A_6: 6:10–11.

Collection E has a couple of internal repetitions and otherwise shares whole verses only with collections B_1 and B_3.

Collection F has no internal repetition and shares no whole verses with any other collection.

Chart 2 shows the location of half-verses repeated (2.0–2.2), by far the most common type of repetition I have isolated. The picture presented is very complex because of this popularity, and every major collection is involved.

Collection A again shows a number of internal repetitions of half-verses. The collection is linked by these repetitions to all other collections except for the shorter sections C_E, D, F_1, F_3, and F_4. There is just one repetition shared between collections A and E, and that case occurs in the extraneous section A_6.

Collection B, like collection A, shows several internal repetitions of half verses, but B_2 has no such repetitions within itself. Several chapters in collection B show an amazing propensity to use internal repetitions when compared, for example, with collection E. Chapter 10 is one such locus, and Skehan's collection B_2, especially chapters 15–16, shows a great deal of affinity with other sections in collection B, as do chapters 18 and 20.

The Egyptian section of collection C (C_E) shows two internally repeated sayings, which are also found in Egyptian. And here (in C_E) is the only instance in collection C in which a half-verse is shared with another collection, collection E. C_H shares half-sayings with all other collections, except E, F, and B_2.

The short collection D shares repeated half-verses with collections B_3, C_H, and E.

Collection E, which has a couple of internal repetitions, has relatively infrequent repetition of half-verses with other collections. But there are three verses related to B_2 and one to the Egyptian part of C. Collection E also has nothing to do with F or with A, except for one half-verse shared with A_6.

Collection F has only one half-verse repeated, and, again, it is from A_6.

There are relatively few cases of half-verses repeated in whole verses (3.0–3.2), as chart 3 shows, and the absence of the phenomenon in collections C and D is probably not significant. But in this light the concentration of such repetitions in chapter 20 (B_3) takes on significance. Both whole and half-verses found elsewhere are also found in chapter 20, along with two cases of internal repetition of half-verses repeated in whole verses.

Chart 4 plots the cases of syntactically related verses (4.0–4.9). The distribution of these verses seems rather random, with perhaps three exceptions. The section of collection B labeled B_3 seems to have quite a few of them. Also, the Egyptian section of collection C (C_E) has one of the most common forms (4.2). Collection F, which has minimal contact with other collections in the other types of repetition, contains two verses linked to verses elsewhere. Both verses are from the "Woman of Valor" section, which has not previously shared any verses in this survey.

The number of verses involved in repetition in Proverbs is substantial. The summary in table 3 omits the possible syntactical resemblances and includes only verses participating one or

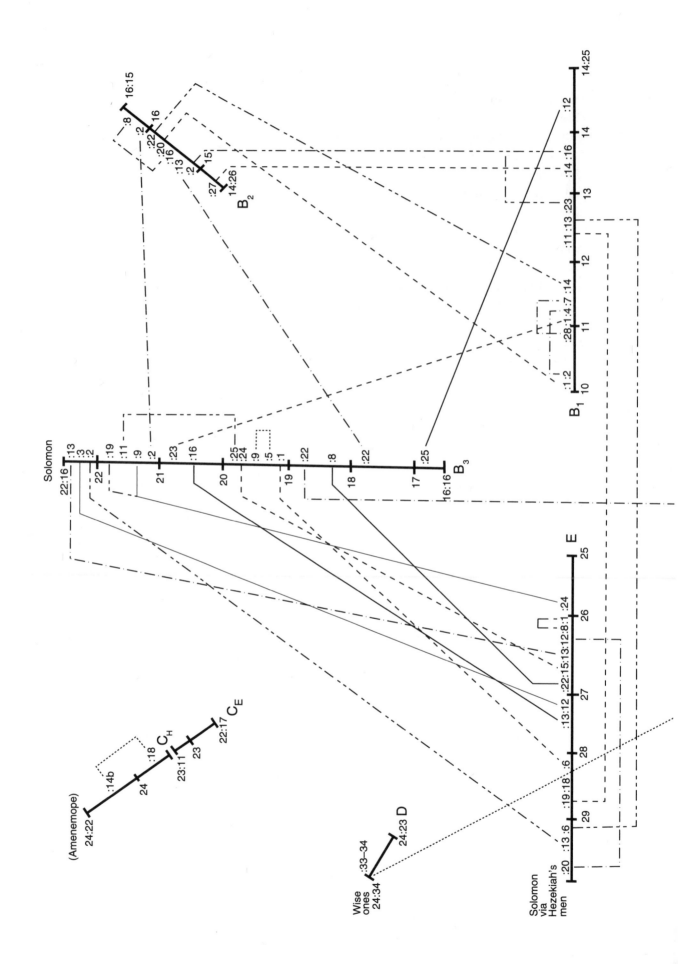

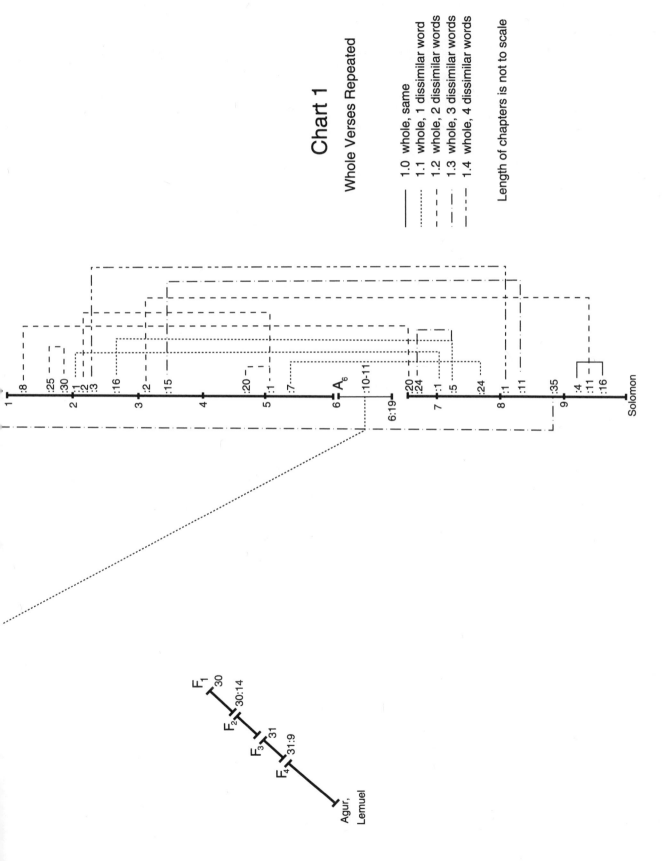

Chart 1

Whole Verses Repeated

1.0 whole, same
1.1 whole, 1 dissimilar word
1.2 whole, 2 dissimilar words
1.3 whole, 3 dissimilar words
1.4 whole, 4 dissimilar words

Length of chapters is not to scale

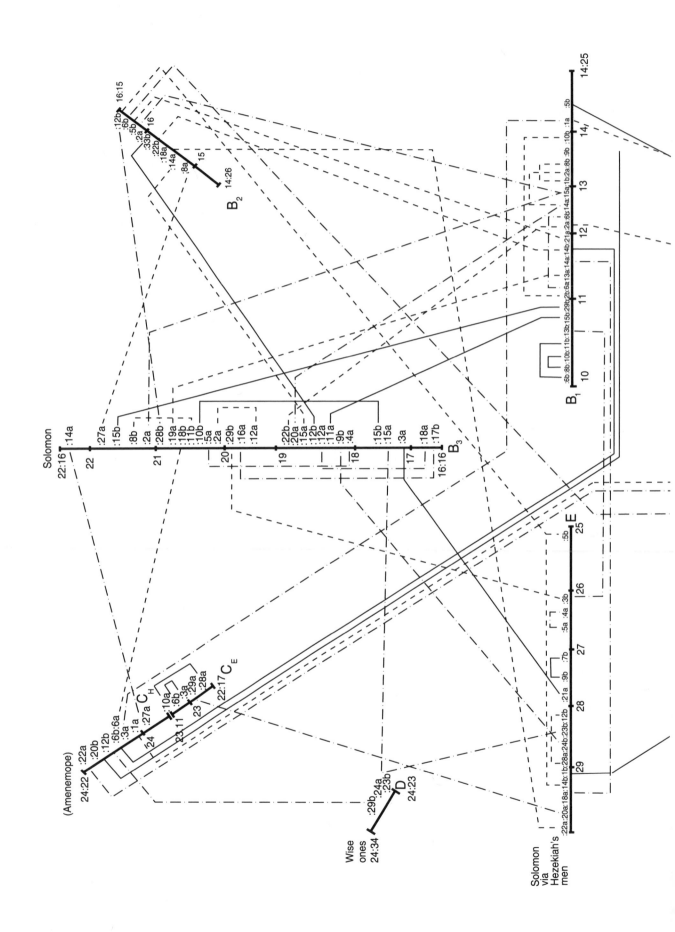

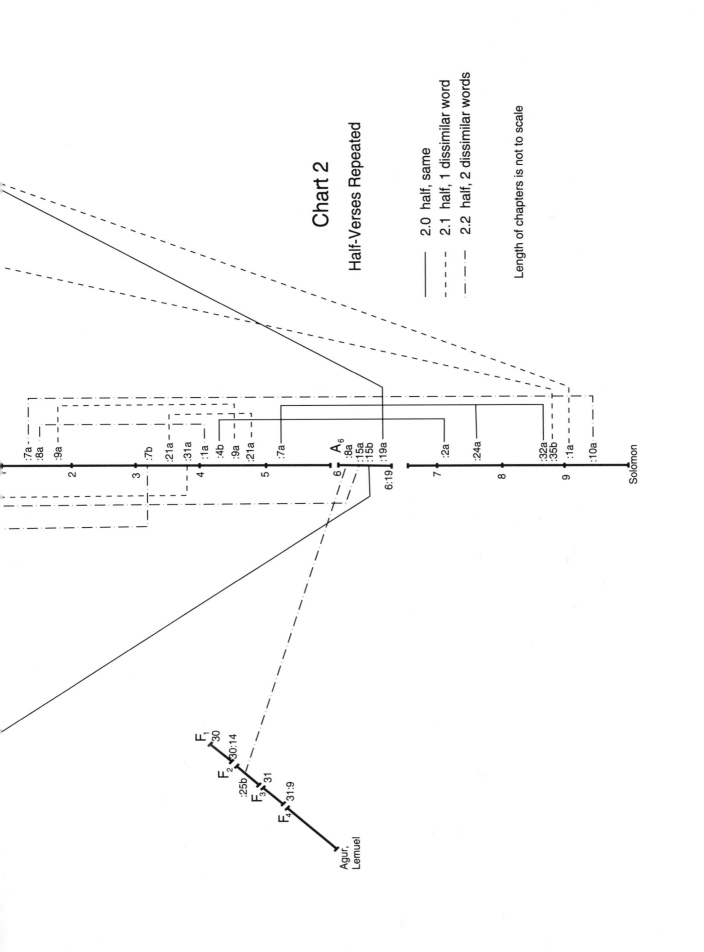

Chart 2

Half-Verses Repeated

2.0 half, same

2.1 half, 1 dissimilar word

2.2 half, 2 dissimilar words

Length of chapters is not to scale

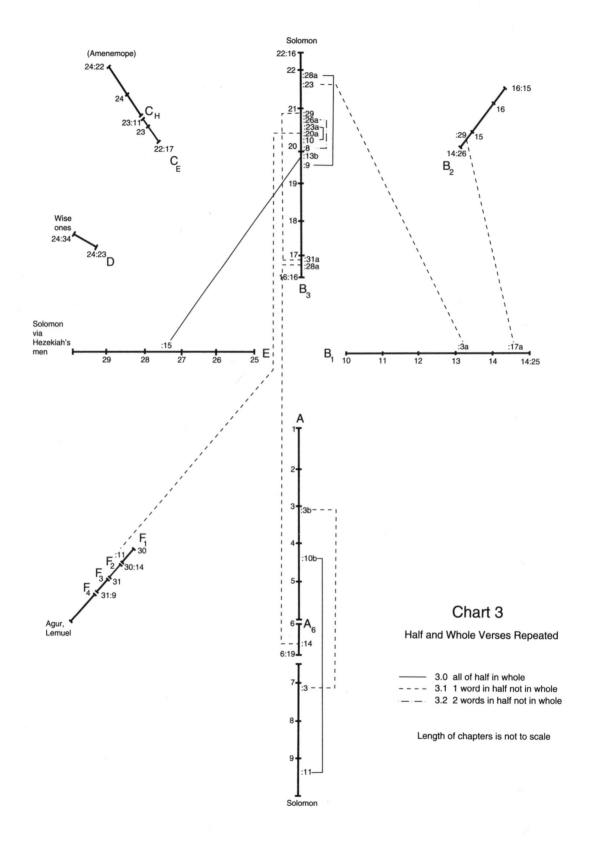

Chart 3

Half and Whole Verses Repeated

3.0 all of half in whole
3.1 1 word in half not in whole
3.2 2 words in half not in whole

Length of chapters is not to scale

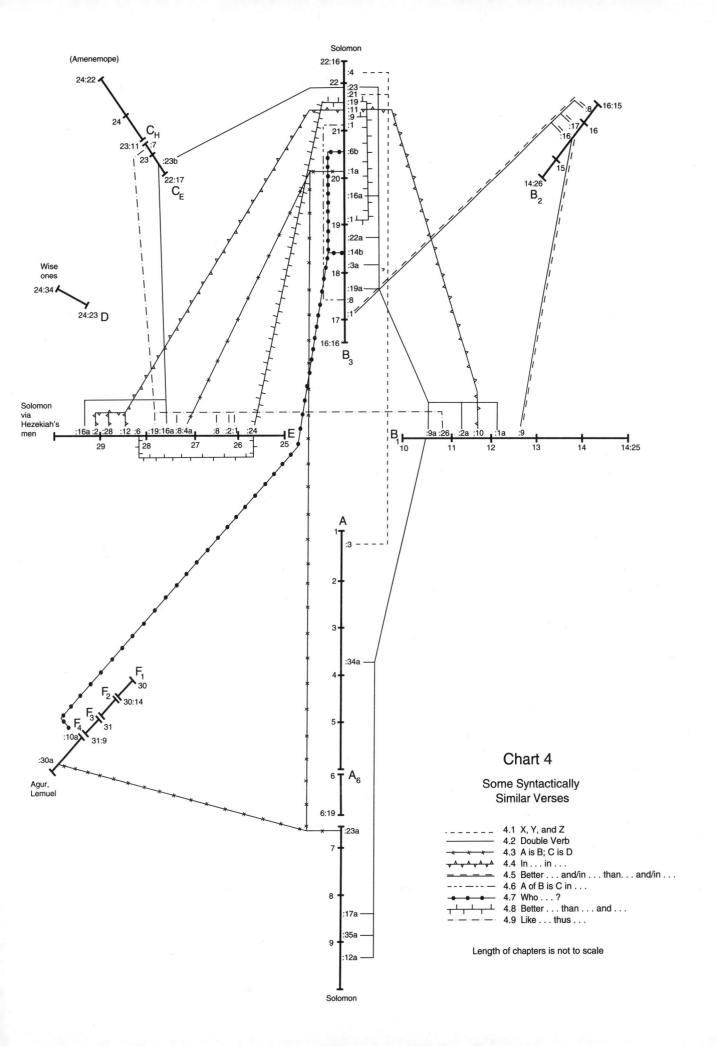

Chart 4

Some Syntactically
Similar Verses

– – – – – – –	4.1 X, Y, and Z
―――――――	4.2 Double Verb
–✳–✳–✳–	4.3 A is B; C is D
–▽–▽–▽–	4.4 In . . . in . . .
══════	4.5 Better . . . and/in . . . than. . . and/in . . .
– · – · – ·	4.6 A of B is C in . . .
–●–●–●–	4.7 Who . . . ?
⊢⊢⊢⊢⊢	4.8 Better . . . than . . . and . . .
–·–·–·–	4.9 Like . . . thus . . .

Length of chapters is not to scale

TABLE 3. *Total Number of Verses Repeated*

Collection	Number of Verses in Collection	Number of Verses Involved in Repetition
A	237	39 = 16%
A_6	19	6 = 32%
B_1	141	37 = 26%
B_2	59	16 = 27%
B_3	175	51 = 29%
C_E	24	5 = 21%
C_H	46	9 = 20%
D	12	5 = 42%
E	138	30 = 22%
F_1	14	1 = 7%
F_2	19	1 = 5%
F_3	9	0
F_4	22	0
Total	915	200 = 22% of the book

more times in the first three types of repetition described above (1.0–3.2). The last column contains the number of verses from each collection involved in repetition, with the percentage that number represents of the total number of verses in the collection.[11] These figures indicate that the types of repetition isolated in this study are a significant factor.

The time has now arrived for deciding whether these data can shed light on the various hypotheses about repetition outlined in chapter 3 above. These hypotheses will be considered in the order in which they were presented before.

The first hypothesis that repetition is due to literary cleavage (see pp. 11–12 above) can in some cases be ruled out on the grounds that repetition of one sort or another frequently occurs in verses within the same collection and in verses very close to each other in the present shape of a book. This is clearly seen in each type of verse repetition isolated, especially in half-verses repeated (see chart 2). This finding does not mean that no repetition is due to literary cleavage. Certainly in individual cases repetition does underline the similarity of materials used and the discreteness of collections, as in the case of the sharing of whole verses in 6:10–11 and 24:33–34 (1.1). But I do believe that literary cleavage in itself is not usually a likely explanation for the phenomena of verse repetitions in Proverbs.[12]

Skehan's hypothesis about the numerological goals of a final editor of the book cannot be proven or disproven, as I pointed out above (p. 13). But some of Skehan's ideas about the

---

11. For a summary of kinds of repetition within collections see table 4 (p. 78 below). I have experimented with a graph form of presenting instances of repetition in order to highlight the use of the different types of repetition in the various collections, but ultimately I decided that such presentation did not add much to the foregoing charts and merely gave a look of scientific precision where little exists.

12. Scott, "Wise and Foolish," 151, saw this already.

occurrences of repetition in the collections can now be seen in the light of the observations above. His view that the beginning of section B_1 and all of B_2 are the places where much repetition occurs is not especially true for whole-verse repetitions (though B_2 has a respectable number of them). There are, however, quite a few half-verses repeated both in the first half of B_1 and in B_2, and there are clusters of them in chapters 18, 20 (B_3), and 24 (C_H), as well.

This concentration of one sort of repetition does, I think, show that part of Skehan's case makes sense. The clustering of repetitions in these chapters is an evidence of intention. Section B_2 is a locus for some sort of authorial-editorial activity, but chapters 18, 20, and perhaps 24 are also. It is not possible now to determine the goal of this activity. It would seem that if an editor had merely been interested in padding, he would have concentrated on copying whole verses from other collections. This clearly was not done to any great extent in B_2.

In the cases of half-verses repeated in whole verses, which would logically seem closely related to half-verse repetitions, there is another clustering of instances, but not in B_2. Chapter 20 in B_3 bristles with this sort of repetition and even has four verses involved in half-whole repetition with each other. This also suggests intentionality. One could perhaps argue that the half-whole repetitions are the results of the activity of a second editor, since they are a slightly different kind of repetition. But I see no reason that the different forms of repetitions should necessarily be perpetrated by different individuals, and Skehan certainly would not have felt that this was so.

The partial survey of syntactically similar verses seems to show a rather general distribution, except that chapter 21 has more of the various types than the other chapters have.

Though Skehan's idea about an editor's interest in numerology cannot be confirmed, it does seem possible that close studies of these chapters, especially with a view to the nature of the connections between verses, may bring to light more information about the authorial or editorial goals at play. This work could best be done in a commentary on the whole book for the purpose of determining whether the way sections B_1 and B_2 were put together differs from the ways in which other sections were composed. It is safe to conclude that some of Skehan's ideas are supported by the systematic study of repetitions, though others remain hypothetical.

The third hypothesis, that verses are repeated for emphasis (p. 13), can at present only be judged subjectively, since we lack a complete subject index to the book. Such an index would allow one to determine whether the subject of a given repeated verse were unusual or not.[13] It seems to me that the repeated sayings are characteristic of the book. In most cases there is no reason to rule out the possibility that sayings or parts of sayings are repeated for emphasis. As noted before, authorial goals cannot be discerned without a closer study of the individual sections, and the goal of emphasizing may have been a major cause for repetition.

The hypothesis that repetition stems from oral formulaic methods of composition (pp. 13–14) could be bolstered by finding successions of different types of repetition. It may be that collection B_2, from which both whole and half-verses are repeated elsewhere, is open to an oral-formulaic

---

13. The subject indexes in W. Gunther Plaut, *Book of Proverbs: A Commentary* (New York: Union of American Hebrew Congregations, 1961) 21–25 (reference courtesy of John Gammie); Scott, *Proverbs*, 130–31, 170; and R. N. Whybray, *The Book of Proverbs* (Cambridge: Cambridge University Press, 1972) 188–89, are very general.

explanation, though of course Skehan's view was that its composition was an entirely literary process. Again, a detailed commentary on the section might show some regularities.

It appears that each of the reasons for repetition proposed by earlier students remains possible. Literary cleavage, however, does not explain the predilection for repetition in all cases. The theory of a numerologically inclined final editor is not adequately supported, but some sort of systematic activity does occur in B_2 where Skehan first observed it and also in other places. Repetition for the purpose of emphasis appears likely, and repetition owing to oral composition, though less likely, also remains a viable hypothesis.

The traditional view of the history of the wisdom tradition in Israel is that it began as an import from Egypt, perhaps during the time of Solomon, but probably during the period of the divided monarchy. Israelite students are presumed to have studied with Egyptian masters and to have absorbed from them the millennia-long tradition of Egyptian and international wisdom literature. The Israelite students then went on to develop this tradition in their own way, perhaps also using some of their local traditions.[14]

This view of wisdom tradition origins may be correct. But it seems rather clear that the incorporation of the Egyptian collection into the Book of Proverbs had little direct effect on the rest of the book. That collection seems to have served neither as the source nor the model for the other compositions that have been preserved. However, there is one facet of repetition that may have been affected by the incorporation of this Egyptian material, and that is the syntax. The double-verb form is found in C_E and elsewhere in the book; indeed it is the most popular form of syntax that I have isolated. And we know that this was a popular form of expression in the Egyptian wisdom tradition.[15] But because the double-verb form seems to be the only affinity between C_E and the other collections, it is likely that the use of this form in the book is not directly due to imitation of section C_E but due rather to a more subtle influence of Egyptian modes of thought at an earlier stage in the development of the Israelite intellectual tradition. To assert this is not to deny that a great deal is shared between the wisdom compositions in Egypt and Israel. For example, it is not unlikely that the instruction form was at some stage borrowed from Egypt by Israelite writers, although it may also have originated in a much less complicated way.[16]

The Egyptian connections, which are strong but not datable, may have come into the book either early or late. These have been most systematically presented by Bryce.[17] However, his three stages of the adoption of Egyptian material are not always convincing. He argues that material in the first stage was borrowed from Egyptian sources and adapted, sometimes with

---

14. See the discussion by R. B. Y. Scott, *The Way of Wisdom* (London/New York: Macmillan, 1971) 12–15; and, more popularly, E. W. Heaton, *Solomon's New Men* (New York: Pica, 1974), esp. 121–26. G. E. Bryce, *A Legacy of Wisdom* (Lewisburg, Pennsylvania: Bucknell University Press/London: Associated University Presses, 1979), is a more detailed statement of this view.

15. C. Kayatz, *Studien zu Proverbien 1–9* (Neukirchen: Neukirchener Verlag, 1966) 101, on the "reziproke Formel," the double-verb form.

16. As suggested by E. Gerstenberger, *Wesen und Herkunft des sogenannten apodiktischen Rechts im alten Testament* (Bonn: Rheinische Friedrich-Wilhelms-Universität, 1961), esp. 95–108, the origin of the prohibitive at least is in family instruction.

17. Bryce, *Legacy of Wisdom*.

words transliterated or translated with Egyptian meanings.[18] An example of this stage, of course, is collection C_E with its clear Egyptian parallels. Also convincing as a representative of adaptation is Prov 15:16, which is closely related to *Amenemope* 9:7–8 and its double *Amenemope* 16:13–14.[19] But the stages of assimilation and integration which Bryce claims to demonstrate are much less obvious and leave fewer traces.[20] In my view the Egyptian influence has been overemphasized, but because the evidence is ambivalent, opinions will continue to differ on the matter.

I think it is clear from the data I have assembled here that the Book of Proverbs is not a slavish extension of Egyptian models. The book shares worldviews and language with comparable Egyptian works, but it is very much an independent book. It is a Hebrew book for Hebrew readers and cannot be understood as an elaboration on the Egyptian collection that has been incorporated within it. The corollary to this finding is important for the uses to which the book is put in modern scholarship. It follows that the book may reflect to a large extent its Israelite milieu when it deals with social problems and when it deals with religion.[21] Many, if not most of the sentiments expressed in the book might have been quite acceptable to a contemporary educated Egyptian. But it is likely that the book stems from a period or periods in the history of Israel when a great many local elements had also been incorporated into the tradition.

These conclusions stand, I believe, regardless of how one chooses to reconstruct the history of the composition of the various collections and of the assembly of the book as it now appears.

---

18. Ibid., 65.

19. Ibid., 71–75. Compare Albrecht Alt, "Zur literarischen Analyse der Weisheit des Amenemope," in *Wisdom in Israel and in the Ancient Near East: Presented to Professor Harold Henry Rowley* (ed. Martin Noth and D. Winton Thomas; Vetus Testamentum Supplement 3; Leiden: Brill, 1955) 19. Alt uses this repetition within the Egyptian along with others to argue for the composite nature of the collection. Grumach's *Amenope* attempts to work out the implications of this suggestion, though not always convincingly, in the view of Ronald J. Williams, "The Sages of Ancient Egypt in Light of Recent Scholarship," *Journal of the American Oriental Society* 101 (1981) 5.

20. Bryce, *Legacy of Wisdom*, 57–58.

21. Compare studies on the religion of Proverbs, including F. D. Kidner, "The Relationship between God and Man in Proverbs," *Tyndale Bulletin* 7–8 (1961) 4–9; M. V. Fox, "Aspects of the Religion of the Book of Proverbs," *Hebrew Union College Annual* 39 (1968) 55–69; and H. D. Preuss, "Das Gottesbild der älteren Weisheit Israels," in *Studies in the Religion of Israel* (Vetus Testamentum Supplement 23; Leiden: Brill, 1972) 117–45—all of which assume that the book does reflect an Israelite milieu. This is also the case in R. Gordis, "The Social Background of Wisdom Literature," *Hebrew Union College Annual* 18 (1943–44) 77–118.

7

Composition of the Book

Turn on the prudent ant, thy heedful eyes,
Observe her labours, sluggard, and be wise.
No stern command, no monitory voice
Prescribes her duties, or directs her choice,
Yet timely provident, she hastes away
To snatch the blessing of the plenteous day;
When fruitful summer loads the teeming plain,
She gleans the harvest, and she stores the grain.
    How long shall sloth usurp thy useless hours,
Dissolve thy vigour, and unchain thy powers?
While artful shades thy downy couch enclose,
And soft solicitation courts repose,
Amidst the drousy charms of dull delight,
Year chases year, with unremitted flight,
Till want, now following fraudulent and slow,
Shall spring to seize thee like an ambushed foe.
    —Johnson, "The Ant" (after Proverbs 6:6–11)

Dr. Johnson put into verse the admonition to diligence in Prov 6:6–11. It is no accident that his interest in the Book of Proverbs should focus on this passage, since he was so continually concerned throughout his life about his own tendencies toward indolence.[1] But will diligence insure a better understanding about the composition of the book? Not, I am afraid, with the certainty that any self-respecting ant might expect. Still we must try not to be sluggards, given the new material we have assembled.

There are features of the book that hint at the relative order of its composition and compilation. Scholars generally agree that there are few indications of the absolute dates when the compositors and editors worked. Since the existence of kings is assumed in some passages, scholars accept the idea that much of the book comes from a time after the establishment of the

---

1. See W. J. Bate, *The Achievement of Samuel Johnson* (New York: Oxford University Press, 1955) 9–11. A focus for Johnson's resolutions was his habit of sleeping in late; his ideal was to get up between 6:00 and 8:00 A.M., and he complained that he sometimes lay in bed until 2:00 P.M. (p. 10)!

Israelite monarchy and perhaps before the divided monarchies were destroyed.[2] This represents a long period from about 1000 B.C.E. to 587 B.C.E., and of course it is possible that either the book or its parts was assembled later than that.

The information about repetition assembled here does not appear to produce a clearer chronology of the collections. The major reason that the data about repetition are not unambiguous on the question of the composition of the book is the impossibility of determining which instance of a repeated verse is the original and which is copied. Earlier scholars thought this was possible to do, but it is not.[3] And, of course, there is no way to rule out oral-formulaic composition; if oral composition played some role, the sayings may all stem from the general cache of oral lore. Thus a given occurrence may not have related directly to any other. The determination of relative originality must be part of a detailed commentary, and the originality probably cannot be determined without commentarylike treatment. I am not totally without hope that detailed, commentarylike studies of the book which pay attention to repetitions could come to firmer conclusions about the direction of borrowing of some of the repeated elements. But at this point all that can be said is that one collection has a greater or lesser affinity for another.

I have attempted to study the contexts, especially of repeated whole verses, to see if some determination about originality can be made. But usually it is only possible to determine that a saying is slightly more closely related to one context than to another. Being firmly related to a context does not necessarily mean that a saying was originally at home there. One could equally well imagine a late editor reorganizing sayings that had circulated without contexts into sections that did argue a point or were held together by assonance and consonance or use of the same words. Recent study has shown that there was a great deal of poetic organization, even in collections that previously have been regarded as incoherent.[4]

Also, we should keep in mind that the distinction between the time of the original compilation of a section and the time that it was worked into the book is potentially an important one. There seems to be no reason for supposing that a collection was composed early or late from the point of view of form or content. But the use of repetition may be a key to determining whether compositors were aware of other parts of the book when they began to work on their own contributions.

---

2. See in general R. B. Y. Scott, *Proverbs, Ecclesiastes* (Anchor Bible 18; Garden City, New York: Doubleday, 1965) xxx–xxxvi.

3. Compare, for example, W. Nowack, *Die Sprüche Salamo's* (2d ed. of E. Bertheau's comm.; Leipzig: Hirzel, 1883) xxviii.

4. See the study by Ted Hildebrandt, "Proverbial Pairs: Compositional Units in Proverbs 10–29," *Journal of Biblical Literature* 107 (1988) 207–24; also relevant is G. Boström, *Paronomasi i den äldere hebreiska maschal-litteraturen* (Lund: Gleerup/Leipzig: Harrassowitz, 1928); and, building on Boström's work, Raymond C. Van Leeuwen, *Context and Meaning in Proverbs 25–27* (Atlanta: Scholars Press, 1988). On the connections among sayings in Proverbs 10–15, see Hans-Joachim Hermisson, *Studien zur israelitischen Spruchweisheit* (Neukirchen-Vluyn: Neukirchener Verlag, 1968) 171–83. S. C. Perry, *Structural Patterns in Proverbs 10:1–22:16: A Study in Biblical Hebrew Stylistics* (Ph.D. diss., University of Texas at Austin, 1987), esp. 250, has found in his computer-based study some unexpected affinities based more on sound than on topics among verses in the part of the book he studies. Hildebrandt notes in a personal communication that he argues for a variegated approach, including Boström's phonetics, Murphy's catchwords ("Assumptions and Problems in Old Testament Wisdom Research," *Catholic Biblical Quarterly* 29 [1967] 407–18), as well as syntactic and rhetorical methods of cohesion within collections. See his valuable unpublished paper, "Strings in Proverbs 10" (1988). John Gammie suggests in a personal communication that the detailed linking of verses in chapters 25–26, shown by Van Leeuwen, indicates a later date of composition, but I am not convinced that it really has chronological implications.

The interest of compositors of the collections in repetition is a potentially valuable tool for showing affinities among collections. And these affinities may serve as a basis for consideration of the method in which the book as a whole was assembled and perhaps even when. It may be thought that trying to date collections only on the basis of repetition is a bit odd, and, of course, a great many other factors ought to be taken into consideration.[5] But such considerations can in my view only properly be judged in detailed commentaries, and such commentaries have in the past ignored to a large extent the phenomenon of repetition. Thus it is advisable at this point to concentrate exclusively on repetition.

In order to obtain an idea of the manner of composition, it seems valuable to summarize the size of the collections and their propensities for repetition. This summary will show how unusual some of the collections are, and these descriptions will lead to some conclusions that will revise some of the current scholarly views about the history of the intellectual tradition in Israel.

Table 4 lists some of the characteristics of the collections and an average percentage, as derived by analyzing the collections in the book. This is the only place I have arranged the collections in order of size instead of the order in which they are found in the book, in order to determine whether there are characteristics that large or small collections share. All the figures in table 4 are restatements of those presented earlier. Again I would caution that my figure for syntactically related verses is at most a sampling of a few remarkable syntactical forms and is not complete.

Row 1 in table 4 shows what percentage of the entire Book of Proverbs each collection constitutes in terms of number of verses. The first collection is by far the longest, but collections B_3, B_1, and E are rather similar in size. These four collections are very likely to influence what we think of as typical in the book, merely because of their bulk.

Row 2 shows the wide variety in the percentages of whole verses repeated in each collection, both within and outside the collections. The larger collections, along with B_2, A_6, and D, show a relatively large percentage of their verses wholly repeated, whereas the rest of the collections mostly lack this kind of repetition.

Row 3 lists percentages of half-verses repeated. This category, containing the largest percentages of all the categories, is represented in more of the collections, especially the Egyptian collection C_E and D.

Row 4 lists the percentage of half-verses repeated in whole verses, which is in each case very small, except, interestingly enough, in B_3 and F_1. F_1 has not been represented in the other categories but in this case has one verse repeated.

Row 5 shows that the percentage of syntactically related verses predominates in sections B_3 and E, though the Egyptian C_E and even F_4 also demonstrate this sort of echoing.

Row 6 gives the percentage of verses that are repeated in any of the three ways (1.0–3.2) within the book, but outside the collections in which the verses are found.

The range of the first three types of repetition with other collections (whole, half, and half-whole verses—that is, excluding syntactically related verses) is from 33% for D to 0% for F_3 and F_4. In descending order, the distribution is as follows (items of equal distribution are bracketed):

---

5. As noted by Leo G. Perdue in a personal communication.

Collections by Percentage of Outside Repetition

$$
\begin{array}{c}
D \\
A_6 \\
B_2 \\
B_1 \\
\left.\begin{array}{c} C_H \\ E \end{array}\right\} \\
B_3 \\
F_1 \\
F_2 \\
C_E \\
A \\
\left.\begin{array}{c} F_3 \\ F_4 \end{array}\right\}
\end{array}
$$

It is possible that in drawing conclusions regarding the composition of the book it is more important to look mainly at whole-verse repetition, because that phenomenon is much more likely to derive from real affinity than is half-verse repetition or any of the other kinds of repetition that edge nearer to the shared cliché.[6] If one lists the collections only by whole-verse repetition, one arrives at the following order:

Collections by Percentage of Whole-Verse Repetition

$$
\begin{array}{c}
D \\
B_2 \\
\left.\begin{array}{c} A \\ A_6 \\ B_3 \\ E \end{array}\right\} \\
B_1 \\
C_H \\
\left.\begin{array}{c} C_E \\ F_1 \\ F_2 \\ F_3 \\ F_4 \end{array}\right\}
\end{array}
$$

The last five collections in this list have no whole-verse repetition whatsoever. In general this ordering is similar to the preceding one, which included all kinds of repetition except syntactical. The major difference between these two methods of ordering is that collection A's abundance of whole-verse repetitions (the second method) makes A appear much more typical than do its overall repetitions (the first method).

The implications of these orderings are far-reaching. They argue that the Egyptian collection (containing no whole-verse repetitions) has less to do with repetition outside itself—a cardinal feature of the book—than any other collection except the self-contained A and the short F_3 and F_4.

---

6. As suggested by Edward Greenstein in personal correspondence.

TABLE 4. *Comparison of Collections (in Order by Size)*

Categories	A 1:1–5:23 6:20–9:18	B₃ 16:16–22:16	B₁ 10:1–14:24	E 25:1–29:27	B₂ 14:25–16:15	C_H 23:12–24:22	C_E 22:17–23:11	F₄ 31:10–31	F₂ 30:15–33	A₆ 6:1–19	F₁ 30:1–14	D 24:23–34	F₃ 31:1–9	Average Percentage
1. % of Book	26	19	15	15	6	5	3	2	2	2	2	1	1	8
2. % of Whole-Verses Repeated (1.0–1.4)	10	10	9	10	14	4	0	0	0	10	0	17	0	6
3. % of Half-Verses Repeated (2.0–2.2)	7	15	16	12	15	15	21	0	5	16	0	25	0	11
4. % of Half-Verses Repeated in Whole Verses (3.0–3.2)	2	7	1	1	2	0	0	0	0	5	7	0	0	2
5. % of Syntactically Related Verses (4.0–4.9)	2	10	4	9	5	0	8	9	0	0	0	0	0	4
6. % of Verses Repeated Outside of collections	2	16	19	17	26	17	4	0	5	32	7	33	0	14

Now it is time to explore what other implications the various levels of repetition might have for the questions regarding the compilation of the book. The one thing that seems undeniable is that the collections with less than an average percentage (A: 2%; C_E: 4%; F_1: 7%; F_2: 5%; F_3: 0%; F_4: 0%) were composed in relative isolation from the other collections. This does not necessarily mean that their compositors were later in time than the people who put together the other collections. But it would seem that, even though these collections may have existed somewhere in Israel at an early date, they were joined to the book after the other collections had been formed.

If one uses only whole-verse repetition, then the collections C_E (0%), F_1–F_4 (all 0%), and C_H (4%) seem isolated because of their lack of repetition. All of these collections can be form-critically isolated from the rest of the book since they are in the instruction form, except perhaps F_4, the acrostic poem, and it may be argued that this kind of isolation was predictable given the form-critical distinctiveness of these collections. But it is remarkable that there is not more borrowing among these collections since they presumably have similar situations in life.

At the other end of the spectrum are the collections that show a greater percentage of repetition (D: 33%; A_6: 32%; and B_2: 26%). If one uses only whole-verse repetition, then the significant collections are D (17%) and B_2 (14%). Skehan proposed that B_2 was a late and imitative collection and that D and A_6 were short and possibly derivative. But, it could be argued that these were actually the earliest and that later compositors borrowed heavily from them. It is also possible to see collections D, B_2, and A_6 as the latest efforts of compositors who were aware of some of the other collections currently in the book. It is not easy to decide how to date these collections relatively, but it may be better to view them as late and *imitative* than as early and *imitated*. Collection B_2 has no headline to indicate its relationship to its context (only Skehan sees it as a distinct entity). But A_6 was obviously inserted into its present position, since it incorporates a series of one- and two-line sayings in the midst of verses in the instruction form of collection A. Collection D has a headline that stresses its secondary nature: "Also these are of/for [the] wise ones" (24:23a).

What is to be concluded about the collections that are only average in the amount of repetitions in comparison with other collections (B_3: 16%; B_1: 19%; E: 17%; and C_H: 17%—if one uses only whole-verse repetition, then the average collections include A: 10%; A_6: 10%; B_1: 9%; B_3: 10%; and E: 10%)? An average collection was either an early collection *from* which people borrowed moderately, or it was a late collection *into* which people borrowed moderately. In either case it may be average because it was lengthy and had more verses to influence overall totals.

Skladny has argued on grounds of content and style that 10:1–22:16 and chapters 25–29 are the oldest collections in the book. He wishes to divide chapters 25–27 from 28–29, and, on the basis of content, argues that the former is aimed at peasants, while the latter is addressed to princes.[7] Van Leeuwen believes that the whole is really court-oriented; the so-called peasant-ethnic passages in his view are images of royal power.[8] Skladny's view is that a court-created phenomenon was

---

7. U. Skladny, *Die ältesten Spruchsammlungen in Israel* (Göttingen: Vandenhoeck & Ruprecht, 1962) 76–82 (on dating); he prefers a chronological order of chapters 10–15, 28–29, 16:1–22:16, and 25–27 (p. 79). Skladny uses the term *Bauernethik* 'peasant ethic' on p. 56. He makes clear that he thinks chapters 28–29 are borrowed from the court (p. 57). Compare also Hermisson, *Studien zur israelitischen Spruchweisheit*, 16–18, who argues that 10:1–22:16 and chapters 25–29 date from before the Exile, perhaps as early as the Early Monarchy.

8. Van Leeuwen, *Context and Meaning in Proverbs 25–27*, 133, on Prov. 27:23–27.

popularized in chapters 25–27, but I am unsure if that is still a legitimate view, since some now doubt that royalty has a corner on wisdom. F. W. Golka has studied attitudes toward kings in African proverbs, which he finds paralleled in the Book of Proverbs, and he concludes that the book does not come from the court but from the "little people," who appear only rarely in the Hebrew Bible.[9] I am wary of dating by content, but if Skladny is right that in chapters 25–27 we have somehow a peasant ethic, perhaps that should identify chapters 25–27 as the earliest collection of Israelite sayings.[10]

It may be that the other collections with a similar amount of repetition are old. The only hesitation about dating them all early is that C_H is couched in the imperative mood and is in the instruction form. It is more closely connected to the rest of the book than C_E is, and it does not share repeated verses with C_E. Thus it is clear that C_H is not an elaboration on the Egyptian translation.

On the basis of these considerations, I suggest that there were four stages to the book's assembly. First, collection E was brought together, perhaps soon followed by the other average collections, B_3, B_1, and C_H. Then the repetitive collections were elaborated to join these, that is, D, A_6, and B_2. In the third stage the less repetitive collections were brought together, perhaps with A as an introduction to B_{1-3} and C_E as an introduction to C_H and E. Finally the miscellaneous collections in F were joined at the end, possibly with F_1 slightly earlier, in view of its arrangement in the Septuagint between C_H and D.

---

9. F. W. Golka, "Die Königs- und Hofsprüche und der Ursprung der israelitischen Weisheit," *Vetus Testamentum* 36 (1986) 13–36, esp. 34. Golka also suggests (p. 36) that the concentration of modern scholars on the role of the Israelite king and court has more to do with political views of scholars in Wilhelmine Germany than with the Israelite data, and he suggests that it is time to seek elsewhere besides the court for the *Sitz im Leben* of Proverbs. See, in general, the interesting comparative material assembled from Birkina Faso, formerly Upper Volta, in L. Naré, *Proverbes salomoniens et proverbes mossi: Étude comparative à partir d'une nouvelle analyse de Pr 25–29* (Frankfurt am Main: Lang, 1986), with his extensive and valuable bibliography on the Book of Proverbs as well as African materials. Compare also R. N. Whybray, *The Intellectual Tradition in the Old Testament* (Berlin/New York: de Gruyter, 1974), esp. 69–70, who argues that wealthy farmers such as Job were the most likely purveyors of wisdom.

10. Note, nonetheless, that the headline of collection E (25:1), like that of D in 24:23, indicates that a compositor sensed he was adding chapters 25–29 to something else: "Also these are proverbs of Solomon, which the men of Hezekiah, king of Judah, copied." The difficulty of the last verb should be emphasized; this is the only clear instance of the verb in any literary sense, and elsewhere it means 'to move forward, to remove, to break camp' and 'to grow old.' Whybray, *Intellectual Tradition in the Old Testament*, 51–52, notes that expressions such as *men of Hezekiah* elsewhere always refer to military groups, but here it clearly does not. He suggests (p. 51 and n. 163) translating the verb "edited" but admits its usage here is unique. The Septuagint adds an adjective and sees the "men" as friends:

> Αὗται αἱ παιδεῖαι Σαλωγῶντος αἱ ἀδιάκριτοι,
>   ἃς ἐξεγράψαντο οἱ φίλοι Εζεκιου τοῦ βασιλέως τῆς Ιουδαίας.
> These are the miscellaneous instructions of Solomon,
>   which the friends of Hezekiah, king of Judah, copied out.

As J. P. Mathieu suggests, the word *miscellaneous* is clearly secondary ("Les deux Collections salomoniennes [Proverbs 10:1–22:16; 25:1–29:27]," *Laval théologie et philosophie* 19 [1963] 175 n. 1), and P. Stadter (in a personal communication) notes that the plural of παιδεία is unusual. The Targum and Syriac use the more normal word for "proverbs" here, but also add an adjective, "deep." M. A. van den Oudenrijn proposes that ἀδιάκριτοι means, not that there was no particular order, but that sayings by authors other than Solomon were included ("Prov xxv, 1," *Angelicum* 5 [1928] 566–67). My guess is that the headline, whatever it may mean in Hebrew, is secondary to the assemblage of the collection.

And so my ordering of the collections is this:

$$
\begin{array}{l}
\text{E} \\
\text{B}_1 \\
\text{B}_3 \\
\text{C}_\text{H} \\
\text{D} \\
\text{A}_6 \\
\text{B}_2 \\
\text{A} \\
\text{C}_\text{E} \\
\text{F}_1 \\
\text{F}_2 \\
\text{F}_3 \\
\text{F}_4
\end{array}
$$

Again, the actual order of the joining of the bracketed collections is unknown. The problem with this reconstruction is that A_6 cannot be placed, since collection A may not have existed when it was composed.

If this order of assembly of the book is supportable, one can be precise about when the book began to be compiled. Collection E, the earliest, in my view, is dated by its headline to Hezekiah, therefore at the latest 686 B.C.E. This dating jibes with R. B. Y. Scott's judgment, partly because of this headline and partly because of his analysis of the stories about Solomon in the Book of Kings that the wisdom tradition began to flourish during his reign.[11]

Some would argue that E might be later than B (or part of B), since Hezekiah lived long after Solomon. This is possible, but E lacks the repetition patterns that are important in B, and it could be that E's random relations to other collections result from its availability to the compilers.

Crenshaw sensibly objected that Hezekiah's time was hardly one in which international contacts flourished or in which court-connected worthies would be likely to have turned for enlightenment to Egyptian texts.[12] There are two answers to his objection. First, though wisdom material is not markedly nationalistic in any of the cultures of the Near East, neither is it markedly international. The reason it travels so well is that it does not say much about, for example, polytheism or idolatry or the cult of the dead. Or rather, some Egyptian works do mention especially the latter,[13] but the material borrowed into Hebrew does not. Wisdom material does not, therefore, by its nature, work against any king's pious reforms. At best it simply argues mildly in Proverbs that kings and God should be obeyed. Second, if the book began to come together

---

11. R. B. Y. Scott, "Solomon and the Beginnings of Wisdom in Israel," in *Wisdom in Israel and in the Ancient Near East: Presented to Professor Harold Henry Rowley* (ed. Martin Noth and D. Winton Thomas; Vetus Testamentum Supplement 3; Leiden: Brill, 1955) 262–79; repr. in *Studies in Ancient Israelite Wisdom* (ed. J. L. Crenshaw; New York: Ktav, 1976) 84–101. An opposite view is taken by N. Shupak, "The *Sitz im Leben* of the Book of Proverbs in the Light of a Comparison of Biblical and Egyptian Wisdom Literature," *Revue Biblique* 94 (1987) 98–119, esp. 118.

12. James L. Crenshaw, "Method in Determining Wisdom Influence upon 'Historical' Literature," *Journal of Biblical Literature* 88 (1969) 129–42; repr. in *Studies in Ancient Israelite Wisdom* (ed. J. L. Crenshaw; New York: Ktav, 1976) 481–94, esp. 487.

13. See the survey by Leo G. Perdue, *Wisdom and Cult* (Missoula: Scholars Press, 1977) 19–84, esp. 62–64.

under Hezekiah and if its history was as suggested here, the incorporation of the Egyptian collection may have happened later, maybe even in times when educated Hebrews actually were looking toward Egypt for help of other kinds.[14]

---

14. Compare Jeremiah 37, from the difficult days before the exile. But Shupak points out that Hezekiah was leader of a pro-Egyptian faction opposed by Isaiah ("*Sitz im Leben* of the Book of Proverbs," 118). In connection with Jer 17:5–8 it has been suggested that there is some dependence on an image in *Amenemope* of the good man as a fruitful tree (also found in Psalm 1 and 92:13–16, as noted by Ronald J. Williams, "The Sages of Ancient Egypt in Light of Recent Scholarship," *Journal of the American Oriental Society* 101 [1981] 11). But, of course, this Egyptian connection may not date to Jeremiah's time, since Jeremiah 17 could be secondary to Jeremiah's compositions.

Note that Donald B. Redford says that the Late Egyptian dialect was "full of technical and literary terms borrowed either from classical Hebrew or the West Asian dialect ancestral to it" and that it was used as a literary dialect from 1300 "to well after 700 B.C.E." ("The Relations between Egypt and Israel from El-Amarna to the Babylonian Conquest," in *Biblical Archaeology Today: Proceedings of the International Congress on Biblical Archaeology, Jerusalem, April 1984* [Jerusalem: Israel Exploration Society and Academy of Sciences and Humanities in cooperation with the American Schools of Oriental Research, 1985] 197). This kind of borrowing shows continued close contact throughout the relevant period. Note, however, that Redford (p. 198) rejects the usual equation of חכם 'wisdom' with $m3^c t$ 'order, right-dealing, truth'.

8

Conclusion

I fancy mankind may come, in time, to write all aphoristically, except in narrative; grow weary of preparation, and connection, and illustration, and all those arts by which a big book is made.

—Johnson

It has not quite come to pass that aphorism has taken over everything, though a case can be made that it has taken over advertizing and politics. And yet in the Book of Proverbs we have a relatively large book that—although it was certainly prepared, connected, and illustrated—does not easily reveal by what arts it was made. A number of important questions remain open, including the questions of why verses are repeated and to what extent proverbial clichés can be used to study affinities within the book.

But I am finally in a position to evaluate Grintz's conclusions, reviewed in chapter 2 above. First, Grintz suggested that collections A (Proverbs 1–9) and B (Prov 10:1–22:16) are closely related. My study of whole verses repeated does not support that idea at all. Only one wholly repeated verse is shared by these two collections. But there are a number of shared half-repeated verses, one half-whole verse repetition, and several syntactically related verses. Since it seems that whole-verse repetition is most likely of the various kinds of repetition to show affinity, I conclude that Grintz's conclusion is not supported by this study.

Grintz also suggested that collection A (Proverbs 1–9) is closely related to collections C_E (Prov 22:17–23:11) and C_H (Prov 23:12–24:22). That is certainly not true of whole-verse or half-whole repetition, slightly more true with regard to half-verse repetition and syntactically related verses. In spite of the form-critical similarity, Grintz's suggestion is not supported by my findings.

Grintz further suggested that collection B (Prov 10:1–22:16) was close to collection E (Proverbs 25–29). This observation appears to be correct in whole-verse and half-verse repetition, and perhaps also of half-whole repetition and syntactically related verses. Thus Grintz's idea is supported both by the form-critical similarity of the two sections and by the patterns of repetitions.

Grintz denied a relation between collections A (Proverbs 1–9) and E (Proverbs 25–27); he is certainly right with regard to all four types of repetition. I can say that this idea is strongly supported by the results presented here.

Grintz also said that almost no relation exists between collection B (Prov 10:1–22:16) and collections C_E, C_H, and D (Prov 22:17–24:34). This is true in regard to whole-verse and half-whole repetition, less true in regard to half-verse repetition and syntactically related verses. The collections are small and the validity of Grintz's assertion may be questioned on this basis, but in general he seems to have been right.

Finally, Grintz denied a relation between collection E (Proverbs 25–29) and collections C_E, C_H, and D (Prov 22:17–24:34). He was correct in regard to whole-verse and half-whole repetition, less decisively so with regard to the other two types of repetition.

It should be clear from the discussion in chapter 7 that I do not share Grintz's conclusions. But in spite of my disagreement on several points of detail, Grintz's observations have value beyond their importance in the history of scholarship and they ought to be considered individually in their own right.

The uncertainty we have attained is not a bad thing if we therefore manage to see a little more clearly what exactly we do not know. From the perspective of this study, I think a great deal can now be done that will lead first to firmer understandings and then to cleverer speculations about the history of the book and its use in Israel.

As I survey the prospects for further study, it appears to me that we are only at the very beginning of an understanding of the Book of Proverbs and its composition. Several projects that grow from the present study seem worthy of the attention of scholars.

First, a logical next step would be to test the list of proverbial clichés against the so-called wisdom books, Job and Ecclesiastes, and against other passages that are generally accepted as having something to do with wisdom. This might be done most fruitfully in the contexts of studies on those works and might also lead to the development of lists of clichés not necessarily shared with Proverbs but which can be identified within them.

Further, it may be possible to make some progress in giving rough absolute dates for proverbial collections by testing the present list of clichés against non-wisdom books that are more or less datable. Even if the clichés turn out to be only "common cultural stock," as Crenshaw termed it, it stands to reason that over time this common stock changed. Fashions in word usage may or may not have been shared between people who wrote down the Book of Ezra and people who wrote down Proverbs. But the question is worth investigation.

Clearly, no commentary ever written on Proverbs takes repetitions, clichés, and the shapes of the collections seriously.[1] The task of writing such a commentary, which with luck would be useful to other students and would not merely reflect one's own pet ideas, is likely to be lengthy and difficult. It should probably be undertaken by an older scholar who already has an accumulation of wisdom, not to speak of file cards, on the many problems of the book. As I noted, I failed in my own fledgling attempts to determine, in the case of repeated verses, which of a pair of them had a chance of being original and which copied. But I think that such verses studied in

---

1. Compare the complaint of C. Begg, reviewing L. Alonso Schökel and J. Vilchez Lindez's *Proverbios*: "An obvious characteristic of the book of Proverbs is its repetitiveness, in which the same or similar thoughts keep recurring. Given this state of affairs, any verse-by-verse commentary on the book such as the one offered here will inevitably partake of a like repetitiveness. Accordingly, one wonders if there might not be an alternative approach to doing a commentary specifically on Proverbs which would permit a more compact and focused presentation" (*Journal of Biblical Literature* 105 [1986] 712).

their contexts, and studied along with the clichés identified here, could help to define further traces of intentionality or unintended affinity on the part of compositors or editors. Perhaps some visual method of charting in detail sections with their repeated verses, clichés, and subject affinities could lead to further clarity.

There are other features one might look for in a truly original commentary, including a thorough restudy of the later versions. It is not by chance that the most useful commentary currently available is still the 1899 volume by C. H. Toy who had control of the versions available in his day.[2] But of course a good Proverbs commentary would take a lifetime to develop, though it might have a chance of being useful through another ninety years.

I cannot resist a final quotation from Samuel Johnson on the art of making a commentary. Discussing his own work on Shakespeare, he said, "A commentary must arise from the fortuitous discoveries of many men in devious walks of literature."[3] Some women, too, one would hope, in these days, but the emphasis on the fortuitous and the devious underlines the vast array of knowledge needed that is not directly connected to the subject.

There are still a great many things that we do not know about the Book of Proverbs. But it does not appear likely that, barring the discovery of new comparative material or older biblical texts, one can hope to answer the important questions of how and when the book was set down without close attention to the verses that have come down to us twice-told.

---

2. For a very helpful bibliography of commentaries, including medieval ones, see L. Naré, *Proverbes salomoniens et proverbes mossi* (Frankfurt am Main: Lang, 1986) 413–18, updating F. Vattioni, "Studi sul libro dei Proverbi," *Augustinianum* 12 (1972) 121–68 (pp. 150–53 on commentaries).

3. James Boswell, *The Life of Johnson* (New York: Modern Library, 1964) 200.

Appendix

"The Proverbs of Solomon"

Clarifications on the Question of the Relation between the Three Collections in the Book of Proverbs Attributed to Solomon

by Jehoshua M. Grintz
[First published in *Lešonēnu* 33 (1968), pp. 243–69]

TRANSLATOR'S INTRODUCTION

Grintz's prose is difficult to render into English because it is full of digressions, and so I have frequently simplified his sentence structure. Likewise, I have altered the paragraphing to accord with English usage, since Grintz's paragraphs are very long. I have retained Grintz's use of 'ה (abbreviation of השם). The few clarifications that I have added are enclosed in double square brackets. Page numbers of the original publication are handled in a like manner. Hebrew words in single square brackets are retained from Grintz's original wording.

So many of the biblical references in his article were wrong that Grintz published a list of corrections and omissions the following year (in *Lešonēnu* 34 [1969] 159–60). I have incorporated these corrections into the translation without noting where I have done so.

I have omitted Grintz's reproduction of verses outside of Proverbs, but I have checked and corrected such references wherever they are cited. When citing such passages, Grintz did not list all instances—not even all instances in Proverbs. I doubt that he was trying to skew his results, but his references must nonetheless be checked against a concordance if the total list is desired.

Grintz, who lived from 1911 to 1976, was a student of Umberto Cassuto's. For an appreciation of Grintz, see the Festschrift edited by Benjamin Uffenheimer in his honor in 1982: גרינץ עיונים במקרא: ספר זכרון ליהושע מאיר (Tel Aviv: University of Tel Aviv, 1982), especially pp. 9–14. The editors of *Lešonēnu* have kindly granted their permission to include this translation here.

—Daniel C. Snell

* *
*

In this article we will attempt to analyze in a new way the relation between the three collections attributed to Solomon in the Book of Proverbs—according to the linguistic material and the subject matter.[1]

The Book of Proverbs in its entirety is not attributed simply to Solomon but just a part of it. The book is explicitly divided into nine collections (which we will call here collections A: Prov 1–9, B: 10:1–22:16; C: 22:17–24:22; D: 24:23–34; E: 25:1–29:27; F: 30:1–14; G: 30:15–33; H: 31:1–9; and I: 31:10–31). These collections can be recognized by the headlines that stand at the beginning of each.

In the headlines the name of the compiler is stated clearly in most cases (1:1, 10:1, 25:1—all Solomon; 30:1—Agur son of Jakeh; 30:15—Aluqah;[2] 31:1—Lemuel, king of Massa; 22:17, 24:23—both attributed to "the wise ones"). But out of the nine collections, only three were attributed to Solomon.[3] Of these three, two came right after each other, and the third (collection E) comes after the words of various "wise ones." These latter two collections (C and D) appear as

---

1. A short study by Heinrich Ewald was done about this matter by Ewald in K. F. Keil, *Manual of Historico-Critical Introduction* (trans. George C. M. Douglas; Edinburgh: T. & T. Clark, 1869; reprinted 1952) 1:474–75. At any rate this effort stands alone and has no reference to what preceded on the subject. It is the product of a course that I conducted on the Book of Proverbs during the year 1962–63 at the University of Tel Aviv. From all the students who participated, first place goes to three female students without whose help perhaps this essay would not have seen the light: Yonah Levy, Daliah Benyamini, Eldah Atir. Many thanks.

2. See in this matter my words in תרביץ 28 (1958–59) 135–37, and in brief in פרקי מבוא לס׳ משלי [[*Chapters of Introduction to the Book of Proverbs*]] (Jerusalem, 1968) 30. [[עלוקה is not commonly understood as a proper name.]]

3. The headline at the head of the book does not attribute the whole book to Solomon (as T. Fritsch writes in *The Interpreter's Bible*, 1955). If it were so, the name of Solomon would not be repeated at the beginning of chapter 10, and there would be no mention of at least three other proverb-makers besides Solomon. The truth is, however, that the headline at the beginning of the book is connected only to the first collection (see the additional evidence on this within this article and at its end).

Indeed, in the Septuagint translation the headline at the beginning of chapter 10 is missing. But this translation has in this regard a whole system that extends throughout all the book, the object of which is to erase any memory of another proverb-maker besides Solomon. For this purpose the headline at the beginning of chapter 10 is deleted; and the headlines at the head of collections F (30:1), G (30:15), and H (31:1) are explained not as names of individuals but as words with epigrammatic meaning. "Words of Agur son of Jakeh, the Massaite" is translated [[in Greek]]: "Fear my words, my son; take them and return an answer"; "of Ithiel" becomes "for those trusting God" (apparently the meaning of "of Ithiel" is understood as "these who are with God"); "words of Lemuel" becomes "my words are said by God" (interpreting למואל?). This also is the explanation of the translations of 22:17 ("Incline your ear to words of wise ones and hear my words") and 24:23 ("Also these I say to you, to hear wise ones"). These translations are not obvious from the Hebrew, since the things discussed here are actually "words of wise ones" and new compositions.

Also, the order of the collections is changed. The order in the Septuagint is A (including B), C, F, D, G, H (all of them, except A, without a headline), and only after them comes collection E ("Proverbs of Solomon which the men of Hezekiah copied"), and after it the poem "A Woman of Valor" (31:10–31).

The whole book is thus divided according to this system into two parts, and all of it is attributed to Solomon. Indeed, there is no reason to say that the translators invented this system. Certainly they received these explanations and this text from tradition (that is, one without the headline at the beginning of chapter 10), from teachers that preceded them in the land of Israel, and from a text that was in the hands of those teachers.

That is how it is explained in the Midrash: "Words of Agur, etc.—Rabbi Hiyya bar Abba said, Why is his name called *Agur*?—because he collected [אגר] the Torah; *Ben-Jakeh*—because he vomited it [הקיאה]; *Leithiel*—since it is written in the Torah: 'And let him not increase for himself women, so that his heart not swerve' [[Deut 17:17]]; *and Ucal*—Solomon said: 'I will increase but I will not swerve.' Another interpretation . . . (see, for all sorts of other explanations, ילקוט to Proverbs 30).

It is reasonable to assume that the men of the united congregation, who attributed more sacred songs to David than proverbs and songs were attributed to Solomon (1 Kgs 5:12), had a Hebrew text without the headline "Proverbs of Solomon" at the head of chapter 10, and in the same order given in the translation of the Septuagint.

two separate collections, and they stand between "the Proverbs of Solomon" attributed directly to the king (collection B) and the collection about which it is said at its head that the men of Hezekiah copied it (collection E).

The assumption to be derived from this division is that the Book of Proverbs as it lies before us was not formed at one time, but in two stages at least. In the first stage people assembled together all of the "proverbs" that were attributed to Solomon, collections A and B, and added to them some of the words of the various "wise ones" (22:17–24:22, collection C). In the second stage they added [[244]] to the first words of the wise ones another collection from other wise ones ("these also are of the wise ones"—24:23–34, collection D). And so they were obliged to have a separate headline.

These editors set that other small collection [[D]] next to the first collection [[C]], and beside it they set collection E, which they had copied from "the proverbs of Solomon" and which had not been arranged in the first stage. They also added some new "appendixes" from various compilers: Agur, Aluqah, and Lemuel. The last section, "the woman of valor," if one judges according to its contents, is a glorification of the woman of valor, Wisdom, who knows how to supply her house. It is possible that already in the first stage of the arrangement it served as a conclusion to the collection done then, including only A and B. For in its contents, the woman of valor, the antithesis to the strange woman, serves as a contrast to the woman of noisy foolishness, who wastes what "her husband" assembled—a major theme in collection A.

At any rate, to return to the subject under discussion, even if the headlines were confirmed as historical as they are, we still would not know what is the nature of the arrangement of "Solomon" or of "the men of Hezekiah." It is clear that there is a difference in style, form, and contents between collections A and B. We do not need to dwell on this below, but let us note it briefly here. In collection B we get the polished artistic proverb, and each verse is a world of its own; with enough effort one can find some association that has prompted the proverb collectors to put the verses together as they did. In contrast, in collection A the language is fluent, pouring out essay and reproof, connecting all the sections almost as one block in the framework of several closely connected ideas, which are repeated one after another.

To the clear difference in form between collections A and B there are accompanying differences in semantics. For example, there is a different meaning for the word מזמות/מזמה, which in collection A means "becoming wise" in a good sense and in collection B in a bad sense. And more important than this are differences in ways of life reflected [[245]] in the collections. Collection B addresses initially and essentially the man who is lord among his people. But collection A initially and essentially addresses the simple lad. Collection B focuses on the man whose work is in the field, while collection A focuses on the lad whose work is in the city.

When we turn to the other "Solomonic" collection, collection E, we find that there is a great deal of similarity between collections B and E. This similarity extends to both style and form, since both of them collect sayings. It also extends to their contents since in both of them the life of the village is the important thing.

But in spite of this similarity, a difference in the arrangement of material is obvious. Collection B is entirely composed of isolated verses. But in collection E not all the sayings have simple parallelism of the verse halves. There are some that are extended a great deal, and there are others in which there is a cluster of sayings dealing with one subject. In collection E there is also a variegation of view; for example, there seems to be more emphasis on the ass as opposed

to the king. There also is some sort of change between collections B and E in the way of making proverbs and in the way of making a connection between the proverb and the thing that is compared. (We will give more detail below in the conclusion).

What is early here, and what is late? If we turn away for a brief time to the non-Jewish research that comes from the end of the eighteenth century, the beginning of the nineteenth, and up to our day, there are studies that raise the date of the arrangement of the Book of Proverbs and others that lower the date. The first and natural inclination was to affirm the historicity of the headlines according to their plain meanings with regard to the collections as wholes or with regard to parts of them.

Nevertheless, the claim still arose that collection A was later than collection B. And scholars proposed that the long headline at the beginning of the book was not intended as a beginning to collection A, but to the whole of the book, or to its first edition, which contained 1:1–24:22 (see above).

A recurring claim (since Ewald) was, and still is, that the long, connected speech of collection A is a later form than the condensed language of the collections like collection B with one-line sayings. With the tendency of Wellhausen's followers to date things later as much as possible, and with a scale of lowered dates, which this tendency introduced into the world of biblical research, the whole of the Book of Proverbs was dated later in order forcefully to obliterate its period; it was dated to the most distant parts of the Second Temple period. Its fate was like the fate of the Torah, and also the whole Bible. It was seen as part of a world of late forgeries, which had been attributed to earlier people.[4]

The new discoveries—in Egypt at first, and in our own generation at Ugarit—and the renewed understanding of the wisdom of the peoples of the East changed the evaluation of matters a great deal. Scholars now have the Aramaic Proverbs of Ahiqar, which were discovered at Elephantine and were published at the beginning of this century, and the proverbs of Babylonia and Sumer in our days, and especially the Egyptian Proverbs of Amenemope [[246]]. The renewed recognition that the wisdom tradition [[gnoma]] had ancient sources in the lands of the Bible that bordered Israel has again recently reinvigorated the belief among scholars in the possibility that collection B was from the days of Solomon[5] or from a time near to his,[6] though not everyone shares this belief.

---

4. In its essentials this view still lives today among the remnant of scholars who follow Wellhausen. For Arthur Weiser (in his introduction, *Einleitung in das Alte Testament*, 1957), collection A (Proverbs 1–9) is still the latest in time, and on no account is it from before the fourth century ("wohl kaum vor dem 4. Jahrhundert"): "Similar to the arrangement of the Torah and to the collection of the sacred songs of Psalms, in this case also people set at the beginning what was relatively late."

The long sentences in this collection are adjudged by him to be the fruit of the influence of Greek style, and warnings in it are the fruit of the prophetic vision; and from prophecy came also the words about wisdom, the fear of the Lord, and the warnings against the strange woman, etc. (ibid., pp. 239–40). But see p. [[93]] below. Compare against this Y. Kaufman, תולדות האמונה הישראלית [[*History of Israelite Religion*]] 2:631–46, and my words in לס׳ משלי פרקי מבוא [[*Chapters of Introduction to the Book of Proverbs*]] (1968), chaps. 6–7, pp. 75–92. On the antiquity of the motifs and language in collection A see W. F. Albright, "Some Canaanite-Phoenician Sources of Hebrew Wisdom," *VTSup* 3 (1955) 1–15; and the essay by K. A. Kitchen, "Some Egyptian Background to the Old Testament," *Tyndale [House] Bulletin* 5–6 (1960) 4–18.

5. C. Kuhl, *Die Entstehung des Alten Testaments*, 268–79.

6. B. Gemser, *Sprüche Salomos* (HAT; Tübingen, 1963): "About a hundred and fifty years after Solomon" (p. 4). The author does not reveal to us how he arrived at this precise date. But as he continues, he tells his readers (p. 5) that the same economic struggle reflected in the prophets and in the Book of Deuteronomy (i.e., in the days of Isaiah

Scholars saw that the old Hebrew-Canaanite language ("West Semitic") found at Ugarit provided witnesses and ancient parallels to the rich language of the proverbs in the Book of Proverbs. They also discovered other parallels with regard to the contents of the words of the wise ones of old, for example, about wisdom personified as a woman, about the strange women, and so on. Of course, the headline about "the men of Hezekiah" at the beginning of collection E was then accepted as appropriate.[7]

But there is a tendency still current (and it is almost universal) to consider some parts of the book late, even though this is not in accordance with what is clearly stated in the headline at the beginning, Prov 1:1. This tendency toward late dating is still prevalent, especially with regard to collection A. Over time all the proofs that were said to make this collection late have been found invalid. Nevertheless, the custom of considering it late is still accepted. The reason for this is its form as a connected discourse, which is seen as an obvious indication that it cannot be early. And so it is dated later than the rest of the collections. Because Wellhausen's method considers prophecy to be the beginning of every kind of literature in Israel, collection A is still judged as being influenced by prophecy [[and thus is later than the eighth-century prophets at least]].

In this article we will make an experiment—as we said at the beginning—and try to judge the collections of the Book of Proverbs—initially and in principle the three collections attributed to Solomon—not according to forced descriptions designed to accommodate the demands of a certain system, and not according to external supporting texts. We will try to judge the collections according to their mutual relation in terms of language and style. And only after that we try to evaluate the collections according to an understanding of their content and plan.

In collection B we have a series of verses that are repeated with some changes, or parts of verses that are repeated in different places in the same collection, and this partial repetition is the case for the majority of repeated verses. Similar to this we have a series of verses repeating in the same way in two places remote from each other; one (or more) is to be found in collection B [[247]] and another in collection E. It is a question in itself how this duplication arose since we are not dealing here with popular sayings, which may be changed through their perambulation for one reason or another. But here we are dealing with artistic proverbs, which were adapted and polished from the beginning by the wise men from the people, and not by the people themselves. At any rate it is obvious from the fact of repetition that the material from which the verses were fashioned came out of a similar or, sometimes, out of an equivalent background. We also have an obvious similarity of another sort—the contents of collections B and E (just as we have said).

---

according to Gemser's viewpoint)—that is, an agricultural situation devoid of hope(!)—is also found in collection B. According to Gemser it was worthwhile at first glance to bring the date down at least to the days of the destruction of the temple, except that he is apparently influenced by the new current [[to date it even later]], and, thus, he abstains.

With regard to collection A, he repeats all the "proofs" that earlier students listed (see p. 4 in Weiser), and he even takes pains to add, "Die Sammlungen mit längeren Sprucheinheiten—die ein bestimmtes Thema verfolgen, sind wie in Ägypten jüngeren Datums" [[The collections with longer proverbial units, which follow a definite theme, are as in Egypt of a younger date]]. This statement, I fear, proves that this author kept himself from looking at any Egyptian collection of proverbs, since the complete opposite of this is in fact the case (compare my pamphlet mentioned above).

7. The belief in this headline is almost universal—it is to be found in older studies about the new discoveries. Apparently the desire here is to find support just as the reforms of Josiah have been seized for the same need for some specific date, near in time, to serve as a formative period for the Law. Apparently it was for this reason (but not only for this reason) that researchers later came to the point of dating this collection [[E]] before collection B.

All this obliges one at first glance to say that there was a fashioning, not only of the material but also of the collections as wholes, that occurred near the time of writing. In spite of this, the truth of the matter is not thus, since the Bible does not present the two collections as having been created in one generation, at least not from the point of view of the arrangement. Instead, the Bible sees similarity in composition between collections A and B: both of them are literally attributed directly to Solomon. At first glance they seem absolutely dissimilar from each other to such an extent that non-Jewish research for about a hundred years and more judged collection B as earlier and collection A as later, as we have said above. We do not say that the contentions of these non-Jewish researchers have no value at all, but it remains nevertheless an obvious fact that the form and the stylistic arrangement of each of collections A and B seem different in purpose.

What then is the truth? Did the Writings err in attributing these collections to Solomon? Or is there no "error" to be attributed to the Bible but only an *apparent* one, nothing but a first impression? In the linguistic analysis, which we will provide after this introduction, there is, to a great extent, an answer to this question.

But this was not our intention from the beginning of our research. On the contrary, the conclusions put forward here arose as if from themselves, after the analysis. The conclusions were also something of a surprise to the present writer. Indeed our initial intention was to understand clearly the mutual relation between the three collections attributed to Solomon. The fact that the conclusions arose later is no reason not to suggest them. But first we shall present the material of which the conclusions are only a product.

A. EXPRESSIONS UNIQUE TO THE DIFFERENT COLLECTIONS

1. Expressions Unique to Collection A (according to the order of their appearance in the text)

מוסר השכל   1:2, 3

ערמה (in a positive sense)   1:4, 8:5, 8:12, and Job 5:13

מזמה (in a good sense)   1:4, 2:11, 3:21; מזמות 8:12 (but in collection B מזמות is negative; 12:2 מחשב להרע לו בעל־מזמות יקראו 24:8; ואיש מזמות ישׂנא 14:17; איש מזמות ירשיע; and thus also Job 21:27; 10:2, 10:4; and also Jer 11:15, 23:20, 30:24, 51:11; compare also Job 42:2)

לוית־חן   1:9, 4:9

(ל)גרגרתיך   1:9, 3:3, 3:22, 6:21

ענקים   1:9

מזרה (חרשׁת)   1:17

בראשׁ המיה   1:21

[[248]]

לדמים יארבו   1:18 (in B: ארב דם 12:6); and also in Mic 7:2

צפן ~ ארב   1:18

בפתחי שׁערים   1:21

ותפרעו (כל) עצתי   1:25 (פרע with the meaning 'to leave off'; also 4:15, 8:33)

פחד ~ איד   1:26   (compare also 1:27 בבא כשׁאה פחדכם, where שׁאה stands in place of איד)

משׁובה (with the meaning of 'misbehaving')   1:32 (also thus in Jer 2:19)

יאתה   1:27 (ואידכם כסופה יאתה; compare Job 3:25; Job 37:23 is not related to this)

צוקה   1:27 (also Isa 30:6)

שׁחר את (ישׁחרנני)   1:28, 8:17 (in a positive sense, and thus Isa 26:9 and Hos 5:15 similar to the matter in Proverbs)

אל־תבא 1:10 לא־אבו (לעצתי) 1:30, לא־יאבה 6:35,

ישׁכן בטח   1:33 (but see שׁכן ארץ in list B below)

שׁאנן   1:33

ככסף . . . כמטמונים   2:4

דעת אלהים ~ יראת ה׳   2:5 (it is found thus throughout all the Scriptures, but in Hos 6:6 it is only דעת אלהים)

דעת קדשׁים ~ יראת ה׳   9:10 (דעת קדשׁים alone occurs again in Prov 30:3, but the concept itself as a noun and a verb is found elsewhere a great deal; compare Hos 4:6 or Jer 22:16)

מעגל(ות)   2:9, 2:15, 2:18, 4:26, 5:6, 5:21

מעגלי ישׁר   4:11 (compare Ps 23:3)

רפאים . . . שׁאול (מות ~ רפאים)   2:18, 9:18

ארח(ות) צדיקים   2:20, 4:18 (compare ארח in list B below)

מצוה ~ תורה   3:1, 6:23 (in accord with Exod 24:12, Josh 22:5, and 2 Kgs 17:37)

שׁקוי ~ רפאות
עצמותיך ~ שׁרך   } 3:8 (שׁקוי Hos 2:7 and Ps 102:10)

יפיק תבונה   3:13

חפצים . . . פנינים . . . (לא) ישׁוו   3:15, 8:11 (in Job 28:16–19 there is the subject, but not the verb שׁוה)

שׁמים ~ שׁחקים   3:19–20 (but there is Deut 33:26 and elsewhere)

ילזו ילוזו   3:21, 4:21

(רשׁעים) שׁאת   3:25

כסלך   3:26

יליץ   3:34

מרים קלון   3:35 (also compare 14:29 in collection B: מרים אולת)

יתמך־דברי   4:4

סלסלה   4:8 (unique in Scripture; in *Lamentations Rabba* 81:4 the sages asked the maid of Rabbi to explain the word's true meaning and she said that in Arabic the comb is called *mesalselah*). [[Compare Talmud Bavli *Roš Haššana* 26b]]

תמגנך   4:9

תאשׁר   4:14

[[249]]

שׁטה (ישׁט)   4:15, 7:25 (the verb occurs elsewhere only in the Pentateuch, Num 5:12, in a context similar to Prov 7:25)

תוצאות חיים   4:23

עקשׁות פה   4:24, 6:12 (and nowhere else)

לזות שׁפתים   4:24 (only here)

פלס   4:26, 5:6, 5:21 (with a similar content, Isa 26:7)

בליעל ~ אדם   6:12 (A Canaanism? The usual expression is son of, sons of, or man of בליעל. Only in the language of the sages [[in Mishnaic Hebrew]] is the expression used with אדם. Compare אדני שׁדה. In Canaanite-Sidonian the plural of אדם is אדמם = אדמים. בליעל in essence is a Babylonianism, the translation of [*erṣet*] *lā târi* '[the land] of no return,' a

name for Sheol. בליעל(איש־)אדם means he is a man deserving Sheol. Compare 2 Sam 22:5. This is apparently the meaning in Ps 41:9)

בשׂרך ושאָרך   5:11 (this combination occurs in Leviticus in a similar meaning)

מורי מלמדי   5:13

קהל ועדה   5:14 (compare 14:5, and see עדה with the verb קהל in Exod 35:1 and especially in Numbers in several places, including 1:18, 16:19, and elsewhere)

בארך ~ בורך   5:15

פלגי מים ~ מעין   5:16

אילת אהבים ויעלת־חן   5:19

אמרי־פיך   4:5, 5:7, 6:2, 7:24, 8:8 (outside Proverbs this occurs only one time in Deuteronomy, twice in Job, and twice in Psalms)

התרפס   6:3 (the root is also in Ps 68:31, but in a different meaning, apparently)

רהב   6:3 (in the *Qal* also in Isa 3:5 with a different content and apparently also with another meaning)

אשׁנבי   7:6 (only elsewhere in Judg 5:28)

נפתי ~ רבדתי   7:16 (also מרבדים, only in collection A and in the song on the "woman of valor")

חטבות אטון מצרים   7:16

מר אהלים וקנמון   7:17

(התעלס) עלס   7:18 (and nowhere else)

יום כסא   7:20

עכס   7:22   (elsewhere only in Isa 3:18, as an ornament, עכסים)

חדרי מות   7:27

בית נתיבות   8:2

נגידים   ('fine, noble language')   8:6

מפתח שפתי   8:6 (compare 31:26 פיה פתחה בחכמה)

נפתל ועקש   8:8

גאה וגאון   8:13

עצה ותושיה   8:14 (as a comparison see also Isa 28:29)

נסכתי   8:23

ארץ וחוצות   8:26 (Lam 2:21)

מעינות ~ תהומות   8:24

[[250]]

חוללתי   8:25 (compare Isa 66:8, 51:2; Deut 32:18; and Job 15:7)

גבעות ~ הרים   8:25

אמון   8:30

מרמי קרת (על־גפי)   9:3, 9:14 (גפי is unique; [[קרת]] only elsewhere in 8:3, 9:14, [[11:11]], and Job 29:7)

פתיות   9:13 (not found elsewhere)

Synonymous Expressions in Two Parts of the Verse

נתיבה ~ מעגלה ~ מעגל ~ ארח

מולל ~ דבר ~ אמר (with nothing else)

כל שׁפטי ארץ ~ שׂרים ונדיבים (Ps 148:11)

פתאום ~ פתע (Num 6:9)

שואה ~ פחד

7:9 בערב יום באישון לילה ואפלה ~ בנשף

1:3, 2:9 צדק משפט ומישרים

קצין שטר ומשל

1:2, 1:7 (there is also חכמה ומוסר ובינה . . . אמת קנה in 23:23) חכמה ומוסר

1:4 דעת ומזמה

1:6 משל ומליצה

3:2 ארך ימים ושנות חיים ושלום

2. Expressions Unique to Collection B (in alphabetical order)

אבוס   15:17

אוטם   17:28

אוזל   20:14

אויל שפתים   10:8, 10:10

אונים (in the sense of 'evil ones')   11:7

אך־למחסור   11:24, 14:23, 21:5, 22:16

אש צרבת   16:27

אכף פיהו   16:26

יאנה   12:21

אץ ברגליו   19:2

ארח ישרים   15:19

ארגיעה   12:19

מבאיש (from ביש)   13:5

בן מביש   10:5, 17:2, 19:26

בוטה   12:18

גהה   17:22

גרם   17:22

דרך אויל   12:15

דרך בוגדים   13:15

דרך לא טוב   16:29

דרך עקש   22:5

דרך עצל   15:19

דרך רשע   15:9

דברי פי איש (אמרי פי)   18:4

הוה   10:3, 11:6

הפכפך   21:8

התגלע (ריב)   17:14, 18:1, 20:3 (no other parallels); special use of התפעל: מתכבד 12:9; מתעשר 14:16 מתעבד; 18:8 מתלהמים; 13:7; מתרושש 13:7

זמה   10:23, 21:27, 24:9

חדרי בטן   18:8, 20:27, 20:30 (found also in 26:22, but the ⟦251⟧ saying is equivalent to 18:8)

חנף   11:9

חצץ   20:17

יחפיר (from חפר)   13:5

חיי בשרים   14:30

טמן ידו בצלחת   19:24

יד חרוצים   10:4, 12:24

יד ליד   11:21, 16:5 (no other parallels)

יש (at the beginning of a saying)   11:24, 12:18, 13:6, 13:23, 14:12, 16:25, 18:24, 20:15 (the usage in collection A differs from this, as does its usage in two other passages in this collection: 23:18 and 24:14; compare also Num 9:20–21; Ezra 10:44; Neh 5:2; Eccl 1:10, 2:21, and 7:15)

יורא   11:25

כסה   12:16, 12:23

ילבט   10:8, 10:10

לקח מצות   10:8

מקור חיים   10:11, 13:14, 14:27, 16:22

מזמות (in a negative sense)   12:2, 12:17, 24:8

מחתה   10:14–15, 10:29, 13:3, 14:28, 18:7, 21:15

מקשי מות   13:14

מגורה   10:24

מלקוש   16:15

מצרף   17:3

מערכי לב   16:1

משכת חדק   15:19 (Mic 7:4)

מצה   13:10 . . .

נרגן   16:28, 18:8

ניר   13:23

נר (used of 'bad ones') = אור (used of 'righteous ones')   13:9

סלף   11:3, 15:4; סלף   13:6, 19:3, 21:12, 22:12 (aside from this there is Exod 23:8, Deut 16:19, and Job 12:19)

עצב (toil)   14:23

עצבת לב   15:13

עצה עינו   16:30

ערום ('wise one')   12:16, 12:23, 13:16, 14:8, 14:15, 14:18, 22:3, 27:12 (compare Job 5:12 and 15:5)

פלס   16:11

פתה שפתים   20:19

צנים פחים   22:5

קר רוח   17:27

קריה   11:10

קרץ שפתיו   16:30

רוח נכאה [[correcting Grintz's misprint]]   15:13 . . .

רמיה ('laziness')   12:27

ירוע (from רעע)   13:20

שוחה עמוקה   22:14, 23:27

שחר טוב   11:27

תוגה   17:21

תחלת   10:28, 11:7, 13:12

3. Expressions Unique to Collections C and D

קשט   22:21 (elsewhere only in Ps 60:6)
תאלף   22:25
לע   23:2 (only here)
חכללות עינים   23:29 (in the good sense see Gen 49[[:12]])
חבל   23:34 (only here)
ראמות   24:7 (apparently not with this meaning in Job 28:18 and Ezek 27:16; and, if so, then it is unique)
פיד   24:22 (also several times in Job)
[[252]]

4. Expressions Unique to Collection E

הגו   25:4
אפניו   25:11
חלי כתם   25:12
שן רעה   25:19
דליו   26:7
מרגמה   26:8 (unique in Scripture)
מתלהלה   26:18 (unique)
משאון   26:26 (unique)
דכיו (from דך)   26:28 (unique)
נעתרות   27:6 (unique)
סגריר   27:15 (unique)
נשתוה   27:15 (a *Nithpael*—no others exist [[in Proverbs]])
נשך ... תרבית   28:8 (elsewhere only in Lev 25:36 and more recently four times in Ezekiel)
מנון   29:21 (unique)
מטר סוחף   28:3
מכתש   27:22; in the metaphorical meaning only in Judg 15:19
ריפות   27:22 (unique)
עֱלי   27:22 (unique)
נזר   27:24
נערות, עתודים, כבשים)   27:26–27)

B.   SHARED EXPRESSIONS

1. Expressions Shared (or Nearly So) by Collection A (chapters 1–9) and Collection B (10:1–22:16)

אגר   6:8 ~ 10:5
אויל   1:7 ~ thirteen instances in collection B

אולת 5:23; in collection B sixteen times (also in collection D at 24:9 and in collection E at 26:4, 26:5, 26:11, 27:22)

איד 1:26, 1:27, 6:15 ~ 17:5 (in another context)

איש חמס 3:31 ~ 16:29 (also in collection E)

 A: איש און 6:12

 B: איש חסד 11:17 (also 20:6); (איש בליעל 16:27; איש אמונים 20:6; איש חמה 15:18; איש רשע 21:29 18:24; איש רעים 21:9; איש מדונים

 C: איש חמות 22:24; איש מחסור 21:17; איש מהיר במלאכתו 22:29

 D: איש עצל 24:30

 E: איש חכם 26:12; איש עשיר 28:11; איש אמונים 28:20; איש רע עין 28:22; איש תוכחות 29:1; 29:13 איש תככים 29:22; איש אף 29:20; איש אץ בדבריו 29:6; איש רע 29:3; איש אוהב חכמה

אישון (used of 'night') 7:9 ~ 20:20 ('dark')

ארב דם לדם 1:11, 1:18 ~ 12:6

דרך ~ ארח 2:8, 2:13, 2:20, 4:14, 4:18, 4:19, 9:15 ~ 12:28, 15:19

ארח(ות) חיים 2:19, 5:6 ~ 15:24

ארח ישרים 2:13 ~ 15:19 ארחות ישר

ארחות משפט 2:8 ~ 17:23

[[253]]

ארח צדקה 8:20 ~ 12:28; only in collection A: ארח(ות) צדיקים 2:20, 4:18; ארח רשעים 4:14; נתיבה / דרך A 1:15, 8:2

דרך איש 5:21 ~ 21:2

דרך רשעים 4:19 ~ 12:26, 15:9

 only in collection A:

  דרך בינה 9:6

  דרך חסידים, טובים 2:8, 20

  דרך חכמה 4:11 (3:17)

  דרך חשך 2:13

  דרכי נעם 3:17

  דרך רע 2:12, 8:13

  דרך רעים 4:14

  דרך חיים 6:23

 only in collection B:

  דרך לא טוב 16:29

  דרך אויל 12:15

  דרך בוגדים 13:15

  דרך עצל 15:19

  דרך השכל 21:16

 synonyms of דרך ~ ארח:

  A: נתיבות 3:17, 8:20

   מעגל(ות) for collection A see list A above [[p. 93]]

  B: מסלת ישרים 16:17

בינה see חכמה

בליעל A: אדם בליעל 6:12; B: איש בליעל 16:27

דעת see synonyms of חכמה

זרה   2:16, 5:3 ~ 22:14 (זרות)

חוץ ~ רחבות   A: 7:12 (about the strange woman) ~ B: 22:13 (about the lazy one)

חדר, חדרי בטן   7:27; B: חדרי בטן 18:8, 20:27, 20:30

חיים

עץ חיים   3:18 ~ 11:30, 13:12, 15:4

ארח חיים   2:19, 5:6 ~ 15:24

A: דרך חיים   6:23; תוצאות חיים 4:23

B: מקור חיים   10:11, 13:14, 14:27, 16:22 (see Ps 36:10)

חָכַם   6:6, 8:33 (present), 9:9, 9:12 (past) ~ 13:20, 19:20, 20:1, 21:11

חכמה   1:7, 2:2, 2:6, 3:13, 3:19, 4:5, 4:7, 4:11, 5:1 ~ 15:33, 18:4, 5:1, 8:1, 8:12

　חכמות   1:20, 9:1

　synonyms of חכמה:

　　בינה   1:2, 7:4 ~ 16:16

　　תבונה   2:6, 3:19 . . . ~ 10:23, 18:2, 21:30

　　מוסר   1:2, 1:7 ~ 15:32, 19:27 (see also combinations)

　　פרע מוסר   8:33 ~ 15:32

　　תוכחה ~ מוסר   A: (B has תוכחת) 3:11 ~ 2:1 (תוכחת ~ מוסר דעת), 15:32

　　תוכחה   1:23, 1:25, 1:30

　　תוכחת   5:12 ~ 12:1, 13:18, 15:31–32

　　לֶקַח   4:2, 7:21 ~ 16:21 (besides Proverbs this occurs in Deut 32:2 and Isa 29:24)

[[254]]

　　יוסיף לקח   1:5, 9:9 ~ 16:21, 16:23

　　ערמה (in the positive meaning)   for collection A see list A above [[p. 92]]; in collection B
　　　　there is a positive meaning for ערום (13:16, 14:15, 14:18) as a noun and also as a verb
　　　　(19:25, 21:11)

　　תושיה   2:7, 3:21, 8:14 ~ 18:1

　　תורה   1:8, 3:1, 4:2 ~ 13:14 (and another ten times); in collection A the law is the law of a
　　　　father (and the teacher?) and a mother; in B the law of the wise one is religious com-
　　　　mandment: 3:1, 6:20, 6:23 ~ 10:8 [[מצוה]], 13:13, 19:15, 19:16

　　מזמה   for collection A (in the positive meaning) see list A [[p. 92]]; for collection B (also
　　　　C) in the negative meaning (12:2, 14:17) see list A above [[pp. 92, 96]]

　　עצה   frequently in A ~ 19:20

　　דעת   frequently in A ~ 19:25, 19:27

　　תחבלות   1:5 (positively) ~ 11:14, 12:5 (positively), 20:18 (among bad ones)

　combinations with חכמה *and* מוסר:

　　קנה בינה, קנה חכמה   4:5, 4:7 ~ 17:16, קנה דעת 18:15

　　עצה ~ תבונה ~ חכמה   21:30

　　תוכחה ~ דעת ~ מוסר   12:1

　　תוכחת ~ מוסר   3:11 ~ 13:18, 15:5, 6:23

　　חסד ואמת   3:3 ~ 14:22, 16:6, 20:28

　　מוסר אב   1:8, 4:1 ~ 13:1, 15:5

　　מוסר ה׳   3:11, only in collection A

　　מצות אב   6:20, only in collection A

　　תורת אם   1:8, 6:20, only in collection A

(B) 10:8 ~ לקחת מצות   8:10 (A) ~ לקחת מוסר

15:32 ~ 8:33   פרע מוסר

13:15 ~ 3:4   מצא חן, חן

3:4 (A)   נתן חן

חסר לב   6:32, 7:7, 9:4, 9:16 ~ 10:13, 10:21, 11:12, 12:11, 15:21, 17:18 (also in collection D at 24:30, but nowhere else)

חרש רעה (singular and plural)   3:29, 6:14 ~ 12:20, 14:22

חרש טוב   14:22

חרש מחשבות און   6:18

(כזבים, ~ שקרים, ~ שקר ~) 19:9, 19:5, 14:25, 14:5, 12:17, 6:19   עד ~ יפיח

יראת ה'   1:7, 2:5 ~ 14:26, 14:27, 15:16, 15:33, 16:6, 19:23, 22:4

יקר מפנינים   3:15, 8:11 (better than) ~ 20:15

(ויכוכו מחשבותיך) 16:3 ~ 4:26   יכונו דרכיך (כין)

כסיל   in collection A four times; in collection B thirty times; also in collections C (23:9) and E

חרוץ כסף   3:14, 8:10, 8:19 ~ 16:16

נלוז (לוז)   2:15; 3:32 ~ 14:2 (it is also found elsewhere in all of Scripture in Isa 30:12 perhaps in accord with Prov 3:32: נלוז ה' (ותועבת)

לזות שפתים   4:24

[[255]]

מדון   6:14 ~ 16:28, 17:14, 22:10

מד(ו)נים   6:14, 6:19 ~ 10:12, 18:18, 18:19, 19:13 (מדינים), 21:9, 21:19 (מדונים), 23:29, 25:24, 26:21, 27:15 (also in collection E)

מרפא   4:22, 6:15 ~ 12:18, 13:17, 14:30, 15:4, 16:24; 4:22: חיים ~ מרפא; 15:4: מרפא לשון עץ חיים; also in collection E (29:1)

מרים קלון   3:35 ~ 14:29 מרים אולת

נסח   2:22 ~ 15:25

צפן ~ נצר   usually with both of them

לא ינקה   6:29 ~ 11:21, 16:5, 17:5, 19:5, 19:9 (also once in collection E)

העז   7:13 ~ 21:29 (פנים) (בפנים)

תפארת ~ עטרת   4:9 ~ 16:31

תקע ~ ערב   6:1 ~ 17:18

פח   7:23 ~ 22:5

פיק (מצא =)   3:13 (יפיק תבונה) / (יפיק רצון מה') הפיק רצון מה' 8:35 ~ 12:2, 18:22

פרי

מפרי דרכם ישבעו   1:31

מפרי פי איש ישבע טוב   12:14, 13:2

פתי   in collection A seven times; in collection B five times (once in collection E at 27:12; another time at Ezek 45:20; one to three times in Psalms)

צדק   1:3, 2:9, 8:15 ~ 12:17, 16:13 (also in collection E at 25:5)

צדק ומשפט   1:3, 2:9 ~ צדקה ומשפט 8:20, 21:3 (as in collection A, so also in Hos 2:21 and Ps 72:2; in Psalm 119 צדק is used most of the time for 'righteousness'; as in collection B, so also צדקה is frequently used in Genesis, Psalms, and Jeremiah)

צדיק   for synonyms of צדיק see the end of this section

קלון   3:35, 6:33, 9:7 ~ 11:2, 13:18, 18:3

קרץ‎   (with eyes) 6:13 ~ 10:10, (with lips) 16:30
קרת‎   8:3; 9:3; 9:14 ~ 11:11
ראשית‎   1:7 ~ 17:14
רפאים‎   2:18, 9:18 ~ 21:16
שׂכל טוב‎   3:4 ~ 13:15
שכן ארץ‎   2:21 ~ 10:30
שלח מדון‎ 16:28 ~ שלח מדנים‎   6:14, 6:19
תהפכות‎   2:12, 2:14 ~ 10:31, 10:32
תחבלות‎   see under words synonymous to חכמה‎ [[p. 99 above]]
תמים(ים)‎   1:12, 2:21 ~ 11:5, 11:20 (also in collection E)
תועבת ה׳‎   3:32 ~ 11:20, 12:22, 15:8, 15:9, 15:26, 16:5, 17:15, 20:10, 20:23
צדיק(ים) ~ טוב(ים)‎   2:20 ~ (איש מזמה ~ טוב‎ (12:2‎); 13:22, and compare 12:13, 12:14, 11:23
   (צדיקים‎) 11:28, and (תאות צדיקים אך טוב‎), 11:27 (דורש רעה ~ טוב‎), and 11:28
תמימים ~ ישרים‎   2:21 ~ 11:5–6 (in v. 5 also תישר ~ תמים‎)
ישרים ~ צדיקים‎   2:20–21 ~ 11:9–11, 12:5–6
בוגדים ~ רשעים‎   2:22 ~ 11:6 [[actually ישרים‎]]
[[256]]

2. Expressions Shared by Collection A and Collections C–D

6:10–11 ~ 24:33–34:   see list C.4 below [[p. 106]]
All the proverbs [[in collections C–D]] are in direct address, 'I' and 'you' (except perhaps 24:23–26)
חכם ~ (בני‎)   6:6 (ראה . . . וחכם‎) ~ 23:15 (אם חכם לבך‎), 23:19 (וחכם ~ שמע‎)
בני(ם)‎   usual in both collections
אב ~ אם‎   4:3 (in Numbers besides here) ~ 23:22, 23:24–25 (in direct address)
מוסר ~ (ל)דעת‎   4:1 ~ 23:12
דעת ~ תבונה ~ חכמה‎   5:1–2 ~ 24:3–4
בינה ~ מוסר ~ חכמה‎   1:2 (4:1), 4:5, 4:7 (בינה ~ חכמה ~ מוסר‎) ~ 23:23
אחרית‎   5:4 ~ 23:18, 24:14
הון יקר‎   1:13 ~ 24:4
יראת ה׳‎   1:7, 1:29, 2:5 (3:7 [[as a verb]]) ~ 23:17
זונה ~ נכריה‎   2:16, 5:3 [[זרה‎ only]], 5:20, 6:24–25 ~ 23:27
ערב ~ תקע‎   6:1 ~ 22:26 (also in collection B)
מצות‎   1:31 ~ 22:20
לחם‎ ('to eat')   4:17, 9:5 ~ 23:1
מישרים‎   2:10, 8:6 ~ 23:16
שפתים(ות) ~ הגה‎   8:7 ~ 24:2
לץ‎   9:7, 9:8 ~ 24:9
נפת‎   5:3 ~ 24:13
נוה צדיק(ים)‎   3:33 ~ 24:15
ארב‎   7:12 ~ 24:15
כי פתאם יקום אידם/ו‎   6:15 ~ 24:22
תהפוכות‎   2:12 ~ 23:33
שבעה‎   9:1 ~ 24:6

נכח 8:9 ~ 24:26
אשר 4:14 ~ 23:19
Also, compare 6:6–11 with 24:33–34 (see p. 106)

3. Expressions Shared by Collection A and Collection E

מרפא 6:15 = 29:1 ~ 4:22, 6:15 (פתע ישבר ואין מרפא)
לא ינקה 6:29 ~ 28:20 (also in collection B)
מדנים 6:14 ~ 26:21, 27:15 (also in collection B)
(The following examples are listed according to the order of verses in collection E)
6:7 אשר אין לה קצין שטר ומשל ~ 25:15 בארך אפים יפתה קצין
6:27 היחתה איש אש בחקו ~ 25:22 כי גחלים אתה חתה על ראשו
6:28 אם יהלך איש על גחלים ורגליו לא תכוינה ~ 26:21 פחם לגחלים ועצים לאש
8:24, 8:25 באין תהומות חוללתי ('I was created') ~ 25:23 רוח צפון תחולל ('holds back!') גשם
  (לפני גבעות חוללתי)
5:3 כי נפת תתפנה שפתי זרה ~ 27:7 נפש שבעה תבוז נפת
7:23 כמהר צפור אל פח ~ 27:8 כצפור נודדת מקנה
1:26 גם אני באידכם אשחק ~ 27:10 ובית אחיך אל־תבוא ביום אידך
1:12 כיורדי בור ותמימים ('whole ones') ~ 28:10 תמימים ('upright ones') ינחלו טוב
3:33 מארת ה' בבית רשע ~ 28:27 ומעלים עיניו רב מארות
3:13 אשרי אדם מצא חכמה ~ 29:18 ושומר תורה אשריהו

4. Expressions Shared by Collection B and Collections C–D

בעל מזמות 24:8 ~ איש מזמות 12:2, 14:17
טוב עין 22:9 (B) ~ רע עין 23:6 (C); also 28:22 (E)
[[257]]

5. Expressions Shared by Collection B and Collection E

איש with a descriptive noun:
 איש חמה 15:18
 איש אמונים 20:6
 איש בליעל 16:27
 איש חכם 16:14
 איש חמס 16:29
 אשת מדנים 21:19
 אשת חן 11:16
 29:22 (בעל חמה) איש אף
 איש חכם 26:12
 איש רע 29:6
 איש תוכחות 29:1
 איש תככים 29:13
 איש אץ־בדבריו 29:20
 אשת מדנים 25:24

איש מדונים 26:21

(see also [[list B.1]], p. 98 above)

אֵיד (שָׂמֵחַ לְאֵיד) 17:5 ~ (בְּיוֹם אֵידְךָ) 27:10

אָץ 19:2 (and (אָץ בְּרַגְלָיו) ~ (וְאָץ לְהַעֲשִׁיר) 28:20, 29:20 (אִישׁ אָץ בִּדְבָרָיו)

אֶרֶךְ־אַפַּיִם 14:29 (אֶרֶךְ־אַפַּיִם) ~ 25:15 (בְּאֹרֶךְ־אַפַּיִם)

אִוֶּלֶת sixteen times ~ five times

אֱוִיל thirteen times ~ four times

דָּשֵׁן (as praise) 13:4 ~ 28:25

חֶסֶד (in the negative meaning) 14:34 (חֶסֶד לְאֻמִּים) ~ 25:10 (פֶּן יְחַסֶּדְךָ)

חוֹנֵן דַּלִּים 19:17 ~ 28:8

כְּחֹמֶץ 10:26 ~ 25:20

חֹסֶן 15:6 ~ 27:24

חַדְרֵי בֶטֶן in a repeated saying 18:8 = 26:22

כְּסִיל thirty times ~ fourteen times

כָּרָה (שָׁחַת) 26:27 ~ (רָעָה) 16:27

מוֹקֵשׁ 12:13 ~ 29:6

מַשְׂכִּית 18:11 ~ 25:11

מְדָנִים (אִישׁ מְדָנִים) 21:9, 21:19 ~ 25:24 (in a repeated saying [[compare above, p. 102]]); 26:21

מָדוֹן (גֵרָה) 15:18 ~ 28:25, 29:22

נֶזֶם זָהָב (as a comparison) 11:22 ~ 25:12

לֹא יִנָּקֶה 11:21 = 16:5, 17:5, 19:5 ~ 28:20 (also in collection A at 6:29)

נִרְגָּן 16:28, 18:8 ~ 26:20, 26:22

נָדִיב 19:6 ~ 25:7

מִתְעַבֵּר 14:16 ~ 26:17

עָצֵל eight times ~ three times

עִקֵּשׁ ~ נַעֲקָשׁ דְּרָכִים 10:9 ~ 28:6, 28:18

כִּי עָרַב זָר 11:15, 20:16 ~ 27:13

פֶּרַע 13:18, 15:32 (פֹּרֵעַ מוּסָר) ~ 29:18

25:5 וְיִכּוֹן בַּצֶּדֶק כִּסְאוֹ ~ 16:12 כִּי בִצְדָקָה יִכּוֹן כִּסֵּא

צִיר אֱמוּנִים 13:17 ~ צִיר נֶאֱמָן 25:13

רָדַף (רִיקִים) 11:19 (רָעָה), 12:11 (רִיקִים), 15:9 (צְדָקָה), 19:7 (אֹמְרִים) ~ 28:19 (רִיקִים)
[[258]]

רֹעֶה (זוֹנוֹת), 29:3 (זוֹלְלִים) ~ 28:7 (כְּסִילִים) 13:20

אַף ~ הֵשִׁיב חֵמָה 15:1 (יָשִׁיב חֵמָה . . . יַעֲלֶה אָף) ~ 29:8 (יָשִׁיבוּ אָף)

שְׁפַל רוּחַ 16:19 ~ 29:23

תֹּמֵךְ כָּבוֹד 11:16 ~ 29:23

שְׁאוֹל וַאֲבַדּוֹן 15:11 ~ 27:20

(שָׂגָב) (וְנִשְׂגָּב) ~ 29:25 (יְשֻׂגָּב) 18:11

תּוֹכַחַת 12:1, 13:18, 15:31, 15:32 ~ 27:5, 29:15

רָשָׁע ~ צַדִּיק
  B: 10:16, 10:24, 10:25, 11:8, 11:31, 12:12, 14:32, 15:6, (15:9), 17:15, 18:5, 21:12, 21:18
  E: 25:26, 28:1, 29:2, 29:7, 29:16, 29:27, 28:1, 28:12

תְּמִימִים 11:5, 11:20 ~ 28:10

6. Expressions Shared by Collection E and Collection C (opposites)

29:20   חזית איש אץ בדבריו
22:29   חזית איש מהיר במלאכתו

C. REPEATED VERSES

1. Repetitions within Collection B

[[Grintz prints the texts of the repeated verses, but in order to save space reference will be given to the category of repetition listed in chapter 5 above, where I have included the Hebrew text and an English translation.]]

a. Equivalent cases:

   14:12 ~ 16:25 [[1.0]]

b. Almost equivalent:

   1.   10:1 ~ 15:20 [[1.2]]
   2.   16:2 ~ 21:2 [[1.3]]
   3.   19:5 ~ 19:9 [[1.1]]
   4.   10:2 ~ 11:4 [[1.3]]
   5.   19:25 ~ 21:11 [[1.4]]
   6.   21:9 ~ 25:24 [[1.0]]
        21:9 ~ 21:19 [[1.4]]
   7.   13:14 ~ 14:27 [[1.2]]

c.   Closely related verses

   8.   10:4   רש עושה כף רמיה ויד חרוצים תעשיר
        12:24   יד חרוצים תמשל ורמיה תהיה למס
   9.   14:20   גם לרעהו ישנא רש ואהבי עשיר רבים
        19:4   הון יוסיף רעים רבים ודל מרעהו יפרד
   10.   10:6b ~ 10:10b [[2.0]]
[[259]]
   11.   20:10 ~ 20:23 [[3.0]]

d. Opposed

   [[(C) indicated verses that complete the thought within the verse; (O) indicates verses that express opposed concepts]]

   12.   16:18 (C) ~ 18:12 (O) [[2.2]]
   13.   10:15 (O) ~ 18:11 (C) [[2.0]]

14. 10:8 (O) ~ 10:10 (C) [[2.0]]
15. 10:27 (O)   יראת ה׳ תוסיף ימים ושנות רשעים תקצרנה
     19:23 (C)   יראת ה׳ לחיים ושבע ילין בל־יפקד רע
16. 11:13 (O) ~ 20:19 (C) [[2.1]]

Nearly the same:

17. (*a*) 11:14 (O) ~ (*b*) 15:22 (O) [[1.4]]
     (*c*) 20:18   מחשבות בעצה תכון ובתחבלות עשֵׂה מלחמה
18. 11:21 (O) ~ 16:5 (C) [[2.1]]
19. 12:14 (C) ~ 13:2 (O) [[2.1]]
20. 14:31 (O)   עשק דל חרף עשֹהו ומכבדו חנן אביון
     17:5 (C)   לעג לרש חרף עשֹהו שמח לאיד לא ינקה
21. 15:33 (C) ~ 18:12 (O) [[2.0]]
22. 19:12 (O) ~ 20:2 (C) [[2.1]]

Near in sense:

23. 11:15   רע ירוע כי ערב זר ושֹנא תוקעים בטח
     17:18   אדם חסר־לב תוקע כף ערב עֲרֻבה לפני רעהו
     20:16   לקח בגדו כי ערב זר ובעד נכרים חבלהו

2. Repetitions within Collection E

     1. 26:12 ~ 29:20 [[1.3]]
     2. 28:12 ~ 28:28 [[2.1]]

3. Repetitions between Collection B and Collection E

a. Equivalent:

     1. 18:8 ~ 26:22 [[1.0]]
     2. 20:16 ~ 27:13 [[1.0]]
     3. 21:9 ~ 25:24 [[1.0]]
[[260]]
     4. 22:3 (read: נסתר) ~ 27:12 [[1.0]]

b. Almost equivalent:

     5. 19:24 ~ 26:15 [[1.2]]
     6. 12:11 ~ 28:19 [[1.2]] (adaptation of B)
     7. 22:2 ~ 29:13 [[1.4]]
     8. 19:1 ~ 28:6 [[1.2]] (adaptation of B)
     9. 16:12 ~ 25:5 [[2.1]]

10. 22:13 (C) ~ 26:13 [[1.3]] (O) (expansion of the first line of the verse in collection B)
11. 17:3 ~ 27:21 [[2.0]] (simplification)
12. 15:18 (O) ~ 29:22 (C) [[2.1]]
13. 19:13 (O) ~ 27:15 (C) (expansion of 19:13b)
14. 10:9   הולך בתם ילך בטח ומעקש דרכיו יודע
      28:18   הולך תמים יושע ונעקש דרכים יפול באחת
15. 15:18   איש חמה יגרה מדון וארך אפים ישקיט ריב
      28:25   רחב נפש יגרה מדון ובוטח על ה׳ ידשן
      13:4   מתאוה ואין נפשו עצל ונפש חרצים תדשן
16. 18:9 ~ 28:24 [[2.2]]

4. Repetitions between Collection A and Collection D

6:10–11 ~ 24:33–34 [[1.1]]

5. Repetitions between Collections C–D and Collection B

1. *a.* 20:8 ~ 24:6 [[2.1]]
  b. 24:6 ~ 11:14 [[2.0]]]
2. 13:9 ~ 24:20 [[2.0]]
[[261]]
3. 22:14 ~ 23:27 [[2.2]]

6. Repetitions within Collection C

1. 22:28a ~ 23:10a [[2.0]]
2. 23:3 ~ 23:6 [[2.0]]
3. 22:22   . . . אל תגזל דל   23 כי ה׳ יריב ריבם
    23:10   . . . אל תסג גבול עולם   11 כי גאלם חזק הוא יריב את ריבם

CONCLUSIONS

Now that we have arranged the vocabulary, rhetoric, and special features of the collections attributed in their headlines to Solomon according to their similarities and differences, we are able to summarize the results of this comparison and to draw some conclusions.

We can say that each collection has its own special vocabulary. In spite of this, each collection has a commonality with one or more other collections. But this commonality is not in its essence equivalent in every instance, and it is not always to be attributed to the same explanation.

First, there exists a certain recognizable connection between collections A and C–D. This connection may be explained by their common background: the school. From this comes their common use of second-person address, the term *my son*, mention of father and mother, combinations of terms connected with wisdom (wisdom–understanding–knowledge, wisdom–discipline–understanding), warnings about whores and "strange" women, making agreements and standing

surety, speaking with directness, [[giving]] advice, the end result of [[one's]] actions, and the guarding of wealth (which is called "dear").

One admonition is repeated in collections A and D (6:10–11 ~ 24:33–34). It is amazing that collection C has the recurring warning against excessive drinking of wine (23:20–21, 23:29–35), even though this subject is completely absent in collection A. Is this due to a difference in historical perspective? Or does this difference reveal a later age with more influence from outside? This is not an empty question since the warning against drinking is the essence of the warning of Lemuel[['s mother]] to the king (31:1–9).

More important than this is what is revealed to us by a comparison of the first two collections. In all its characteristics collection B is different from collection A. Collection B is an aggregation of sayings, while collection A seems to be an aggregation of reproaches and sermons. In collection A the teacher or the father addresses the young man; in collection B the address is to the adult man. In collection A the strange woman seduces the young man and her seduction is the basic obstacle [[262]] for the listener. The strange woman is an important subject in the preaching of wisdom (chapter 2) and in the commands of the father, mother (6:20–35), and teacher (chapter 7), who warn repeatedly about her seduction. In contrast to this, in collection B the talk is about married adult men and women and about different kinds of women—both good (18:22) and bad (19:13), women endowed with grace (11:16) or whose reason has left them (11:22), women of valor (12:4), wise or foolish women (14:1), and irascible women (21:19). The subject in collection B is always about married women in the home.

In collection A peace offerings are mentioned by the woman as a personal vow (7:14). But in collection B the preference for righteousness over sacrifice is stressed (21:3, 27), as it is in prophecy and the Book of Psalms. In collection A there is nothing about the ruler ("by me kings rule" in 8:15 is only a boast in the mouth of Wisdom personified as a woman). In collection B a relation to the king is expressed and the king is evaluated according to his deeds. In collection A there is no real mention of drinking wine ("drink the wine that I have mixed" in 9:5 is rhetoric in the mouth of Wisdom—wine is mentioned only in her praise). In collection B the wine-drinker is condemned (20:1). In collection A "law" and "command" come from the father and mother, but in collection B they are indefinite. The preaching in collection A is above all an admonition to walk in the way of Wisdom; in collection B it is an admonition to walk in the ways of righteousness. In collection A Wisdom personified as a woman is like a cosmic element before creation, and she preaches and speaks on the "top of the walls" like one who admonishes; in collection B wisdom is an object that a man aspires to attain.

Let us examine the description of society given in the Solomonic collections. The society of collection A is the society of the great—people from good families. In A there are schools and teachers who disseminate law, rhetoric, and riddles. The people wear all kinds of jewelry, "a garland of grace," "a crown" for their heads, and "necklaces" for their necks. There is commerce and buying, and there is frequent mention of the city, which has plazas and squares. Husbands go out for weeks at a time to distant places to guide their businesses, and they return only for festivals. Governing is by kings, rulers, nobles, princes, and chiefs, and [[even]] by an officer, a policeman, and a governor.

In collection A there is talk of the village and of the top of the walls ("on the backs of the heights of the village"), about city gates and entrances. People talk about a table of delicacies

on which they mix wine, about vows of peace offerings, about carpets and padded beds in the house, and about serving girls who go forth on errands. People sprinkle their beds with all kinds of spices, myrrh, aloes, and cinnamon, which are brought from the ends of the earth. As is frequent in a life of luxury, there are seductive women at the corners. Dissipated boys, because of the great idleness they enjoy, form gangs of thugs, rob passing merchants, and divide the spoils among themselves. In sum, this is a society of exalted status, one of kings and princes in a magnificent and rich city.

We see the opposite of this situation in collection B. Here we find ourselves among a people working and loving the land. The man and his sons (10:5) cultivate the soil (12:11). There are some people who have a slave to help (12:9). The farmer has bullocks and an ox (14:4). He stores his produce (15:6), and when a year of drought comes, he sells some of his grain to others (11:26). The house is passed from father to son (19:14). Proverbs are created out of experience with creation and agriculture: clouds and dew (16:15; 19:12), overgrown fields (15:19), and damming up water (17:14). There is a warning against false weights, grain measures, and scales ⟦263⟧ (20:10, 23), which must have been a regular concern in any business transactions. There is a graphic image about local buying: "It's bad, really bad, the buyer says, but when he goes away, then he boasts" (20:14). About large-scale commerce there is no talk at all.

There also exists some sort of difference in linguistic usages and meanings. In collections B and E the word *correction* [תוכחת] is always used, whereas in collection A תוכחה is used in all but one instance, which uses תוכחת. In collection A מזמה is positive ('knowledge and insight'); in collection B it is negative (see list A above ⟦p. 92⟧). Collection A usually employs צדק or צדק ומשפט; collection B has צדקה ומשפט.

In spite of all this—as we saw in the synoptic table—there is a great commonality in language, rhetoric, and word combinations, although in collection B synonymous words are paralleled in the two parts of the verse, while in collection A the idea is continued into the second part of the verse and not merely repeated. There is a great difference in the ways wisdom is spoken about: understanding, insight, and acquiring understanding appear in collection A, while collection B refers to the concepts of acquiring knowledge, being simple or a fool or a foolish one, having good sense, getting understanding (increasing understanding), steersmanship, lacking sense, and advising. Collections A and B also differ in the ways they speak of discipline: path(s) of judgment, paths of righteousness, a path of righteous ones, paths of uprightness (upright ones), the ways of a man, the ways of bad ones, laws, commands, discipline, reproof, loving-kindness and truth, perversity, badness, being an abomination to the Lord, fearing the Lord, and the phrase *he will not be found innocent*. There is also an emphasis on life in rhetorical combinations (tree of life, path of life) and in "rich" comparisons (silver, gold, crown, beauty, more expensive than corals).

These usages are not according to the early language; compare Exod 21:14: "And if a man attacks his fellow to kill him with craft [ערמה]. . . ." In collection A "cunning" has a positive meaning, which is also true in collection B with regard to the word *cunning one* (in the meaning of one who keeps his eyes open) and in the verb *to get cunning*. In sum, the common rhetoric of collections A and B is greater than the linguistic distinctiveness of each collection by itself.

In spite of the great similarity between collections B and A, there remains an absence of connection between collections A and E. The comparison between collections B and E is clear.

Both of them are collections of sayings, and in each collection there is a similar division into two parts, one of oppositional sayings (10–15; 28–29) and one of sayings that complete themselves or are synonymous (most of 16–22; most of 25–27). The sayings in both collections are almost always impersonal.

There are also special words found with certain meanings only in collections B and E. Only in these two collections does חסד appear with a negative meaning (14:34: "and חסד to the people is sin"; 25:10: "lest one who hears you shame you"). Also common to both collections is the form תוכחת and idioms like grumbler, depths of the stomach, letting loose of discipline, one who hastens, one who keeps company (in the sense of someone habitually consorting with fools and gluttons), running after, one who pities poor ones, patience, being low of spirit, a man of anger (also: one habituated to anger), a worthless person or man, returning anger (חמה or אף), causing strife, a faithful messenger (נאמן or איש אמונות), laying hold of, a secret conversation, the verb *to be safely inaccessible* [השגב], to dig, the words *storehouse, trap, imagination*, the comparisons for "a ring of gold," vinegar, the rhetorical construction "in righteousness his throne is established," etc.

Above all, it must be noted that the many repeated sayings, whether both parts are repeated or only half of them (about eighteen in number), are in these two collections alone. As in the earlier instances, so in this one, more of collection E is shared with collection B than what is distinctive in it. Some examples in collection E show that there is a reworking of verses found in collection B, either for the sake of simplicity or for the need to produce a precise parallelism. For example, collection B has 19:1: "Better is a poor one going in his integrity than one crooked of lips, he being a fool"—while collection E has [[264]] 28:6: "Better is a poor one going in his integrity than one crooked of ways, he being rich." Similar to this is collection B's 12:11: "One who works his land will have enough bread, and one who chases after empty things lacks sense"—as opposed to collection E's 28:19: "One who works his land will have enough bread, and one who chases after empty things will have enough poverty." In collection B there is maintained in the second line of 19:13 the basic saying; in 27:15 in collection E the basic saying is expanded to a complete verse.

The society in collection E is also somewhat like the society in collection B. The wise one urges the people to worry about sheep and flocks, for from them come both clothing and the price of a field, goat's milk, and the subsistence necessary for all of the people in the household (27:23–27). The one who works the land is praised; he has enough bread (28:19). There is no use in being hasty to try to get rich (28:20). In collection E most of the images are about natural sights, perhaps even more so than in collection B. One hears about clouds, wind, and rain (25:14), the cold of snow on a day of harvest (25:13), the north wind (25:23), cold water (25:25), a muddied spring and a ruined source of water (25:26), a continuous dripping, a stormy day (27:15), the use of iron tools (27:17), and a mortar and pestle (27:22). Bread and water are the basics of life, and when one encounters an enemy, one ought to give bread and water as one would to a friend (25:21). There are some instances of proverbs about honey (25:16, 27). And there are others from nature about a bird and a sparrow (26:2, 27:8), a horse and an ass (26:3), a dog (26:11), and a stone and sand (27:3).

In spite of all of this, there exists a difference in the way in which the half-verse is composed. The verse in collection B is always made of two parts. In collection E it is in most cases composed

of two parts, but never of only one element. It sometimes is tripartite (e.g., 25:8 and 25:20) and occasionally it has even four (25:9–10) or five parts (25:21–22, 26:18–19). In collection B the verses are all either synonymous (complementary) or oppositional in their two parts, but that is not the case in collection E.

There are instances in collection E in which a warning appears in the first verse, and then justifications of it are given in the two following verses (25:8–10). There are instances in which two proverbs appear in the first two verses, and the actual subject of the proverb appears only in the third verse (25:20–22). And there are instances in which there are two warnings in the first verse, and two justifications in the final verse (25:9–10). Elsewhere, the two parts of the first verse are the proverbial image, and the two parts of the second verse contain the thing compared (25:4–5). There is one occasion of three separate sayings—among which there is an affinity—being brought together into one string (27:9–10). This situation is not usually found in collection B, whose similarities with collection E in this regard are few.

There are in collection E whole sections that are concerned only with one subject. Prov 27:23–27 is interested in sheep, 26:3–12 in a fool, 26:13–16 in a sluggard, 26:17–19 in one who is mad, 26:20–23 in the grumbler, 26:24–28 in the hater, 25:2–7 in the king, 25:8–15 in cases of law and dispute, etc. And more than in collection B, collection E usually has a two-part verse that completes its thought and does not repeat it with synonyms in the second half.

The explanation of this state of affairs is that the rhetorical reworking is different in collection E than in collection B, in spite of the fact that in both of them the basic element is the saying. However, the linguistic and rhetorical backgrounds of both are very close.

In spite of all this, there remain the few parallels between collections A and E. If we may give our opinion on the matter, this lack of similarity is most surprising since there exists a great amount of linguistic commonality between collections A and B ⟦265⟧, and collection B is similar in most of its traits and its language to collection E, as we have seen.

The opinion emerges, after all that has been said above, that if there is any comparison to be made, it is between collections B and E. But if, among all the parallels in collections E and A, we were to remove from consideration those idioms that are repeated in collection B ("he will not be found innocent," strifes, disaster, simple, cunning), it appears that almost nothing remains to compare. We are left with the individual words קצין 'officer', not in reference to the life of ants, but as a synonym for an officer [שׁוטר], and משׁל 'he rules', (in an ethical saying about patience). The same thing can be said about similar words: coals (26:21, 6:28), honeycomb (27:7, 5:3), bird, calamity, and pure ones. All of these words appear in completely different—even opposite contexts ("Like a bird wandering from its nest, thus is a man wandering from his place," 27:8—but compare "As a bird hastens to a trap, the seduced young man to the strange woman," 7:23).

In all this lack of similarity there is only one verse that on first glance has a close relationship: 29:18: "And one who keeps the law, happy is he," in contrast to 3:13: "Happy is a man who finds wisdom." But the emphasis in the example from collection E is law, while the example from collection A emphasizes wisdom. Also, "law" is parallel to "prophecy" in 29:18 ("Without prophecy a people is let loose")—thus, it is really *the* law in a general sense. There remains, in fact, only half of one verse that is equivalent ("suddenly he will be shattered, and there is no one to cure," 6:15b ~ 29:1b), and that is little.

What is the conclusion that arises from all of this? It appears clear that:

1. There exists strong linguistic contact between collections . . .
   a. A and B
   b. A and C
   c. B and E (but in a completely different linguistic domain)
2. There is no (or almost no) linguistic contact between collections . . .
   a. A and E
   b. B and C(–D)
   c. E and C(–D)

Thus we propose the following conclusions:

3a. *Collections B and E have a common background*. The similarity or equivalence of language, content, etc., in regard to the repetition of whole and partial verses shows that both collections were formed from the same material. But collection B has one type of arrangement—artistic and polished—and collection E has another type of arrangement—with many free verses and sections.

3b. *Collection A knows collection B (but it does not know collection E)*. The explanation for this is that collection A was composed at the same time as collection B. This equivalence in language shows that we are dealing here with language and style that was acceptable within—or nearly within—a single generation. It is certain that this date was before the main part of collection E was copied and published (for the nearness of collections A and B in language and style, see list B.1 above [[pp. 97–101]]).

3c. *Collection C knows collection A, or both of them were created in a similar milieu—the school*. However, while collection A is a creation finished and polished to an extraordinary extent, collection C is an anthology—according to what is said explicitly in the headline, and according to the word מזמות 'deceit, insight', which is similar to its usage in collection B but not collection A. The proverbs of collection C were drawn from different sources, including the language of preaching and the language of sayings. Note, for example, that collection C's 24:20 ("the light of bad ones will be put out") occurred earlier in collection B at 13:9.

Also, from the point of view of their contents [[266]] there is a change between collections A and E. Collection E stands between collections A and B (more precisely, it stands after both of them). Its material comes from both collections and from words of wise ones that did not appear in either of them, but in its essence collection E is written for schools.

3d. *Collection A does not know collection E* (in contrast to the relationship of collections A and B noted in 3b above). The only explanation for this is as follows. Although collection E emerged from, or was founded on, the same material from which collection B was shaped, collection C was hidden [גנוז] in some manner and had no influence. But when collection E was published, collections A and B were already combined—and included appendix C. Already scholars in the previous generation noted that, if this were not the case, it had to have been the second editor (see below) who attached collection E to this grouping, putting it before collection C, and adding it directly to the earlier "proverbs of Solomon." We know this because, in the days of the Second Temple, the Septuagint translation combined all of the collections attributed to Solomon together and erased all traces of other proverb-makers except Solomon (see n. 3 above).

But the clear fact, which we stressed above, that collection E did not absorb anything from the language of collections A and C, proves that collection E as a whole was published in a later time, after collection C was combined [[with collections A and B]]. Thus collection E has retained its original purity from the linguistic point of view. We do not know what its editors—"the men of Hezekiah"—did to it. It is possible that they structured its sayings and combination of sayings into sections, differently from the structuring in collection B. But the material from which they built is the original material, and from this we have the witness of language for the commonality between collections B and E.

3e. In contrast to this, *the material in collection B—an artful reworking and expansion of individual sayings into verses with two parallel parts—was arranged close to the time of collection A's publication* (see 3b above). In other words, either collection A knew the treasury of sayings that we call collection B, or whoever arranged collection A also arranged collection B. Collection B is arranged in an artful and exact way, similar to the magnificent arrangement of collection A. But collection B was not reworked linguistically in accord with collection A; otherwise we would not have the great similarity between collections B and E and the absence of such similarity between collections A and E. And the whole, parallel verses in collections B and E would not have remained strewn around in the entire book. Furthermore, the material of collection B is situated in village life, which provides an older setting than the setting of collection A—the life of a noisy city. Along with this, there is something of the spirit of collection A in collection B, for example, the many sayings found in collection B praising wisdom (especially chaps. 14–17 but also elsewhere in collection B.) Although the first sections of collection B speak basically about the righteous one and the bad one, the first saying, "A wise son makes a father glad, but a foolish son is a sorrow to his mother" (10:1), has apparently been placed here intentionally in order to connect collection B to collection A.

3f. [[*The information given in the headlines supports the arguments based on linguistic data.*]] Our conclusions so far are based only on the linguistic material without any relation to the headlines. From that alone we have learned that collections A and B were published close together in time; to them collection C was appended after some time, and only later was collection E publicly published. This conclusion is entirely in accord with the headlines in the book. Collections A, B, and E are designated as "Proverbs of Solomon." But while collections A and B are near to each other, collection E is distant from them, and separated from them by [[267]] collections C ("words of wise ones") and D ("these also are of wise ones"). Only in collection E is it said that "the men of King Hezekiah of Judah copied" the proverbs of Solomon (25:1).

The only difference between our conclusions and what can be seen from the headlines is that the headlines precisely identify the time of each collection's publication. Indeed, if we consider the contents of collection A, we can conclude—without being in need of the headline—that there is no other time that accords socially and perhaps linguistically with the stated riches and magnificence than Solomon's time. Contrast this with all that various people (who do not know how to distinguish between the different styles of Hebrew, that magnificent classical language, which is chronologically close to the language of ancients) have said about this.[8]

---

8. Albright speaks of the linguistic closeness of collection A to the language of Ugarit in the article mentioned in n. 4 above.

We would be tempted to conclude the same thing with regard to collection B, which is linguistically close to collection A. And what we could only have guessed at is said explicitly in the book. However, there would have been no way available to us to guess the time of collection E's publication, without the headline at the beginning of chapter 25.

Now that we have drawn these conclusions without resorting to headlines, and have adjusted these conclusions to the evidence from the headlines, we have an obligation to determine with certainty whether the headlines do in fact transmit historical truth. And this seems to be the case. Collections A, B, and E all came from the pen of one creator, or from the pens of several creators working under a common guidance in the same generation (or generations). But collections A and B were published immediately, near their time of composition, in such a manner that they influenced one another. But it seems as if collection E was hidden [נגנז] until the "men of Hezekiah" came and brought it to light.

3g. There still remains one question in regard to all of these matters: *what about the headline at the beginning of the book?* Is this intended to refer only to collection A, or perhaps is it intended to refer to the whole book? The tendency in previous generations was to accept the second possibility and to say that this opening, which includes collection A, is intended for the whole. But the argument that earlier scholars based on the use of the word *proverbs* (the essence of which is that proverbs were regarded as sayings and not as admonitions, as in collection A) is certainly not correct. The definition of the word *proverb* indicates a pictorial comparison with pictorial language. The linguistic commonality between the first two collections is clear, as has been said, and both of them were created in accordance with a unified linguistic design, within a short time, but in a different societal background.

The explanation is that collection A was initially created separately from collection B—as an isolated unit—and never served as an introduction [[to the entire book]]. Its headline existed from the beginning, when the collection stood alone. Thus the opening at the beginning of the book first served collection A alone, and not the rest of the book, as now appears at first glance. We learn from the language of the opening that the work is intended for the simple one and the young man ("to give to simple ones cunning, and to a lad knowledge and insight [מזמה]"—i.e., wisdom—to enable them "to understand a proverb and a saying, the words of the wise and their riddles." This discussion for the youth is found throughout the whole of collection A (see [[268]] above), the essence of which is the words of the wise. To this one must add what we have already adduced above, namely, the very fact that at the beginning of chapter 10 there is again a new headline "of Solomon" also shows that the headline of 1:1 refers only to collection A.

3h. *We therefore conclude from its subject matter that the first book, collection A, comes from the time stated in 1:1.* We saw above that the society described in collection A is the society of the large and rich city, in which merchants, singers, and human pleasures are numerous. But if we are asked which time in biblical history is most fitting for a collection like this, it is difficult to say that we have a time period other than that inscribed at the beginning of the book—the days of Solomon.[9]

---

9. Collection A is connected to the Song of Songs by their common description of the plenty, wealth, and scenes of city life associated with the court of the monarchy. In the Song of Songs spices are to be found in plenty (4:6, 5:3–14, 6:2), and silver, gold (3:10, 8:9), and towers of ivory are recurring images. In Proverbs there is the

The city is noisy and rich, but still this is not the city of the prophets: there is no oppressor of the poor who is heard in its midst, there is no cry of the poor and no robbery of a poor worker, and there is no subversion of judgment. In this there is great similarity to collection B, as well as to collection E. Even collection B, in spite of the fact that it comes from a different societal domain, shows that the working of the land is still entirely successful. And there is still no memory of the subjugation of the many at the hands of the few or of a rule of violence or of exclusion from inheritance, as in the days of Amos.

But it is quite possible that this situation comes to us from the relationship to wisdom. Recent studies about the antiquity of "Wisdom" personified as a woman in general agree about the lateness in other cultures of the personification of human wisdom and beliefs. But after all that has been said about the matter, there is in this book a distinctiveness in its special relation to "Wisdom."

It is possible to say that all of collection A is basically a song in praise of Wisdom. The goal of the collection, as is said at the beginning of the book, is "to know wisdom, understanding, discipline, being smart, . . . [and] to give cunning," and accordingly the teacher gives repeated warnings (chapter 2). Out of this comes the song in praise of Wisdom (3:13–20: "Happy is the man who finds wisdom," v. 13; everything is created through wisdom, vv. 19–20), and on the basis of wisdom the father gives his warnings in chapter 4. The warning about a strange woman comes from the strength of "Wisdom" (chapter 5) and, finally (chapters 8–9), Wisdom herself speaks. All of this indoctrination about Wisdom accords with what is known to us about the unique period of Solomon. Furthermore, it has no peer or example [[269]] in any other collection of sayings, not even in ancient Egypt, where collections of ethical sayings were never lacking. The many things said on this subject in 1 Kings, especially 5:9–14, are enough to serve as a testimony to the distinctiveness in collection A. The question still remains, does not this business about Wisdom as a preexisting being derive from the innovation of this generation?

The end of the matter, if we return to where we started, is that we have an obligation to judge the headlines according to their face value and to see the collections attributed to Solomon as collections that were created in his time. The canonical order of the book is, as it appears, also the historical order. The first edition of the book contained the first two collections attributed to Solomon and an appendix of "words of wise ones," collection C. In a second edition, people added other proverbs of wise ones: collections D and E and, as it appears, also the rest of the appendixes. This second and last edition was made, apparently, by the "men of Hezekiah."

---

image of "the doe of love and antelope of grace" (5:19). In the Song of Songs people are told to swear an oath "by gazelles or antelopes of the field" (3:5 and elsewhere). There are images about "an antelope and a young stag" (2:9 and elsewhere). There are other similarities in language (רבדתי Prov 7:16 ~ רפד Song 2:5, נזלים in Prov 5:15 and Song 4:15, and kinds of spices, etc.). The setting of the Song of Songs is ~ the time of Solomon, at least its earliest form comes from this period (see M. H. Segel, "שיר השירים," *Tarbiz* 8 [1938–39] 121–36, and idem, "The Song of Songs," *Vetus Testamentum* 12 [1962] 470–90). Unlike the language of the Book of Proverbs, the language of the Song of Songs is not connected with the archaic literary language that Israel inherited from antiquity. In fact, it is essentially rooted in contemporary, popular language (perhaps השירים [[in its title]] means 'of the singers'?).

There are many ancient attestations to the imagery and literary symbols of the Song of Songs, both from [[within Israel]] before Solomon's time and from outside Israel; for example: "If you find my beloved, what will you say to him?" (5:8); "What is your beloved more than another beloved?" (5:9); "My beloved is radiant" (5:10); etc.

Bibliography

Albright, William F. "Some Canaanite-Phoenician Sources of Hebrew Wisdom." Pp. 1–15 in *Wisdom in Israel and in the Ancient Near East: Presented to Professor Harold Henry Rowley*. Edited by Martin Noth and D. Winton Thomas. Vetus Testamentum Supplement 3. Leiden: Brill, 1955.

Alonso Schöckel, Luis, and J. Vilchez Lindez. *Proverbios*. Nueva Biblia Española. Madrid: Cristiandad, 1984.

Alster, Bendt. *Studies in Sumerian Proverbs*. Mesopotamia 3. Copenhagen: Akademisk, 1975.

Alt, Albrecht. "Zur literarischen Analyse der Weisheit des Amenemope." Pp. 16–25 in *Wisdom in Israel and in the Ancient Near East: Presented to Professor Harold Henry Rowley*. Edited by Martin Noth and D. Winton Thomas. Vetus Testamentum Supplement 3. Leiden: Brill, 1955.

Alter, Robert. *The Art of Biblical Poetry*. New York: Basic Books, 1985.

Anbar, M. "Proverbes 11,21; 16,5: יד ליד, 'sur le champ.'" *Biblica* 53 (1972) 537–38.

Baumgartner, Antoine J. *Étude Critique sur l'État du Texte du Livre des Proverbes*. Leipzig: Drugulin, 1890.

Behnke, P. "Spr. 10,1. 25,1." *Zeitschrift für die Alttestamentliche Wissenschaft* 16 (1896) 122.

Berezov, Jack L. "Remarks on the LXX Translation of Duplicate Proverbs." P. 65 in *Society of Biblical Literature Abstracts*. Edited by Paul Achtemeier. Missoula: Scholars Press, 1979.

_____. *Single-Line Proverbs: A Study of the Sayings Collected in Proverbs 10[:1]–22:16 and 25–29*. Diss., Hebrew Union College—Jewish Institute of Religion, 1987.

Boman, Thorlief. *Das hebräische Denken im Vergleich mit dem Griechischen*. 7th ed. Göttingen: Vandenhoeck & Ruprecht, 1983.

Boström, Gustav. *Paronomasi i den äldere hebreiska maschallitteraturen*. Lunds Universitets Årsskrift 1/23/8. Lund: Gleerup/Leipzig: Harrassowitz, 1928.

Brown, S. G. "The Structure of Proverbs 10:1–22:16." Paper read at the annual meeting of the Society of Biblical Literature (Rhetorical Criticism Section), 1988.

Bryce, Glendon E. "Another Wisdom-'Book' in Proverbs [25:2–27]." *Journal of Biblical Literature* 91 (1972) 145–57.

_____. *A Legacy of Wisdom: The Egyptian Contribution to the Wisdom of Israel*. Lewisburg, Pennsylvania: Bucknell University Press/London: Associated University Presses, 1979.

Bühlmann, Walter. *Vom rechten Reden und Schweigen: Studien zu Proverbien 10–31*. Orbis Biblicus et Orientalis 12. Freiburg: Universitätsverlag/Göttingen: Vandenhoeck & Ruprecht, 1976.

Carlson, R. A. "Élie à l'Horeb." *Vetus Testamentum* 19 (1969) 416–39.

Crenshaw, James L. "Education in Ancient Israel." *Journal of Biblical Literature* 104 (1985) 601–15.

_____. "Method in Determining Wisdom Influence upon 'Historical' Literature." *Journal of Biblical Literature* 88 (1969) 129–42. Reprinted in *Studies in Ancient Israelite Wisdom*, pp. 481–94. Edited by James L. Crenshaw. New York: Ktav, 1976.

_____ (editor). *Studies in Ancient Israelite Wisdom*. New York: Ktav, 1976.

Dahood, Mitchell. "The Phoenician Contribution to Biblical Wisdom Literature." Pp. 123–52 in *The Role of the Phoenicians in the Interaction of Mediterranean Civilizations*. Edited by William A. Ward. Beirut: American University of Beirut, 1968.

Delitzsch, Franz. *Biblical Commentary on the Proverbs of Solomon*. Translated by M. G. Easton. Grand Rapids: Eerdmans, 1978. Reprint of 1873 edition.

Dundes, Alan. "On the Structure of the Proverb." Pp. 103–18 in his *Analytic Essays in Folklore*. Studies in Folklore 2. The Hague: Mouton, 1975.

Ebeling, Erich. *Die akkadische Gebetsserie "Handerhebung."* Berlin: Akademie-Verlag, 1953.

Eissfeldt, Otto. *The Old Testament: An Introduction*. Translated by Peter R. Ackroyd. New York: Harper & Row/Oxford: Blackwell, 1965.

Finkelstein, Jacob J. "Hebrew חבר and Semitic *ḤBR." *Journal of Biblical Literature* 75 (1956) 328–31.

Fox, Michael V. "Aspects of the Religion of the Book of Proverbs." *Hebrew Union College Annual* 39 (1968) 55–69.

de Fraine, J. "מַרְגֵּמָה (Prov 26,8)." Vol. 1: pp. 131–35 in *Fourth World Congress of Jewish Studies: Papers*. Jerusalem: World Congress of Jewish Studies, 1967.

Gerleman, Gillis. "The Septuagint Proverbs as a Hellenistic Document." *Oudtestamentische Stüdien* 8 (1950) 15–27.

_____. *Studies in the Septuagint 3: Proverbs*. Lunds Universitets Årsskrift 1/52/3. Lund: Gleerup, 1956.

Gerstenberger, Eberhard. *Wesen und Herkunft des sogenannten apodiktischen Rechts im Alten Testament*. Bonn: Rheinische Friedrich-Wilhelms-Universität, 1961.

Golka, Friedemann W. "Die Königs- und Hofsprüche und der Ursprung der israelitischen Weisheit." *Vetus Testamentum* 36 (1986) 13–36.

Gordis, Robert. "The Social Background of Wisdom Literature." *Hebrew Union College Annual* 18 (1944) 77–118.

Gordon, Edmund I. "Sumerian Animal Proverbs and Fables: 'Collection Five.'" *Journal of Cuneiform Studies* 12 (1958) 1–21, 43–75.

_____. *Sumerian Proverbs: Glimpses of Everyday Life in Ancient Mesopotamia*. Philadelphia: University Museum, 1959.

_____. "Sumerian Proverbs: 'Collection Four.'" *Journal of the American Oriental Society* 77 (1957) 67–79.

Grintz, Jehoshua M. "שלמה׳: בירורים בשאלת היחס שבין שלושת הקבצים בס׳ משלי המיוחסים לשלמה משלי.׳" *Lešonēnu* 33 (1968) 243–69; corrections in *Lešonēnu* 34 (1969) 159–60. English translation by Daniel C. Snell on pp. 87–114 above.

Grumach, Irene. *Untersuchungen zur Lebenslehre des Amenope*. Münchener ägyptologische Studien 23. Munich/Berlin: Deutscher Kunstverlag, 1972.

Gutas, Dimitri. *Greek Wisdom Literature in Arabic Translation: A Study of the Graeco-Arabic Gnomologia*. American Oriental Series 60. New Haven: American Oriental Society, 1975.

Heaton, Eric W. *Solomon's New Men: The Emergence of Ancient Israel as a National State*. New York: Pica/London: Thames & Hudson, 1974.

Hermisson, Hans-Jürgen. *Studien zur israelitischen Spruchweisheit*. Wissenschaftliche Monographien zum Alten und Neuen Testament 28. Neukirchen-Vluyn: Neukirchener Verlag, 1968.

Hildebrandt, Ted. "Proverbial Pairs: Compositional Units in Proverbs 10–29." *Journal of Biblical Literature* 107 (1988) 207–24.

_____. "Strings in Proverbs 10." Unpublished paper. 1988.

Hummel, Horace D. "Enclitic *Mem* in Early Northwest Semitic, Especially Hebrew." *Journal of Biblical Literature* 76 (1957) 85–107.

Kaminka, A. "Septuaginta und Targum zu Proverbia." *Hebrew Union College Annual* 8–9 (1931–32) 169–91.

Kayatz, Christa. *Studien zu Proverbien 1–9: Eine form- und motivgeschichtliche Untersuchung unter Einbeziehung ägyptischen Vergleichsmaterials*. Wissenschaftliche Monographien zum Alten und Neuen Testament 22. Neukirchen-Vluyn: Neukirchener Verlag, 1966.

Kidner, F. Derek, "The Relationship between God and Man in Proverbs." *Tyndale [House] Bulletin* 7–8 (1961) 4–9.

Kovacs, Brian W. "Is There a Class-Ethic in Proverbs?" Pp. 171–89 in *Essays in Old Testament Ethics: J. Philip Hyatt, In Memoriam*. Edited by James L. Crenshaw and John T. Willis. New York: Ktav, 1974.

Lang, Bernhard. *Wisdom and the Book of Proverbs: A Hebrew Goddess Redefined*. New York: Pilgrim, 1986.

Lemaire, André. *Les Écoles et la Formation de la Bible dans l'Ancien Israël*. Orbis Biblicus et Orientalis 39. Freiburg: Éditions Universitaires/Göttingen: Vandenhoeck & Ruprecht, 1981.

McKane, William. *Proverbs: A New Approach*. Old Testament Library. Philadelphia: Westminster/London: SCM, 1970.

Mathieu, J.-P. "Les deux collections salomoniennes (Proverbes 10:1–22:16; 25:1–29:27)." *Laval Théologie et Philosophie* 19 (1963) 171–78.

Murphy, Roland E. "Assumptions and Problems in Old Testament Wisdom Research." *Catholic Biblical Quarterly* 29 (1967) 407–18.

_____. *Wisdom Literature: Job, Proverbs, Ruth, Canticles, Ecclesiastes, and Esther*. The Forms of the Old Testament Literature 13. Grand Rapids: Eerdmans, 1981.

Naré, Laurent. *Proverbes Salomoniens et Proverbes Mossi: Étude comparative à partir d'une nouvelle analyse de Pr 25–29*. Frankfurt am Main: Lang, 1986.

Nowack, Wilhelm. *Die Sprüche Salamo's*. Kurzgefasstes exegetisches Handbuch zum Alten Testament 7. 2d edition of 1847 commentary by Ernst Bertheau. Leipzig: Hirzel, 1883.

O'Connor, Michael P. *Hebrew Verse Structure*. Winona Lake, Indiana: Eisenbrauns, 1980.

Oesterley, W. O. E. *The Book of Proverbs*. Westminster Commentaries. London: Methuen, 1929.

Ogden, Graham S. "The 'Better'-Proverb (*Tôb-Spruch*), Rhetorical Criticism, and Qoheleth." *Journal of Biblical Literature* 96 (1977) 489–505.

Perdue, Leo G. *Wisdom and Cult: A Critical Analysis of the Views of Cult in the Wisdom Literatures of Israel and the Ancient Near East*. Society of Biblical Literature Dissertation Series 30. Missoula: Scholars Press, 1977.

Perry, S. C. *Structural Patterns in Proverbs 10:1–22:16: A Study in Biblical Hebrew Stylistics*. Diss., University of Texas, 1987.

Plaut, W. Gunther. *Book of Proverbs: A Commentary*. New York: Union of American Hebrew Congregations, 1961.

Preuss, H. D. "Das Gottesbild der älteren Weisheit Israels." Pp. 117–45 in *Studies in the Religion of Ancient Israel*. Vetus Testamentum Supplement 23. Leiden: Brill, 1972.

Redford, Donald B. "The Relations between Egypt and Israel from El-Amarna to the Babylonian Conquest." Pp. 192–205 in *Biblical Archaeology Today: Proceedings of the International Congress on Biblical Archaeology, Jerusalem, April 1984*. Jerusalem: Israel Exploration Society and Israel Academy of Sciences and Humanities in Cooperation with the American Schools of Oriental Research, 1985.

Scott, Robert B. Y. *Proverbs, Ecclesiastes*. Anchor Bible 18. Garden City, New York: Doubleday, 1965.

_____. "Solomon and the Beginnings of Wisdom in Israel." Pp. 262–79 in *Wisdom in Israel and in the Ancient Near East: Presented to Professor Harold Henry Rowley*. Edited by Martin Noth and D. Winton Thomas. Vetus Testamentum Supplement 3. Leiden: Brill, 1955. Reprinted in *Studies in Ancient Israelite Wisdom*, pp. 84–101. Edited by James L. Crenshaw. New York: Ktav, 1976.

_____. *The Way of Wisdom in the Old Testament*. London/New York: Macmillan, 1971.

_____. "Wise and Foolish, Righteous and Wicked." Pp. 146–65 in *Studies in the Religion of Ancient Israel*. Vetus Testamentum Supplement 23. Leiden: Brill, 1972.

Shupak, Nili. "The *Sitz im Leben* of the Book of Proverbs in the Light of a Comparison of Biblical and Egyptian Wisdom Literature." *Revue Biblique* 94 (1987) 98–119.

Simpson, D. C. "The Hebrew Book of Proverbs and the Teaching of Amenophis." *Journal of Egyptian Archaeology* 12 (1926) 232–39.

Simpson, William K. (editor). *The Literature of Ancient Egypt*. New Haven: Yale University Press, 1972.

Skehan, Patrick W. "A Single Editor for the Whole Book of Proverbs." *Catholic Biblical Quarterly* 10 (1948) 115–30. Reprinted in his *Studies in Israelite Poetry and Wisdom*, pp. 15–26. Catholic Biblical Quarterly Monograph Series 1. Washington, DC: Catholic Biblical Association, 1971. Also reprinted in *Studies in Ancient Israelite Wisdom*, pp. 329–40. Edited by James L. Crenshaw. New York: Ktav, 1976.

Skladny, Udo. *Die ältesten Spruchsammlungen in Israel.* Göttingen: Vandenhoeck & Ruprecht, 1962.

Snell, Daniel C. "Notes on Love and Death in Proverbs." Pp. 165–68 in *Love and Death in the Ancient Near East: Essays in Honor of Marvin H. Pope.* Edited by John H. Marks and Robert M. Good. Guilford, Connecticut: Four Quarters, 1987.

_____. "The Wheel in Proverbs xx 26." *Vetus Testamentum* 39 (1989) 503–7.

Steuernagel, Carl. *Lehrbuch der Einleitung in das Alte Testament.* Tübingen: Mohr, 1912.

Toy, Crawford H. *A Critical and Exegetical Commentary on the Book of Proverbs.* International Critical Commentary. Edinburgh: T. & T. Clark/New York: Scribner, 1899.

Van den Oudenrijn, M. A. "Prov xxv,1." *Angelicum* 5 (1928) 566–68.

Van Leeuwen, Raymond C. *Context and Meaning in Proverbs 25–27.* Society of Biblical Literature Dissertation Series 96. Atlanta: Scholars Press, 1988.

Vattioni, F. "Studi sul Libro dei Proverbi." *Augustinianum* 12 (1972) 121–68.

Whybray, Roger N. *The Book of Proverbs.* Cambridge Bible Commentary. Cambridge: Cambridge University Press, 1972.

_____. *The Intellectual Tradition in the Old Testament.* Beiheft zur Zeitschrift für die Alttestamentliche Wissenschaft 135. Berlin/New York: de Gruyter, 1974.

_____. *Wisdom in Proverbs: The Concept of Wisdom in Proverbs 1–9.* Studies in Biblical Theology 45. London: SCM/Naperville, Illinois: Allenson, 1965.

_____. "Wisdom Literature in the Reigns of David and Solomon." Pp. 13–26 in *Studies in the Period of David and Solomon and Other Studies.* Edited by Tomoo Ishida. Winona Lake, Indiana: Eisenbrauns, 1982.

Williams, Ronald J. "The Sages of Ancient Egypt in Light of Recent Scholarship." *Journal of the American Oriental Society* 101 (1981) 1–19.

Wilson, Gerald H. *The Editing of the Hebrew Psalter.* Society of Biblical Literature Dissertation Series 76. Chico: Scholars Press, 1985.

Wright, C. *The Literary Structure of Assyro-Babylonian Prayers to Ishtar.* Ph.D. diss., University of Michigan, 1979.

Index 1

Repeated Words in Repeated
Verses and Clichés

This index lists words in Proverbs that are related to each other in one of two ways: words that occur more than once in repeated verses, and words that occur more than once with one or more other words (i.e., words that are part of what I have defined as a cliché). Words in repeated verses are marked with an asterisk; the number (e.g., 2.2) after the references refers to the catalog of repeated verses in chapter 5, where the whole verse may be found. Words in verses that seem to be syntactically similar (category 4.0) have not been included here at all unless they also participate in repetition of verses and clichés. Also, parts of repeated verses that are not actually repeated are not included, even if the words are synonyms.

References are arranged by order of occurrence in the catalog above for repeated verses, and by canonical order for clichés.

I hope this index will make it easier to trace proverbial affinities beyond the book. Because of space limitations I have not included each word in a repeated verse under the reference to one of the words. Such clichés may be seen in the full display of each verse presented in the catalog in chapter 5 above. Many repeated verses do participate in clichés that can otherwise be identified, however, and they are entered under such cliché words. An example of this would be the repeated verses 19:1 ~ 28:6 (1.2 in the catalog), which share the cliché עקשׁ 'crooked' ~ דרך/ שׂפה 'way/lip', and so have been entered with the other verses that share this cliché. If, however, no other verse happens to have the cliché, here it will remain buried in its repeated verse.

In a sense this index amounts to an extension of R. B. Y. Scott's list of "wisdom" words, which has been expanded by R. N. Whybray.[1] But this index differs from theirs in that it uses only the Book of Proverbs, which is a cohesive if not totally coherent corpus at the heart of the intellectual tradition. Because of my mechanical criterion for defining clichés, I have come up with some words that do not use what we think of as typical wisdom vocabulary, but which nonetheless do present closely related words. For example, who would have thought the drinking of violence or violent wine (see חמס, שׁתה below) to have been a cliché? It is probably in identifying such atypical word groups that this exercise has been most productive.

---

1. R. B. Y. Scott, *The Way of Wisdom* (New York: Macmillan/London: Collier, 1971) 121–22; R. N. Whybray, *The Intellectual Tradition in the Old Testament* (Beiheft zur Zeitschrift für die Alttestamentliche Wissenschaft 135; Berlin/New York: 1974), esp. pp. 121–49 and 76–120 on the root חכם.

And yet, many of the clichés identified here may not be especially linked with the intellectual tradition. The so-called wise may be more interested in oratory than others in Israel, but they probably said someone "opens his mouth" the same as any other Hebrew speaker would have (see פתח, פה below). Clearly, there is no way to judge whether a cliché would sound proverbial to a native speaker. But the collection even of such clichés may allow us to be more coherent about affinities to the Book of Proverbs than we could have been before. And when we speak of the wisdom tradition, that is perhaps all we can ever mean.

Many of these clichéd words occur in Proverbs and elsewhere in poetic parallelism and are either synonyms or antonyms of one another. And many such poetic parallelisms occur only once in the book and so have not been entered in this index. Again, we cannot say that they are thereby excluded from sounding proverbial.[2]

The use of the root sign ($\sqrt{}$) indicates that the nouns involved come from the same root but do not have the same form. Others might eliminate word groups including such different words, or they might use such affinities more widely, for example, putting together חכם 'wise' and חכמה 'wisdom'. The repetition of verbal roots, which I have studied elsewhere, leads me to think that the proverbialists may have thought of noun roots occasionally as similar.[3]

---

2. See the discussion at the beginning of chapter 4 on the relation between clichés and repetition.

3. D. C. Snell, "Notes on Love and Death in Proverbs," in *Love and Death in the Ancient Near East: Essays in Honor of Marvin H. Pope* (ed. John H. Marks and Robert M. Good; Guilford, Connecticut: Four Quarters, 1987) 165–68.

Index of Repeated Words

אב*
1:8~6:20 (1.2)
10:1~15.20 (1.2)
1.8a~4:1a (2.2)
20:20a~30:11 (3.1)

see also שׂמח and בן, יולד, מוסר

אם ,אב
1:8, 4:3, 6:20, 10:1, 15:20,
19:26, 20:20, 23:22, 23:25,
28:24, 30:11, 30:17

יולדת ,אב
17:25, 23:25

───────────

אבד*
10:28~11:7 (1.3)
19:9~21:28a (3.0)

see also רשׁע

───────────

שׁאול see אבדון/ה
אבה*
1:25~1:30 (1.2)

───────────

שׁור ,אבוס
14:4, 15:17

───────────

עני and חונן see אביון
אבן*
11:1~20:23 (1.2)
20:10~20:23a (3.0)

───────────

אדם*
28:12b~28:28a (2.1)

see also אישׁ

───────────

אדמה*
12:11~28:19 (1.2)

אהב, אהב
8:17, 12:1, 17:19, 21:17

see also פשׁע

On these verses see my article, "Notes on Love and Death in Proverbs."

שׂנא√ ,אהב√
Only 10:12 and 15:17 have nonverbal forms for 'love' and 'hate'.

1:22, 8:36, 9:8, 10:12, 12:1,
13:24, 14:20, 15:17, 27:6

───────────

אהב see אהבה
רוה ,דדים ,אהבים
5:19, 7:18

───────────

אויל*
10:8b~10:10b (2.0)

see also חכם and ערום

───────────

אולת*
12:23~13:16~15:2 (1.4)
26:4a~26:5a (2.2)
14:17a~14:29 (3.1)

כסיל ,אולת
12:23, 13:16, 14:8, 14:24, 15:2,
15:14, 17:12, 26:4, 26:5, 26:11

see also ערום, and מוסר ,דעת

───────────

און*
10:29b~21:15b (2.0)
see also פעל

───────────

עין ,אור√
15:30 has the noun מאור while 29:13 has the verbal form מאיר.

15:30, 29:13

see also נר

───────────

אזן*
2:2~5:1 (1.2)

4:20~5:1 (1.2)

see also נטה

לב ,אזן
2:2, 18:15, 22:17, 23:12

שׁמע ,אזן
5:13 and 28:9 merely have 'ear' with a verbal form from 'to hear', but the other three verses have 'a hearing ear' where the two words are closely related.

5:13, 15:31, 20:12, 25:12, 28:9

───────────

רֵעַ see אח

───────────

אחרית*
14:12~16:25 (1.0)
23:18~24:14b (1.1)

───────────

איד*
6:15a~24:22a (2.2)

see also בוא

פחד ,איד
1:26, 1:27

───────────

אין*
11:14~15:22 (1.4)
6:15b~29:1b (2.0)
11:14a~29:18a (2.2)

אפס/אין ,אין
8:24, 21:30, 25:28, 26:20 (אפס)

רב ,אפס/אין
13:7 and 28:27 have forms from רָב instead of רֹב.

5:23, 11:14, 13:7, 14:4, 14:28
(אפס), 15:22, 28:27

───────────

אישׁ*
14:12~16:25 (1.0)
6:11~24:34 (1.1)
16:2~21:2 (1.3)
26:12~29:20 (1.3)
3.31a~24:1a (2.1)

12:14a~13:2a (2.1)
15:18a~29:22a (2.1)
12:14a~13.2a~18:20a (2.2)
18:4a~20:5a (2.2)
22:29a~29:20a (2.2)

see also בעל and חסר

איש, אדם
12:14, 24:30, 30:2

אך see מחסור

אכל, דבש
24:13, 25:16, 25:27
אכל, דבש, טוב
24:13, 25:27
אכל, לחם
25:21, 31:27
אכל, שבע
1:31, 13:25

אל, תהי, ב
22:26, 23:20

אלהים see יהוה

אלוף see מפריד

אם*
1:8~6:20 (1.2)
10:1~15:20 (1.2)
20:20a~30:11 (3.1)

see also אב and בוז

אמונה, שקר
12:17, 12:22

אמן see ציר

אמץ see עזז

אמר*
9:4~9:16 (1.0)
22:13~26:13 (1.3)

see also קרא and שבע

אמרים*
2:1~7:1 (1.1)
2:16~7:5 (1.1)

5:7~7:24 (1.1)
see also לקח

אמרים, דעת
19:27, 23:12
אמרים, נעם
15:26, 16:24
אמרים, פה
4:5, 5:7, 6:2, 7:24, 8:8

אמת see חסד, שקר

אף*
see 15:18~29:22 (2.1)
14:17a~14:29 (3.1)
see also בעל, חמה, שוב

אף, רוח
14:29, 16:32

אפס see אין

אצל, פנה
7:8, 7:12

ארב, דם
1:11, 1:18, 12:6
ארב, צפן
1:11, 1:18

ארבע see שלוש

ארח, דרך
2:8, 2:13, 2:20, 3:6, 4:14, 9:15, 12:28, 15:19
see also עקש, and עזב, ישר

ארח, דרך, שמר
2:8, 2:20
ארח, חיים
2:19, 5:6, 10:17, 15:24
ארח, ישר√
2:13, 15:19
2:13 has ישר, and 15:19 has ישרים.
ארח, מעגלת
2:15, 5:6
ארח, משפט
2:8, 17:23
ארח, צדיק
2:20, 4:18

ארח, צדקה, נתיבה
8:20, 12:28

ארי*
22:13~26:13 (1.3)

ארץ, שמים
3:19, 25:3
see also שכן and יסד√

אש see עץ

אשה*
21:9~25:24 (1.0)
~21:19 (1.4)
2:16~7:5 (1.1)
6:24~7:5 (1.3)
2:16~6:24 (1.4)
19:13b~27:15 (3.0)
אשה, חיל
12:4, 31:10

את* 'with'
11:2b~13:10b (2.1)

ב

בֶּגֶד*
20:16~27:13 (1.0)

בגד see ישר√, סלף, and רשע

בהל see הון

בוא*
6:11~24:34 (1.1)
בוא, בוא
1:27, 11:2, 18:3
בוא, פחד
1:26, 1:27, 3:25

בוז, אם
23:22, 30:17

בוז, ירא
13:13, 14:2

בוז, לרעהו
11:12, 14:21

see also שכל

בחן see תכן

בטח see הלך

בטן*
18:8~26:22 (1.0)

see also חדר

בין, בין
8:5, 28:5

בין, דעת
Compare also 9:10 with דעת and בינה.
2:5, 19:25, 29:7

see also ידע

בינה see חכמה

ביש, חפר
13:5, 19:26
13:5 has יבאיש, which with BH³ probably should be emended to יביש because of 19:26.

see also משכיל

בית*
21:9~25:24 (1.0)
9:1a~14:1a (2.1)
9:1a~14:1a~24:3a (2.2)

see also בנה and עכר

בית, נערות
27:27, 31:15
The use of 'maids' in parallelism to 'house' is a case of merismus, using a part for the whole.

בל see פנים

בן*
2:1~7:1 (1.1)
5:7~7:24 (1.1)

1:8~6:20 (1.2)
4:20~5:1 (1.2)
10:1~15:20 (1.2)
5:7a~7:24a~8:32a (2.0)
1:8a~4:1a (2.2)

see also יסר

בן, אב
1:8, 3:12, 4:1, 4:3, 6:20, 10:1, 13:1, 15:20, 17:6, 17:25, 19:13, 19:26, 28:7

בן, מביש
Compare 29:15, which has נער 'lad' with מביש.
10:5, 17:2, 19:26

בנה*
9:1a~14:1a (2.1)
9:1a~14:1a~24:3a (2.2)

בנה, בית
9:1a, 14:1a, 24:3a, 24:27b

בנה, בית, כון
24:3, 24:27

בְעד*
20:16~27:13 (1.0)

בעל, אף, איש, חמה
22:24, 29:22

בצע, בצע
1:19, 15:27

בקש see פשע

ברך√, קלל√
30:11 has verbs from each root, but 27:14 has a verb from ברך and the noun קללה.
27:14, 30:11

ברכה, לראש
10:6, 11:26

בשר, עצם
לבשרך is restored from the dubious לשרך 3:8.
3:8, 14:30

see also חיים

ג

גאה√ see רוח

גבה√, שבר
16:18 has the noun גבה while the other verses have verbal forms.
16:18, 17:19, 18:12

גבול*
22:28a~23:10a (2.0)

גג*
21:9~25:24 (1.0)

גו*
19:29b~26:3b (2.1)
10:13b~26:3b (2.2)

גיל see שמח

גלה*
11:13a~20:19a (2.1)

גלה, כסה
11:13, 26:26

גלה, סוד
11:13, 20:19, 25:9

גלע, ריב
17:14, 20:3

גם*
17:15b~20:10b (2.0)

see also יהוה

גערה*
13:1b~13:8b (2.1)

גרגרת see חן

גרה*
15:18a~29:22a (2.1)

מדון ,גרה
15:18, 28:25, 29:22

תהפכות ,דבר
2:12, 23:33

מישרים ,שפה ,דבר
8:6, 23:16

———————————

דָּבָר*
18:8~26:22 (1.0)

see also מענה

———————————

מתוק ,דבש
16:24, 24:13

see also אכל

———————————

אהבים see דדים

———————————

דור ,דור
30:11–14 may not be directly relevant since each verse begins with 'a generation (which). . . .'

27:24, 30:11, 30:12, 30:13, 30:14

———————————

דל see חונן ,עשיר, and עשק

———————————

דלף*
19:13b~27:15 (3.0)

———————————

דם see ארב and שפך

———————————

דעך*
13:9b~24:20b (2.0)

נר see דעך

———————————

דעת*
12:23~13:16~15:2 (1.4)
19:25~21:11 (1.4)
15:14a~18:15a (2.1)

see 1:7~9:10 (2.2)

see also חכם ,בין ,אמרים,
מזמה ,מוסר ,לקח ,ידע ,חכמה,
ערמה ,ערום ,נתן ,נצר ,נבון ,מצא,
and שׂנא

אולת ,דעת
12:23, 13:16, 14:18, 15:2, 15:14

יראת יהוה ,דעת
1:29, 2:5, 9:10

———————————

דֶּרֶךְ*
14:12~16:25 (1.0)
16:2~21:2 (1.3)
12:15a~16:2~21:2 (2.2)

see also פלס ,עקש ,הלך ,ארח,
and תם

דרך ,דרך
3:17, 30:19

מעגלת ,דרך
4:11, 4:26, 5:21

נתיבה ,דרך
1:15, 3:17, 7:25, 8:2

רחק ,דרך
5:8, 7:19, 22:5

———————————

דשן see נפש

הבל see הון

———————————

הגה ,שפה
8:7, 24:2

see also לב

———————————

הון*
10:15a~18:11a (2.0)

see also שבע

בהל/הבל ,הון
13:11, 28:22
I have assumed emendations to achieve a cliché, in 13:11 from מהבל to מבהל. (The related 20:21 lacks הון but probably should be emended from מבחלת to מבהלת.) 28:22 has נבהל.

יקר ,הון
1:13, 12:27, 24:4

כל ,הון
1:13, 6:31, 24:4

מלא ,הון
1:13, 24:4

מצא ,הון
1:13, 6:31

רב ,הון
13:7, 19:4

רבה ,הון
13:11, 28:8

———————————

היה see אל

———————————

הלך*
19:1~28:6 (1.2)
11:13a~20:19a (2.1)

בטח ,הלך
3:23, 10:9

דרך ,הלך
2:13, 2:20, 3:23, 7:19, 8:20, 16:29, 28:6, 28:18

תמים/תם ,הלך
Only 28:18 has תמים.

2:7, 10:9, 19:1, 20:7, 28:6, 28:18

———————————

הנה*
9:4~9:16 (1.0)

זֶבַח*
15:8a~21:27a (2.1)

———————————

זדון*
see 11:2~13:10 (2.1)

———————————

זהב*
17:3a~27:21a (2.0)

see also כסף and נזם

חמה see קנא ,בעל, and שוב

חמה, אף
15:1, 15:18, 21:14, 22:24, 27:4, 29:22

―――

חמס*
10:6b~10:11b (2.0)

see also נפש

חמס, שתה
4:17 has יין חמסים and 26:6 has חמס.
4:17, 26:6

―――

חן*
1:9a~4:9a (2.1)

see also מצא and נתן

חן, גרגרת
1:9, 3:22

―――

חסד, ואמת
3:3, 14:22, 16:6, 20:28

―――

חסר*
9:4~9:16 (1.0)

חסר, לב
6:32, 7:7, 9:4, 9:16, 10:13, 10:21, 11:12, 12:11, 15:21, 17:18, 24:30

חסר, לב, איש, תבונה
11:12, 15:21

―――

חפץ*
3:15~8:11 (1.3)

―――

חפר see ביש

―――

חקר see כבוד and מלך

―――

חרוץ 'gold' see כסף

―――

חרוץ 'diligent' see רמיה

―――

חרף, עשהו
14:31, 17:5

―――

חרפה see קלון

―――

חשב√ see כון

ט

טהור see חכם

―――

טוב*
21:9~25:24 (1.0)
~21:19 (1.4)
19:1~28:6 (1.2)
15:16~16:8 (1.4)
12:14a~13:2a (2.1)
24:23b~28:21a (2.2)

see also אכל ,מצא ,נחל ,פנים, רע, and שמועה

טוב, צדיק
2:20, 13:22, 14:19

טוב, נבחר
16:16, 22:1

טוב, כי, סחרה
3:14, 31:18
The possessive pronoun in 3:14 refers to 'wisdom' and in 31:18 to the 'woman of valor'.

טוב, רעה
11:27, 13:21, 17:13, 17:20

―――

טמן*
19:24~26:15 (1.2)

―――

טרד*
19:13b~27:15 (3.0)

י

יד*
6:10~24:33 (1.1)
19:24~26:15 (1.2)

11:21a~16:5b (2.1)

see also כף

יד, יד
These verses may not really share a cliché since 6:5 does not have the expression יד ליד discussed above under 2.1.
6:5, 11:21, 16:5

―――

ידע, בין
1:2, 24:12, 28:2, 29:7

ידע, דעת
14:7, 17:27, 29:7, 30:3

ידע, צדיק
12:10, 29:7

―――

יהוה*
11:1~20:23 (1.2)
8:35~18:22 (1.3)
~12:2a (2.0)
16:2~21:2 (1.3)
22:2~29:13 (1.4)
17:15b~20:10b (2.0)
1:7a~9:10a (2.2)
3:7b~16:6b (2.2)
20:10~20:23a (3.0)

see also כון ,ירא ,יראה ,דעת, and תועבה

יהוה, אלהים
2:5, 30:9

יהוה, גם, שניהם
17:15, 20:10, 20:12

יהוה, רשע, תפלה
15:8, 15:29

יהוה, שלם
16:7, 19:17, 25:22

―――

יולד, אב
17:21, 23:24

―――

יולדת see אב

―――

יום*
3:2~9:11 (1.2)

יום, יום
8:30, 8:34, 27:1

יום, צרה
24:10, 25:19

Compare also the various other unhappy days, in 6:34 'day of vengeance', 11:4 'day of wrath', 16:4 'day of evil', and 27:10 'day of your disaster'.

שׁנה, יום
9:11, 10:27

יועץ*
11:14~15:22 (1.4)
11:14b~24:6b (2.0)
15:22b~24:6b (2.1)

see also מחשבה

יטב*
15:13~17:22 (1.3)

שׁכר, יין
20:1, 31:4, 31:6

see also מסך, לחם and שׁתה

שׂמאל, ימין
3:16, 4:27

ארץ, יסד√
3:19 has יסד־ארץ with 'the Lord' as subject; the subject of 8:29 is the same, but the relevant phrase is בחוקו מוסדי ארץ.

3:19, 8:29

יסף*
3:2~9:11 (1.2)

see also חכם and עוד

נפשׁ, בן, יסר
19:18, 29:17

יעל*
10:2~11:4 (1.3)

יפיח*
19:5~19:1 (1.1)
6:19a~14:5b (2.0)

שׁקרים/כזבים, עד, יפיח
12:17 has שׁקרים but not כזבים. Compare 25:18 with עד שׁקר.

6:19, 12:17, 14:5, 14:25, 19:5, 19:9

פנינים, יקר
3:15, 20:15

see also הון

פניים in 3:15 must probably be emended to פנינים.

יהוה, ירא
3:7, 14:2, 24:21

see also בוז

ירא*
1:7a~9:10a (2.2)

see also דעת

יהוה, ירא
1:7, 1:29, 2:5, 8:13, 9:10, 10:27, 14:26, 14:27, 15:16, 15:33, 16:6, 19:23, 22:4, 23:17, 31:30

כבוד, ענוה, יהוה, ירא
15:33, 22:4

ירד*
18:8~26:22 (1.0)

see also חדר, עלה, and שׁאול

ישׁ*
14:12~16:25 (1.0)
23:18~24:14b (1.1)

ישׁב*
21:9~25:24 (1.0)
~21:19 (1.4)

ישׁר*
14:12~16:25 (1.0)
20:11b~21:8b (2.1)
11:6a~12:6b (2.2)
see also חכם, ארח

ארח (verb), ישׁר
3:6, 9:15

בגד, ישׁר
11:3, 11:6

נלוז, ישׁר√
3:32, 14:2

3:32 has ישׁרים and 14:2 has בישׁרו. Contrast עקשׁות לזות in 4:24.

רשׁע, ישׁר
11:11, 12:6, 14:11, 15:8, 21:29

תמים, ישׁר
2:21, 28:10

כבד√, כבד√
25:2, 25:27, 27:3

see also שׁמר

25:2 and 25:27 both have forms of the noun כבוד, but 27:3 has the noun כבד and the verb כבד.

כבוד*
26:1~26:8 (1.4)
15:33b~18:12b (2.0)

see also עשׁר, ירא, and תמך

חקר, כבוד
25:2, 25:27

כון*
16:12b~25:5b~29:14b (2.1)
6:8a~20:25b (2.2)

see also בנה and מחשבה

חשׁב√, כון
16:3, 16:9, 20:18
16:3 and 20:18 both have the noun מחשבות while 16:9 has the verb יחשׁב.

יהוה, כון
3:19, 16:3, 16:9, 21:31

שׁמים, כון
3:19, 8:27

כור*
17:3a~27:21a (2.0)

כזב*
19:5~19:9 (1.1)
6:19a~14:5b (2.0)
19:9~21:28a (3.0)

see also יפיח

כי*
20:16~27:13 (1.0)
3:2~9:11 (1.2)

see also טוב and מאן

___

כל*
1:25~1:30 (1.2)
3:15~8:11 (1.3)
16:2~21:2 (1.3)

see also עת and הון

___

כן*
26:1~26:8 (1.4)

___

כסא*
16:12b~25:5b~29:14b (2.1)
16:12b~25:5b~29:14b
~20:28b (2.2)

___

כסה*
10:6b~10:11b (2.0)

see also פשע, ערום, and גלה

___

כסיל*
10:1~15:20 (1.2)
26:12~29:20 (1.3)
12:23~13:16~15:2 (1.4)
26:1~26:8 (1.4)
26:7b~26:9b (2.0)
19:29b~26:3b (2.1)
26:4a~26:5a (2.2)

see also לץ, חכם, דעת, אולת,
מבין, נבון, ערום, and פתי

___

כסף*
17:3a~27:21a (2.0)

זהב, כסף
17:3, 22:1, 25:11, 27:21

כסף, חרוץ
3:14, 8:10, 8:19, 16:16

נבחר, כסף
8:10, 8:19, 10:20, 16:16, 22:1

סיגים, כסף
25:4, 26:23

___

כף, יד
10:4, 31:19, 31:20

see also ערב

___

כפיר*
19:12a~20:2a (2.1)

___

כרם see שדה

___

כרת*
23:18~24:14 (1.1)

___

כשל see נפל

___

כתב*
3:3b~7:3 (3.1)

___

ל

___

לא see פנים, נאוה, משפט, and

___

לאם see עם and קבב

___

לב*
9:4~9:16 (1.0)
15:13~17:22 (1.3)
15:14a~18:15a (2.1)
3:3b~7:3 (3.1)

see also עין, לשון, חסר, אזן,
תכן, קנה, פנים, עקש, and

הגה, לב
15:28, 24:2

נפש, לב
2:10, 27:9

שמח√, לב
12:25, 14:13, 15:13, 15:21,
15:30, 17:22, 23:15, 24:17,
27:9, 27:11
Most of these verses have verb forms
from שמח, but 14:13 and 15:21 both have
שמחה 'joy'.

שפה, לב
10:8, 15:7, 22:11, 24:2

___

לבט*
10:8b~10:10b (2.0)

___

לוז*
3:21a~4:21a (2.1)

___

לוח*
3:3b~7:3 (3.1)

___

לויה*
1:9a~4:9a (2.1)

___

לחם*
12:11~28:19 (1.2)
6:8a~30:25b (2.2)

see also מים and שבע; for לחם
(verb) see אכל

יין, לחם
4:17, 9:5

לָחֶם, לחם
4:17, 9:5, 23:6

שתה, לָחֶם
4:17, 9:5

___

לץ*
19:25~21:11 (1.4)

see also פתי

חכם, לץ
9:8, 13:1, 15:12, 21:11

כסיל, לץ
1:22, 19:29

נבון, לץ
14:6, 19:25

___

לקח*
20:16~27:13 (1.0)

see also חכם

אמרים, לקח
2:1, 4:10

דעת, לקח
8:10, 21:11

שכל√, לקח
1:3 and 21:11 have verbal forms from
לקח, but 16:23 has the noun לֶקַח 'understanding'.

1:3, 16:23, 21:11

___

לב, לשון
10:20, 16:1, 17:20

see also פה, רפא, and שפה

מאזנים*
11:1~20:23 (1.2)

מאן, כי, לעשות
21:7, 21:25

מאס מוסר see

מבטח(ה) see עז

מבין, כסיל
17:10, 17:24

מביש בן, משכיל, and עבד see

מגן*
6:11~24:34 (1.1)

מדון*
25:24~21:9 (1.0)
21:9~21:19~25:24 (1.4)
15:18a~29:22a (2.1)
19:13b~27:15 (3.0)
6:14~16:28a (3.1)

    see also עץ and גרה

מדון, נרגן
16:28, 26:20

מדון, ריב
15:18, 17:14, 26:21

מדון, שבת
18:18, 22:10

מדון, שלח
6:14, 6:19, 16:28

מהר see רוץ

מוט see צדיק

מוסר*
1:8a~4:1a (2.2)

    see also שמר and פרע

מוסר, אב
1:8, 4:1, 13:1, 15:5

מוסר, אולת
5:23, 22:15

מוסר, דעת
8:10, 19:27, 23:12

מוסר, מאס, תוכחת
3:11, 15:32

מוסר, תוכחת
3:11, 5:12, 6:23, 10:17, 12:1,
13:18, 15:5, 15:10, 15:32

מוקש*
13:14~14:27 (1.2)
12:13~29:6 (1.4)

מוקש, נפש
18:7, 22:25

מות*
14:12~16:25 (1.0)
13:14~14:27 (1.2)
10:2~11:4 (1.3)

    see also חדר and חיים

מות, שאול
5:5, 7:27

מותר, מחסור
14:23, 21:5

מזמה, דעת
1:4, 5:2, 8:12

    see also ערמה

מזמה, שמר, נצר
2:11, 5:2

מחסור*
6:11~24:34 (1.1)

    see also מותר

מחסור, ל־ אך
Note that 11:23 has אך־טוב in contrast to
אך־למחסור in 11:24.

11:24, 14:23, 21:5, 22:16

מחשבה, עצה/יועץ, כון/קום
יועצים occurs only in 15:22 in this group;
the other two verses have forms from עצה
'counsel'. 15:22 and 19:21 have forms

from קום, but 20:18 has a form from כון,
which seems to be synonymous.

15:22, 19:21, 20:18

מחתה*
10:29b~21:15b (2.0)

    see also פה

מטעמות*
23:3a~23:6b (2.0)

מי*
9:4~9:16 (1.0)

מים*
18:4a~20:5a (2.2)

    see also פלגים and מעינות

מים, לחם
9:17, 25:21

מישרים see דבר and צדק√

מלא see הון

מלחמה*
20:18b~24:6a (2.1)

מלחמה, תשועה
21:31, 24:6

מלך*
16:12b~25:5b~29:14b (2.1)
~20:28b (2.2)
19:12a~20:2a (2.1)
20:8~20:26a (3.2)

    see also רצון; for מלך (verb),
see עבד

מלך, חקר
25:2, 25:3
25:2 has a verbal form from חקר while
25:3 has the noun חֵקֶר.

מלך, רזן√
8:15, 14:28, 31:4
8:15 and 31:4 have רוזנים, while 14:28
has רזן.

מסך, יין
9:2, 9:5

see ארח ,דרך, and פלס מעגל

מעט*
6:10~24:33 (1.1)
15:16~16:8 (1.4)

מים ,מעינות
5:16, 8:24

דבר ,מענה
15:1, 15:23

אלוף ,מפריד
16:28, 17:9

מצא*
8:35~18:22 (1.3)
see also הון and שחר

דעת ,מצא
2:5, 8:9, 8:12

חיים ,מצא
4:22, 8:35, 21:21

חכמה ,מצא
3:13, 10:13, 24:14

חן ,מצא
3:4, 28:23

טוב ,מצא
3:4, 16:20, 17:20, 18:22, 19:8

פוק ,מצא
3:13, 8:35, 18:22

מצוה*
2:1~7:1 (1.1)
4:4b~7:2a (2.0)

see נצר ,שמר ,תורה מצוה

מצרף*
17:3a~27:21a (2.0)

מקור*
13:14~14:27 (1.2)

חיים ,מקור
10:11, 13:14, 14:27, 16:22

מרמה*
11:1~20:23 (1.2)

see also עד

קרת ,על ,מרמים
9:3 has על־גפי מרמי קרת while 9:14 has
על־כסא מרמי קרת. Compare also
קרת תרום in 11:11.
9:3, 9:14

מביש ,משכיל
10:5, 14:35, 17:2
see also עֶבֶד

מָשָׁל*
26:7b~26:9b (2.0)

עֶבֶד see מָשַׁל

בְּלֹא ,משפט
13:23, 16:8
see also פנים ,עשה ,ארח,
רשע, and √צדק

נפש ,מתוק
16:24, 27:7

נפת ,מתוק
24:13, 27:7
see also דבש

מתלהמים*
18:8~26:22 (1.0)

נ

ל־ ,לא ,נאוה
17:7, 19:10, 26:1

תוכחת ,נאץ
1:30, 5:12, 15:5

נבון*
15:14a~18:15a (2.1)
see also חכם and לץ

דעת ,נבון
14:6, 15:14, 18:15, 19:25

כסיל ,נבון
14:33, 15:14

see טוב and כסף נבחר

see צפור נדד

נהם*
19:12a~20:2a (2.1)

see צפור נוד

צדיק ,נוה
Compare 21:20 נוה חכם 'the pasture-
ground or abode of a wise one'.
3:33, 24:15

זהב ,נזם
11:22, 25:12

טוב ,נחל
13:22, 28:10

נטה*
2:2~5:1 (1.2)
4:20~5:1 (1.2)
see also רשע and שמע

אזן ,נטה
2:2, 4:20, 5:1, 5:13, 22:17

קשב ,נטה
1:24, 2:2, 4:20, 5:1

נכא*
15:13~17:22 (1.3)
see also רוח

בְּשֵׁבֶט ,נכה
23:13, 23:14

נכר* (verb)
24:23b~28:21a (2.2)

נכרי*
20:16~27:13 (1.0)

see זר נכרי

נכריה*
2:16~7:5 (1.1)
6:24~7:5 (1.3)
2:16~6:24 (1.4)

see also זרה

נלוז   see   ישר

נסג*
22:28a~23:10a (2.0)

נעם   see   אמרים

נער   see   פתי

נערות   see   בית

נפל, כשל
24:16, 24:17

נפל, בְּרִשְׁעָה/בְּרָע(ה)
11:5 has בְּרִשְׁעָתוּ and 13:17 has בְּרָע; the rest have בְּרָעָה, all synonymous.

11:5, 13:17, 17:20, 24:16, 28:14

see also שׁוחה

נפשׁ*
16:17b~19:16a (2.2)
13:3a~21:23 (3.1)

see also מתוק, מוקשׁ, לב, יסר, נצר/שׁמר and

נפשׁ, דשׁן
11:25, 13:4

נפשׁ, √חמס
8:36 has the verbal form יֶחֱמֹס while 13:2 has the noun חמס.

8:36, 13:2

נפשׁ, רעב
10:3, 19:15, 27:7

נפת, חֵךְ
5:3, 24:13

see also מתוק

נצל*
10:2~11:4 (1.3)
11:6a~12:6b (2.2)

נצר, דעת
5:2, 22:12

נצר, מצוה
3:1, 6:20

נצר, שׁמר
2:8, 2:11, 4:6, 4:23, 5:2, 13:3, 16:17, 27:18

נצר, תורה
3:1, 6:20, 28:7

see also מזמה and שׁמר נפשׁו

נקה*
19:5~19:9 (1.1)
11:21a~16:5b (2.1)

נר*
13:9b~24:20b (2.0)

נר, אור
6:23, 13:9

נר, דעֵךְ
13:9, 20:20, 24:20

נרגן*
18:8~26:22 (1.0)

see also מדון

נשׂגב   see   עז

נשׁר, שׁמים
23:5, 30:19

נתיבה   see   ארח and דרך

נתן*
2:3~8:1 (1.4)

see also צדיק

נתן, דעת
1:4, 2:6

נתן, חכמה
1:20 has חכמות; the rest have חכמה, but 8:1 and 13:10 may have little to do with

---

a cliché 'giving wisdom' since the two words are in separate clauses.

1:20, 2:6, 8:1, 13:10, 29:15

נתן, חן
4:9 may be less directly related than the other two since it speaks of giving a 'garland of grace'.

3:34, 4:9, 13:15

נתן, קול
1:20, 2:3, 8:1

נתשׁ*
1:8~6:20 (1.2)

סבא, זלל
23:20, 23:21

סוד*
11:13a~20:19a (2.1)

see also גלה

סור*
9:4~9:16 (1.0)
13:14~14:27 (1.2)
3:7b~16:6b (2.2)

סור, מֵרע
3:7, 4:27, 13:19, 14:16, 16:6, 16:17

סחר   see   טוב

סיגים   see   כסף

סלף√, בגד
11:3 has the noun סלף and 22:12 the verb יְסַלֵּף.

11:3, 22:12

סתר*
22:3~27:12 (1.0)

עבד* (verb)
12:11~28:19 (1.2)

עֶבֶד, מַשְׂכִּיל/מֵבִישׁ
14:35, 17:2

עֶבֶד, מֹשֵׁל/מֶלֶךְ
Only 30:22 has a form from the verb מלך; the rest have forms from the synonymous משל.

17:2, 19:10, 22:7, 30:22

עבר*
22:3~27:12 (1.0)

עד*
19:5~19:9 (1.1)
6:19a~14:5b (2.0)
19:9~21:28a (3.0)

see also יפיח

עֵד, מִרְמָה
Note that both verses also have nouns from the root אמן: אמונה in 12:17 and אמת in 14:25.

12:17, 14:25

עוֹד, יֹסֵף
9:9, 11:24, 19:19

עוֹלָם*
22:28a~23:10a (2.0)

עֹז*
10:15a~18:11a (2.0)

see also עזז and קריה

מִבְטַח(ה), עֹז
14:26, 21:22
14:26 has מבטח while 21:22 has מבטחה.

נִשְׂגָּב, עֹז
18:10, 18:11

עֹזֵב, אֹרַח
2:13, 10:17, 15:10

עֹזֵב, תּוֹרָה
4:2, 28:4

עֹזֵב, שֹׁמֵר
10:17, 28:4

√ עזז, אמץ
8:28, 24:5, 31:17
8:28 has the verbal form יעזוז; the others have the noun עז.

עֹז, פָּנִים
7:13, 21:29
This expression may not really be completely similar in both verses since 21:29 has הַעֵז... בְּפָנָיו, while 7:13 lacks the preposition before 'face'.

see also עֹז

עטרת see תפארת

עַיִן*
16:2~21:2 (1.3)
~12:15a (2.2)
3:21a~4:21a (2.1)

see also חכם (טהור, יָשָׁר),
√אור, רום, קרץ, and רע

עַיִן, לֵב
4:21, 21:4, 23:26, 23:33

עַיִן, עַפְעַף
4:25, 6:4, 30:13

עֹכֵר, בֵּיתוֹ
11:29, 15:6, 15:27

עֹלֶה, יֹרֵד
21:22, 30:4

עלץ see צדיק

עַם*
11:14a~29:18a (2.2)

עַם, לְאֹם
14:28, 24:24

עָמֹק*
18:4a~20:5a (2.2)
22:14a~23:27a (2.2)

עֹנֶה*
26:4a~26:5a (2.2)

עֹנֶה*
15:33b~18:12b (2.0)

ענוה see יראה

עָנִי, אֶבְיוֹן
30:14, 31:9, 31:20

עני see חנן

ענשׁ*
22:3~27:12 (1.0)

עפעף see עין

אֵשׁ, מָדוֹן, עֵץ
26:20, 26:21

עֵץ, חַיִּים
3:18, 11:30, 13:12, 15:4

עצה*
1:25~1:30 (1.2)

see also מחשבה

עצל*
19:24~26:15 (1.2)
22:13~26:13 (1.3)

עצם see בָּשָׂר, √רפא, and רקב

עקשׁ*
19:1~28:6 (1.2)

עקשׁ, אֹרַח/שָׂפָה/דֶּרֶךְ
2:15, 10:9, 19:1, 22:5, 28:6, 28:18
19:1 is the only verse here with שפתים, but I include it because it is directly related to 28:6 (see category 1.2). BH[3] even suggests, on the basis of some manuscripts, emending 19:1 to read דרכים, but that seems unnecessary. 2:15 has ארחתיהם instead of דרכיהם.

עקשׁ, לֵב
11:20, 17:20

תמים/תם ,עקש
10:9, 11:20, 19:1, 28:6, 28:18
11:20 and 28:18 have forms of תמים; the rest have תם.

פה ,עקשות
4:24, 6:12

---

*ערב
20:16~27:13 (1.0)

זר ,ערב
6:1, 11:15, 20:16, 27:13

תקע ,ערב
6:1, 11:15, 17:18, 22:26

---

*ערום
22:3~27:12 (1.0)
12:23~13:16 (1.4)

אולת/אויל ,ערום
12:16, 12:23, 13:16, 14:8, 14:18
Only 12:16 has אויל; the rest have אולת.

בין ,ערום
14:8, 14:15

דעת ,ערום
12:23, 13:16, 14:18

אולת/אויל ,כסה ,ערום
12:16, 12:23
12:16 has אויל and 12:23 has אולת.

אולת ,כסיל ,ערום
12:23, 13:16, 14:8

פתי ,ערום
14:15, 14:18, 19:25, 22:3, 27:12

מזמה ,דעת ,ערמה
1:4, 8:12

see also פתי

---

*עשה
20:18b~24:6a (2.1)

see also שמח ,מאן ,חרף, and

משפט ,עשה
21:3, 21:7, 21:15

---

*עשיר
10:15a~18:11a (2.0)

see also רש√

דל ,עשיר
10:15, 22:16, 28:11

דל ,עשק
14:31, 22:16, 28:3

(ו)כבוד ,עשר
Only 11:16 lacks the 'and'.
3:16, 8:18, 11:16, 22:4

see also רש√

בְּכל־ ,עת
5:19, 6:14, 8:30, 17:17

---

*עתה
5:7~7:24 (1.1)
~8:32a (2.0)

---

*פגש
22:2~29:13 (1.4)

---

*פה
5:7~7:24 (1.1)
19:24~26:15 (1.2)
10:6b~10:11b (2.0)
26:7b~26:9b (2.0)
12:14a~13:2a (2.1)
~18:20a (2.2)
13:3a~21:23 (3.1)

see also עקשות ,אמרים,
and פתח

לשון ,פה
10:31, 15:2, 21:23, 26:28, 31:26

מחתה ,פה
10:14, 13:3, 18:7

שפה ,פה
4:24, 10:32, 13:3, 16:23, 18:6,
18:7, 18:20, 27:2

פוח   see   יפיח

---

*פוק
8:35~18:22 (1.3)
8:35~18:22~12:2a (2.1)

see also מצא

שׁאה ,פחד
1:27, 3:25

see also איד and בוא

מים ,פלג
5:16, 21:1

מעגל ,פלס
4:26, 5:6, 5:21

---

*פנה
21:9~25:24 (1.0)

see also אצל

---

*פנים
24:23b~28:21a (2.2)

see also עזז

לפני→פנים*
14:12~16:25 (1.0)
15:33b~18:12b (2.0)
16:18a~18:12a (2.2)

בְּמשפט ,טוב ,פנים
18:5, 24:23

לב ,פנים
15:13, 15:14

---

*פנינים
3:15~8:11 (1.3)

see also יקר

---

*פעל
10:29b~21:15b (2.0)

און ,פעל
10:29, 21:15, 30:20

*פֹּעַל
20:11b~21:8b (2.1)
24:12b~24:29b (2.2)

---

*פרי
12:14a~13:2a (2.1)
~18:20a (2.2)

תבואה ,פרי
8:19, 18:20

מוסר ,פרע
8:33, 13:18, 15:32

שמר ,פרע
13:18, 29:18

see also שמע

פשע*
12:13~29:6 (1.4)

אהב√ ,בקש ,פשע
17:9, 17:19

17:9 has אהבה while 17:19 has אהב.

כסה ,פשע
10:12, 17:9, 28:13

פתאם*
6:15a~24:22a (2.2)

שפה ,פתה
The expressions in these verses are slightly different since 24:28 has ב 'with' before 'lips', and 20:19 has the verb in the *Qal* while 24:28 has it in the *Hiphil*.

20:19, 24:28

פה ,פתח
24:7, 31:8, 31:9, 31:26

פתי*
9:4~9:16 (1.0)
22:3~27:12 (1.0)
19:25~21:11 (1.4)

see also ערום

כסיל ,פתי
1:22, 1:32, 8:5

לץ ,פתי
1:22, 19:25, 21:11

נער ,פתי
1:4, 7:7

ערמה ,פתי
1:4, 8:5

פתע*
6:15b~29:1b (2.0)

צדיק*
12:13~29:6 (1.4)
17:15a~24:24a (2.2)

see also ידע ,טוב ,חכם ,ארח,
שרש ,רשע ,רע ,רדף ,רבה ,נוה,
and תאוה

חטא√ ,צדיק
11:31, 13:21

11:31 has חוטא and 13:21 has חטאים.

חלץ ,צדיק
11:8, 11:9

מוט ,צדיק
10:30, 12:3, 25:26

נתן ,צדיק
9:9, 10:24, 12:12, 21:26

9:9 is less related than the others since the verb and noun are in different clauses.

רשע ,עלץ ,צדיק
11:10, 28:12

שמח√ ,צדיק
10:28, 13:9, 21:15, 23:24, 29:2, 29:6

10:28 and 21:15 have שמחה, while the other verses have forms of the verb שמח.

משפט ,צדק√
1:3 and 2:9 have צֶדֶק; 8:20, 16:8, and 21:3 have צדקה; 12:5 and 21:16 have forms from צדיק.

1:3, 2:9, 8:20, 12:5, 16:8, 21:3, 21:16

צדקה*
10:2~11:4 (1.3)

see also ארח and רדף

אמן√ ,ציר
13:17 has אמונים and 25:13 has נאמן.

13:17, 25:13

צלחת*
19:24~26:15 (1.2)

נדד/נוד ,צפור
26:2 has לנוד and 27:8 has נודד(ת). These are from different verbs, but they sometimes seem to be synonymous, and they are similar in sound.

26:2, 27:8

צפן*
2:1~7:1 (1.1)

see also ארב

צרה   see יום

לאם ,קבב
11:26, 24:24

חכמה and דעת   see קדש

קול*
2:3~8:1 (1.4)

see also נתן

קום
28:12b~28:28a (2.1)

see also מחשבה

קיץ*
6:8a~30:25b (2.2)

קציר ,קיץ
6:8, 10:5, 26:1

חרפה ,קלון
6:33, 18:3

קלל*
20:20a~30:11 (3.1)

see also ברך√

קנא*
3:31a~24:1a (2.1)

חמה, קנאה
6:34, 27:4

חכמה, קנה
4:5, 4:7, 16:16, 17:16, 23:23
4:5, 4:7, and 16:16 each have two forms from the verb קנה. 4:5, 4:7, 16:16, and 23:23 each also has בינה as a synonym for 'wisdom'.

לב, קנה
17:16, 18:15, 19:8

קציר see קיץ

קצר*
14:17a~14:29 (3.1)

אמר, קרא
1:21, 7:4

רחק, קרב
5:8, 27:10

קריה*
10:15a~18:11a (2.0)

עז, קריה
10:15, 18:11, 18:19

עין, קרץ
6:13, 10:10, 16:30

קרת see מֹרֹמים

קשב*
2:2~5:1 (1.2)
4:20~5:1 (1.2)

קשב see נטה and שמע

קשר*
3:3b~7:3 (3.1)

ר

ראה*
22:3~27:12 (1.0)

ראש*
1.9a~4:9a (2.1)

ראש see ברכה

רֹב*
11:14~15:22 (1.4)
11:14b~24:6b (2.0)
15:22b~24:6b (2.1)

see also אין

רב see הון

רבה*
4:10b~9:11 (3.0)

see also הון

רשע, צדיק, רבה
28:28, 29:2, 29:16

רדף*
12:11~28:19 (1.2)

צדקה/צדיק, רדף
11:19, 15:9, and 21:21 have צדקה; 13:21 and 28:1 have צדיקים.

11:19, 13:21, 15:9, 21:21, 28:1

רוה see אהבים

רוח*
15:13~17:22 (1.3)

see also אף and תכן

גאה√, רוח
16:18, 16:19, 29:23
16:18 has גָאוֹן, 16:19 has גאים, and 29:23 has גאות. Also, 16:19 and 29:23 share the phrase שפל־רוח 'lowly of spirit'.

נכאה, רוח
15:13, 17:22, 18:14

עין, רום
6:17, 21:4, 30:13

לרע(ה), מהר, רוץ
1:16 has לרע and 6:18 has לרעה.

1:16, 6:18

רזן√ see מלך

רחבות*
22:13~26:13 (1.3)

see also חוץ

רחק see דרך and קרב

ריב, ריב
22:23, 23:11, 25:9

see also גלע and מדון

ריק*
12:11~28:19 (1.2)

ריש*
6:11~24:34 (1.1)

see also רש√

רכיל*
11:13a~20:19a (2.1)

חרוץ, רמיה
10:4, 12:24, 12:27

אח, רֵע
17:17, 18:24, 19:7, 27:10

see also בוז and רש

רָע*
12:13~29:6 (1.4)
3:7b~16:6b (2.2)

see also נפל, סור, רוץ, and רשע

טוב, רע
14:22, 15:3, 31:12

עין, רע
23:6, 28:22
Compare 22:9 which has the opposite expression, טוב עין.

צדיק, רע
11:21, 12:13, 29:6

רעב see נפש

רעה*
22:3~27:12 (1.0)

רעה ,נפל and טוב, see רוץ

רפא*
6:15b~29:1b (2.0)

see also חיים

רפא ,לשון
12:18, 15:4

רפא√ ,עצם
3:8 has רפאות; the others have מרפא.
3:8, 14:30, 16:24

רצון*
8:35~18:22 (1.3)
8:35~18:22~12:2a (2.1)

see also תועבה

רצון ,מלך
14:35, 16:13, 16:15

רקב ,עצם
12:4, 14:30

רש*
19:1~28:6 (1.2)
22:2~29:13 (1.4)

רש√ ,עשר√
10:4, 10:15, 13:7, 13:8, 14:20,
18:23, 22:2, 22:7, 28:6, 30:8
10:4 has ראש and a *Hiphil* verb from
עשר. 13:7 has a *Hithpael* from עשר and a
Hithpolel from רוש. 10:15 has עשיר 'a
rich person' and רֵישׁ 'poverty'; 13:8 has
עשר 'wealth' and רש 'a poor person'; 30:8
has עשר 'wealth' and ראש 'poverty'. The
rest have עשיר 'rich' and רש 'poor'.

רש ,שנא ,רעהו
14:20, 19:7

רשע*
10:28~11:7 (1.3)
10:6b~10:11b (2.0)
13:9b~24:20b (2.0)
15:8a~21:27a (2.1)
28:12b~28:28a (2.1)
17:15a~24:24a (2.2)

see also רבה ,צדיק ,ישר ,יהוה,
and תועבה

רשע ,אבד
10:28, 11:7, 11:10, 28:28

רשע ,בגד
2:22, 21:18

משפט ,נטה ,רשע
17:23, 18:5

רשע ,צדיק
3:33, 10:3, 10:6, 10:7, 10:11,
10:16, 10:20, 10:24, 10:25,
10:28, 10:30, 10:32, 11:8,
11:10, 11:23, 11:31, 12:3, 12:5,
12:7, 12:10, 12:12, 12:21,
12:26, 13:5, 13:9, 13:25, 14:32,
15:6, 15:9, 15:28, 15:29, 17:15,
18:5, 21:12, 21:18, 24:15,
24:16, 24:24, 25:26, 28:1,
28:12, 28:28, 29:2, 29:7, 29:16,
29:27
As one would have expected, this pair
constitutes the most popular cliché in the
book. The odd thing is the heavy concentration of occurrences in the collection
here called B₁; more than half of the instances are in chapters 10–13.

רשע ,רע
4:14, 14:19, 24:20

נפל see רשעה

שבע*
12:11~28:19 (1.2)
12:14a~18:20a (2.2)

see also אכל and שאול

שבע ,אמר הון
30:15, 30:16

שבע ,לחם
12:11, 20:13, 28:19, 30:22

שבע שבע
18:20, 27:20, 28:19

שדה ,כרם
24:30, 31:16

שחק ,שעשוע
8:30, 8:31

שיבה*
16:31a~20:29 (3.1)

שכל ,בוז
12:8, 23:9

see also משכיל√ לקח and

ימין see שמאל

שמח*
10:1~15:20 (1.2)
15:13~17:22 (1.3)

see also חכם ,לב, and צדיק

שמח ,אב
10:1, 15:20, 17:21, 23:24,
23:25, 29:3

שמח ,גיל
2:14, 23:24, 23:25, 24:17

שמח√ ,לעשות√
2:14, 21:15
2:14 has השמחים and 21:15 has שמחה.

שמח√ ,תוגה
10:1 and 17:21 have verbal forms from
שמח and 14:13 has שמחה.
10:1, 14:13, 17:21

שנא ,דעת
1:22, 1:29, 12:1

שנא ,תוכחת
12:1, 15:10

see also רש ,אהב, and שקר

אהב see שנאה

שפה*
10:8b~10:10b (2.0)

see also עקש ,לב ,הגה ,דבר,
and פתה ,פה

שפה ,חך
5:3, 8:7

שפה ,לשון
12:19, 17:4

פחד see שאה

ואבדון/ה, שָׁאוּל
15:11, 27:20
15:11 has אבדן, and 27:20 has אבדוה.

ירד, שָׁאוּל
1:12, 5:5, 7:27

שׁבע, שָׁאוּל
27:20, 30:16

see also מות

שֵׁבֶט*
10:13b~26:3b (2.2)

see also נכה

שׁבר* (verb)
6:15b~29:1b (2.0)

שֶׁבֶר*
16:18a~18:12a (2.2)

see also גבה

שׁבת מדון see

שׁוּב*
19:24~26:15 (1.2)
24:12b~24:29b (2.2)

חמה/אף, שׁוּב
24:18 and 29:8 have forms of אף and 15:1 has אף in the second clause but חמה with the *Hiphil* of שׁוּב.

15:1, 24:18, 29:8

שׁוה*
3:15~8:11 (1.3)

שׁוחה*
22:14a~23:27a (2.2)

שׁור see אבוס

חיק, שׁחד
17:23, 21:14

שׁוחה/שׁחת/שׁחות, נפל
22:14 has שׁוחה, 26:27 has שׁחת, and 28:10 has שׁחות. These are different nouns, but they all mean 'pit' and are also similar in sound.

22:14, 26:27, 28:10

שׁחות see שׁוחה

שׁחר, מצא
1:28, 7:15, 8:17

שׁחת 'pit' see שׁוחה

שׁחת*
18:9b~28:24b (2.2)

שׁכב*
6:10~24:33 (1.1)

שׁכב, שֵׁנָה
3:24, 6:9, 6:10, 24:33

שׁכח see שׁתה

שׁכן, ארץ
2:21, 10:30

שׁכר see יין

שׁלוש, ארבע
30:15, 30:18, 30:21, 30:29

שׁלח*
6:14~16:28a (3.1)

see also מדון

שׁלם see יהוה

שׁמועה, טובה
15:30, 25:25

שׁמים see כון, ארץ, and נשׁר

שׁמע*
5:7~7:24 (1.1)
~8:32a (2.0)
13:1b~13:8b (2.1)
1:8a~4:1a (2.2)

see also אזן

שׁמע, חכם
8:33, 23:19

שׁמע, נטה
5:13, 22:17

שׁמע, פרע
8:33, 15:32

שׁמע, קשׁב
4:1, 7:24

שׁמר*
6:24~7:5 (1.3)
4:4b~7:2a (2.0)
16:17b~19:16a (2.2)
13:3~21:23 (3.1)

see also ארח, נצר, עזב, and פרע

שׁמר, כבד
13:18, 27:18

שׁמר, מצוה
4:4, 7:1, 7:2, 19:16

נצר/נפשׁו, שׁמר
13:3, 16:17, 19:8, 19:16, 21:23, 22:5, 24:12
13:3 and 16:17 have both שׁמר and נצר. 19:8, 19:16, 21:23, and 22:5 have only שׁמר, and 24:12 has only נצר.

שׁמר, שׁמר
19:16, 21:23

מוסר, תוכחת, שׁמר
13:18, 15:5

תורה, שׁמר
7:2, 28:4, 29:18

שֵׁנָה*
3:2~9:11 (1.2)
4:10b~9:11 (3.0)

see also יום

שֵׁנָה*
6:10~24:33 (1.1)

see also שׁכב

תנומה, שֵׁנָה
6:4, 6:10, 24:33

שְׁנַיִם*
17:15b~20:10b (2.0)

see also יהוה

שׁחק see שׁעשׁוע

דם, שׁפך
1:16, 6:17

שׁפל   see רוח

*שׁקר
19:5~19:9 (1.1)
6:19b~14:5b (2.0)

see also אמונה and יפיח

שׁקר, אמת
11:18, 12:19

שׁקר, שׂנא
13:5, 26:28

שׁרשׁ, צדיק
12:3, 12:12

שׁתה, יין
4:17, 9:5, 31:4

שׁתה, שׁכח
31:5, 31:7

see also לחם and חמס

*תאה
23:3a~23:6b (2.0)

תאוה, צדיק
10:24, 11:23, 21:26

תבואה see פרי

*תבונה
2:2~5:1 (1.2)
2:3~8:1 (1.4)

see also חכמה and חסר

*תהפכות
6:14~16:28a (3.1)

see also דבר

שׂמח√ see תוגה

*תוחלת
10:28~11:7 (1.3)

*תוכחת
1:25~1:30 (1.2)

see also שׂנא, נאץ, מוסר, and שׁמר

*תועבה
11:1~20:23 (1.2)
17:15b~20:10b (2.0)
15:8b~21:27a (2.1)
20:10~20:23a (3.0)

see also זמה

יהוה, תועבה
3:32, 6:16, 11:1, 11:20, 12:22,
15:8, 15:9, 15:26, 16:5, 17:15,
20:10, 20:23

רצונו, יהוה, תועבה
11:1, 11:20, 12:22, 15:8

רשׁע, תועבה
15:8, 16:12, 21:27, 24:27

תפלה, תועבה
15:8, 28:9

*תורה
1:8~6:20 (1.2)

see also עזב, נצר, and שׁמר

מצוה, תורה
3:1, 6:20, 6:23, 7:2

*תחבלות
11:14~24:6 (2.0)
20:18b~24:6a (2.1)

תחת, תחת
The last two references have only one instance of the word, but the verses are
clearly parallel.

30:21, 30:22, 30:23

*תכן
16:2~21:2 (1.3)

רוחות/לבות, בחן/תכן
17:3 has בחן; the rest have תכן. 16:2 has
רוחות; the rest have לבות. תכן means 'to
estimate', and בחן 'to examine', but I
think this is really just one cliché. תכן

occurs once in Isa 40:13 with רוח, but
בחן occurs several times in Jeremiah and
in Psalms in this sense. S. G. F. Brandon
("The Weighing of the Soul," in *Myths
and Symbols: Studies in Honor of Mircea
Eliade* [ed. J. M. Kitagawa and C. H.
Long; Chicago: University of Chicago,
1969] 91–110) studied the Egyptian origins of this general idea, which occurs
first in the Coffin Texts from the Middle
Kingdom. There the weighing is not necessarily after death. Brandon does not
discuss the Proverbs or analogous
passages.

16:2, 17:3, 21:2, 24:12

*תם
19:1~28:6 (1.2)

see also הלך and עקשׁ

דרך, תם/תמים
10:29, 11:5, 11:20, 13:6
10:29 and 13:6 have תם־דרך, 11:20 has
תמים... דרכו, and 11:5 has תמימי דרך.

תם, עקשׁ, ישׁר, הלך and תמים   see

כבוד, תמך
11:16, 29:23

*תנומות
6:10~24:33 (1.1)

see also שׁנה

*תפארת
16:31a~20:29 (3.1)

עטרת, תפארת
4:9, 16:31, 17:6

תפלה   see יהוה and תועבה

*תקוה
23:18~24:14 (1.1)
10:28~11:7 (1.3)
26:12~29:20 (1.3)

תקע   see ערב

*תשׁועה
11:14b~24:6b (2.0)

see also מלחמה

Index 2

Repeated Verses and Verses with Clichés
(in the Canonical Order of the Book of Proverbs)

This is a key to index 1 above, the index of repeated words. To find verses with affinities, first find the verse here and its repetitions and then check its suggested clichés in index 1. This procedure may be circuitous, but it seems more efficient than repeating the verse references to clichés here.

Numbers in parentheses refer to the categories of repetition sketched in chapter 4 above; repeated verses may be found in the catalog in chapter 5 under their category numbers. Semicolons separate repetitions and clichés. If a verse is repeated and also has a cliché, the information about repetition is given first.

Whole words in brackets indicate words under which one should seek the suggested cliché in index 1 above. Brackets around parts of words indicate probable restorations.

1:2	בין, ידע	
1:3	~ 21:21 (4.0), 22:4 (4.1); לקח, משפט צדק; שׂכל	
1:4	ערמה, דעת, נתן, מזמה; ערמה, פתי, נער, פתי; דעת	
1:5	נבון, חכם; לקח, יסף, חכם	
1:7a	~ 9:10a (2.2); יהוה, יראה	
1:8	~ 6:20 (1:2); 1:8a ~ 4:1a (2.2); אב, מוסר; אב, בן; אם, אב	
1:9a	~ 4:9a (2.1); גרגרת, חן	
1:11	צפן, דם, ארב; דם, ארב	
1:12	שׁאול, ירד	
1:13	מלא, הון, הון, הון, כל, יקר, הון; מצא, הון	
1:15	נתיבה, דרך	
1:16	דם, שׁפך, לרע, מהר, רוץ	
1:18	צפן, דם, ארב; דם, ארב	
1:19	בצע, בצע	
1:20	נתן, חכמה, נתן, רחובות, חוץ; נתן, קול	
1:21	קרא, אמר	

1:22	פתי, כסיל, לץ; שׂנא, אהב, פתי; לץ, פתי, דעת; שׂנא, דעת, כסיל	
1:24	קשׁב, נטה	
1:25	~ 1:30 (1.2)	
1:26	פחד, בוא, איד; פחד, בוא, איד	
1:27	בוא, בוא, בוא, פחד, איד; שׁאה, פחד; פחד	
1:28	מצא, שׁחר	
1:29	דעת, שׂנא, יהוה, יראה, דעת	
1:30	~ 1:25 (1.2); תוכחת, נאץ	
1:31	שׂבע, אכל	
1:32	כסיל, פתי	
2:1	~ 7:1 (1.1); אמר, לקח	
2:2	~ 5:1 (1.2); חכמה, לב, אזן; חכמה, קשׁב, נטה, אזן, נטה, תבונה	
2:3	~ 8:1 (1.4)	
2:5	דעת, יהוה, יראה, דעת, בין; דעת, מצא, אלהים, יהוה	
2:6	תבונה, חכמה, דעת, חכמה; חכמה, נתן, דעת, נתן	
2:7	תם, הלך	

2:8	שׁמר, דרך, ארח, דרך, ארח; שׁמר, נצר, משׁפט ארח	
2:9	משׁפט צדק	
2:10	נפשׁ, לב, דעת, חכמה	
2:11	נצר, שׁמר, מזמה	
2:12	תהפכות, דבר	
2:13	עזב, ישׁר, ארח, דרך, ארח; דרך, הלך, ארח	
2:14	עשׂה, שׂמח, גיל, שׂמח	
2:15	ארח, עקשׁ, מעגל ארח	
2:16	~ 7:5 (1.1); ~ 6:24 (1.4); זרה, נכריה	
2:19	חיים, ארח	
2:20	שׁמר, דרך, ארח, דרך, ארח; צדיק, טוב, צדיק, ארח; דרך, הלך	
2:21	ארץ, שׁכן, תמים, ישׁר	
2:22	בגד, רשׁע	
3:1	תורה, תורה, נצר; מצוה, נצר, מצוה	
3:2	~ 9:11 (1.2)	